D0102820

"WE WANT THIS HOUSE!"

Money magazine knows that owning a home you love is still the American dream. But today more than ever, you need help—not just in finding the perfect house, but in making the deal go through at a price that won't put you in the poor house.

- When is the best time of year to shop for a house?
- How much home can I afford?
- How can I decide if a house is likely to rise in value?
- Should I get a fixed- or adjustable-rate mortgage?
- Is there a way to keep closing costs low?
- Is a condo ever a good investment?
- What is my seller's bottom line?

Your Dream Home

Money® magazine

Alternate selection of Money® Book Club™

Other books in the
Money® America's Financial Advisor series:

How to Retire Young and Rich

401(k) Take Charge of Your Life

Paying for Your Child's College Education

The Right Way to Invest in Mutual Funds

Dollar Pinching: A Consumer's Guide to Smart Spending

Car Shopping Made Easy

Starting Over: How to Change Careers or Start Your Own Business

Your Dream Home

A Comprehensive Guide to Buying a House, Condo, or Co-op

Marguerite Smith

WARNER BOOKS

A Time Warner Company

If you purchase this book without a cover you should be aware that this book may have been stolen property and reported as "unsold and destroyed" to the publisher. In such case neither the author nor the publisher has received any payment for this "stripped book."

A NOTE FROM THE PUBLISHER

This publication is designed to provide competent and reliable information regarding the subject matter covered. However, it is sold with the understanding that the author and publisher are not engaged in rendering legal, financial, or other professional advice. Laws and practices often vary from state to state and if legal or other expert assistance is required, the services of a professional should be sought. The author and publisher specifically disclaim any liability that is incurred from the use or application of the contents of this book.

Copyright © 1997 by MONEY magazine
All rights reserved.

Warner Books, Inc., 1271 Avenue of the Americas, New York, NY 10020
Visit our Web site at
http://pathfinder.com/twep

 A Time Warner Company

Printed in the United States of America
First Printing: May 1997
10 9 8 7 6 5 4 3 2 1

Library of Congress Cataloging-in-Publication Data

Smith, Marguerite.
    Your dream home : a comprehensive guide to buying a house, condo, or co-op / Marguerite Smith.
        p. cm.
    Includes index.
    ISBN 0-446-67245-9
    1. House buying—United States. 2. Residential real estate—United States—Purchasing. 3. Mortgage loans—United States.
    I. Title.
HD255.S684 1997   96-43899
643'.12—dc20   CIP

Book design and text composition by L & G McRee
Cover design by Bernadette Evangelist © 1997 by Robert Anthony, Inc.
Cover illustration by Peter Hoey

ATTENTION: SCHOOLS AND CORPORATIONS
WARNER books are available at quantity discounts with bulk purchase for educational, business, or sales promotional use. For information, please write to: SPECIAL SALES DEPARTMENT, WARNER BOOKS, 1271 AVENUE OF THE AMERICAS, NEW YORK, NY 10020

To J.W.B.
with fond appreciation

ACKNOWLEDGMENTS

Many people and organizations provided information, data, and advice that greatly enriched this book. In particular I would like to thank the American Homeowners Foundation; the Building Research Council of the University of Illinois at Urbana-Champaign; Robert Clarfeld and Paul Wrobleski of Clarfeld & Co.; Hugh Siler of Coldwell Banker; Ana Maria da Hora of the East Boston Ecumenical Community Council; Helen Szablya of the Fannie Mae Foundation; Marci R. Schneider of the Federal Reserve; Jeanne Salvatore of the Insurance Information Institute; Pamela Baldwin of the Joint Center for Housing Studies at Harvard University; Andrew Kochera and Jay Shackford of the National Association of Home Builders; Elizabeth Johnson of the National Association of Realtors; Jane DeMarines, David Fried, and Kathleen Luzik of the National Cooperative Bank; Lee Pickett; and Heloisa Souza.

At **MONEY** magazine, thanks to managing editor Frank Lalli, who has helped me at several stages of my career. Many of my **MONEY** coworkers made valuable contributions, including Caroline Donnelly, Richard Eisenberg, Carla Fried, and Lani

Luciano. Book editor Dan Green was most attentive to the project. My agent Jim Charlton showed faith in me and the book from the beginning.

At Warner Books, I am fortunate in my editor, Rick Wolff, a coach of diverse talents. He has enhanced the performance of the Cleveland Indians and myriad writers. I am pleased to be one of the latter; I wish I could be one of the former.

And most of all, warm thanks to my loved ones on the domestic front: my husband, Larry, and stepchildren Erik and Flavia. They sometimes make my house a wreck, but they always make it my home. I wouldn't have it any other way.

CONTENTS

CONTENTS

CONTENTS

INTRODUCTION

The Market You Are about to Enter

At 33 cents a pound—about the same price as 16 ounces of watermelon—you could argue that it's a bargain. But of course, a typical single-family detached home weighs in at 339,000 pounds, so it's probably the most expensive (and weightiest) single purchase you will ever make. If it was built in recent years, that house most likely comprises 2,000 square feet of living space, four bedrooms, two and one-half baths, and a two-car garage. Median price: $133,000 for a new model, $112,900 for a used one. (For the components that make up today's median house, see Table 1.)

TABLE 1

Components of a 2,085-Square-Foot Single-Family Home

- 13,127 board feet of lumber
- 6,212 square feet of sheathing
- 13.97 tons of concrete

- 2,325 square feet of exterior siding material
- 2,427 square feet of roofing material
- 3,061 square feet of insulation
- 6,144 square feet of interior wall material
- 120 linear feet of ducting
- 15 windows
- 13 kitchen cabinets; two other cabinets
- one kitchen sink
- 12 interior doors
- five closet doors
- five exterior doors (four hinged, one sliding)
- two garage doors
- one fireplace
- three toilets
- two bathtubs
- one shower stall
- three bathroom sinks
- 2,085 square feet of flooring material
- one range, refrigerator, dishwasher, garbage disposer, range hood
- one washer, one dryer

Source: National Association of Home Builders

In the old days—when houses cost more like a nickel a pound—it might never have occurred to anyone to read a book of practical advice on the subject of home buying. There wasn't all that much you needed to know. Today, however, you had best know a great deal—how to work with a broker, possibly including a buyer's broker; how to evaluate other kinds of housing, such as condominiums and cooperatives; how to assess the physical structure; and most especially, how to obtain a mortgage and what kind to choose.

This book starts with the basic decision to buy, helping you determine if that's the path for you. The following chapters are road maps, intended to guide you through the twists and turns of the home-buying process. If you know where the most dangerous curves and deepest pitfalls may be situated, you can choose the best route around them—and, we hope, end up at the door of your dream house.

A home search traditionally begins at the kitchen table, with the hopeful buyers assembling pay stubs, check records, and the like to determine what they can afford. While computers and the Internet can play a role, home buying remains essentially a low-tech process. The key point is not just how much home you can pay for, but how you and your family want to live and work within the home—and humans must decide that.

That's the conclusion of Marietta L. Baba, an anthropology professor at Michigan's Wayne State University, who started out studying how the kitchen has evolved over the centuries. Now she sees broad historical forces at play in new home layouts that feature large "great" rooms, where families gather for cooking, eating, playing, and relaxing. It's almost a throwback to Colonial times, says Professor Baba, when the centerpiece of the home was the central room, where all family activities took place. "Just as the family was a multifunctional team that worked together," she says, "so the heart of the home was a multipurpose room where the entire family lived together."

In your home search, she suggests, figure out "who you are as a family, or as an individual. Think about what you love to do, what you don't like, what you want to become." Consider how space sets up barriers or enhances togetherness. Do you want to encourage more privacy or less? Does your household want large common rooms for family activities or large bedrooms where people can go off by themselves? Professor Baba herself applauds the trend of walls coming down between kitchen and living areas. "People are running around all day," she notes. "They want to be *together* when they're at home, not isolated in separate rooms."

Her message underscores the point that the search for the dream home is complicated, a process in which you must consult your head, your heart—and the rest of your household. Ultimately, of course, it can be a lifelong search: as your life changes, so does your dream and with it your dream home. What you need and desire may well be different tomorrow from what it is today and almost certainly will be different the decade after that.

In 1926 Sears Roebuck sold its Honor–Bilt kit houses for as little as $474, shipping the precut pieces by train from factory to homesites for owners to assemble. After World War II William J. Levitt's Cape Cod–style tract homes offered 750 square feet of interior space for $6,990—and the baby boomers were born there. Those were yesteryear's dreams, however. Now it's time for you to find your own.

SECTION I

DEFINING THE DREAM: THE ASSESSMENT PROCESS

CHAPTER 1

Is It Time for You to Buy a House?

You think you want to buy a house—a place of your own. You're probably excited and a bit nervous at the prospect, especially if you're a first-time shopper. Is this the right time? Mortgage interest rates seem to jump around like bunny rabbits. Housing markets seem to go from hot to cool to . . . well, how's a person ever to know the right moment?

The right moment, in truth, depends almost entirely on you. Don't torture yourself trying to predict future trends. The time to enter the housing market is when you decide you want to buy a home and when you estimate that you can afford the cost. If you feel drawn to make such a decision—and to analyze your personal finances to that end—you probably have reached a certain level of personal and financial stability. Almost certainly you feel secure in your job. You can see yourself staying in the same place for several years to come. Perhaps your family is getting larger—or you hope it soon will be.

At the same time, you've discovered through experience and reflection that you want the style of life that homeownership provides. After all, it's a powerful tradition, a cornerstone of American life, a reward for thrift and industry.

If you decide it's time to stop renting, you won't be alone. In just the last few years the national homeownership rate has jumped from 64.1% to 64.7% as an additional 2.3 million households made the transition to becoming homeowners. Thanks in part to lower down payments, homes are more affordable for first-time buyers than they were in the '80s and early '90s. In 1995 the average down payment was 13% of the purchase price, down from 18% percent in 1976, according to surveys by the Chicago Title and Trust Company, a major title insurer.

In a significant change, those making low down payments were not all low-income shoppers buying in urban areas. Many moderate-income families are using such mortgages to finance first homes in suburbia. Low down payments free young couples from the traditional catch-22 of paying so much for rent that they cannot save enough money for a down payment so that they can stop paying so much in rent. Lenders eager for deals have found ways to live with down payments of 10%, 5%, or even 3%. In 1995 nearly 45% of all home buyers put less than 10% down on their homes. "And most of this group are first-time buyers," says John Pfister, vice president in charge of marketing research for Chicago Title. About 15% of the new buyers had household incomes of $30,000 or less.

Traditionally, first-time homeowners are drawn from the ranks of young married couples, mostly in the 25–44 age range, that have been renting. This group expresses a near universal preference to become homeowners. But other groups, including immigrants, minorities, and lower-income households, are supplementing the demand for entry-level homes.

And these groups are obtaining credit as never before. From the suburbs of Los Angeles to New York's South Bronx, mortgage lenders are making loans in unprecedented numbers to blacks, Hispanics, and immigrants—the very groups that long were underserved by banks and mortgage companies. Indeed,

Federal Reserve officials say, in many cities low-income borrowers can now find mortgage credit on better terms than affluent whites. A *Wall Street Journal* computer analysis of millions of mortgages showed that home loan approvals to blacks soared more than 38% in 1994 from 1993, while approvals of loans to whites rose about 12%. Loan approvals for Hispanics jumped a steep 31%, with approvals for Asians up 17%.

So if you have been hesitant to approach a lender, now may be a good time to try. Chief among the excellent reasons to buy is housing quality. Rental properties are traditionally smaller, in poorer neighborhoods and inferior school districts. And they are often in run-down physical shape.

A second reason to buy is financial. The average monthly mortgage payment for a typical first home ($372 in 1994) is close to the median rent ($351), the Harvard University Joint Center for Housing Studies says in its annual report, "State of the Nation's Housing: 1995." Moreover, both mortgage interest costs and property taxes are deductible, cutting further the relative costs of ownership. In addition, homeowners keep the equity that builds with mortgage payments, so ownership provides a source of long-term savings lost to renters. Price appreciation over the years is the final extra kicker for owners.

Sometimes, Though, It Pays to Rent . . .

If you're a first-time shopper, however, don't just assume that renting is a bad deal. When your life is changing rapidly, it's often smarter to rent than to buy. Singles pair up, recent graduates take new jobs elsewhere, young couples split—and any of these life changes become only more complicated if you have to unload a house or condo in the bargain. Or you may have a terrific deal: perhaps you're living at home with Mom and Dad and saving every penny for graduate school; maybe you have a great rent-controlled apartment you could never replace. If that's the case, why mess up a good deal?

In other cases the financial benefits of ownership are simply unclear. To clarify your own situation, estimate the size of the tax break you would get for buying. It's true that mortgage interest is generally fully tax-deductible—but for a lot of people that doesn't mean very much. Depending on your tax bracket, each $1 of mortgage interest may be worth only 15 or 28 cents of tax savings. And for more than 70% of tax filers, the interest is utterly useless since they take the standard deduction, which recently was $6,700 for a couple filing jointly.

To help your private calculations, fill in the worksheet on page 12. You'll also need to estimate the rate of return you could earn by investing the cash you would save by not buying—the so-called opportunity cost. Then consider the following two points, the first one financial, the second subjective.

THE KEY DECISION: RENT OR BUY

This chart analyzes the rent/buy decision for a prospective homeowner who is considering buying a $150,000 house with a $30,000 down payment. He can obtain a 30-year, fixed-rate mortgage at 8.25% to finance the remaining $120,000 of the purchase price. His total tax rate, including federal, state, and city taxes, is 35%.

In this hypothetical case, the cost of renting turns out to be $3,915 cheaper than the after tax cost of owning in the first year—a difference that works out to 2.6% of the price of the $150,000 house. If the house were to appreciate in value by at least that amount every year, the owner would come out ahead financially when he sells the house, and also would have enjoyed the emotional benefits of homeownership. You'll find a blank version of this chart on page 12 for you to fill in.

Is It Time for You to Buy a House?

Item	Buy	Rent	Comment
1. Annual income	$60,000	$60,000	
2. Annual rent		$8,400	
3. Mortgage payments	$10,818		$9,865 is tax-deductible interest; $953 is principal.
4. Real estate taxes	$1,500		
5. Heat, other extra costs of ownership	$3,000		
6. Pretax cost of housing	$15,318	$8,400	Sum of items 3 + 4 + 5. Renting is $6,918 cheaper before taxes.
7. Tax deductions	$11,365		Interest paid plus real estate taxes
8. Tax savings	$3,978		Item 7 times his 35% tax rate
9. Taxes due without housing deductions	$21,000	$21,000	Item 1 times his 35% tax rate
10. Taxes due with housing deductions	$17,022	$21,000	Item 9 minus item 8
11. Income after housing and taxes	$27,660	$30,600	Item 1 minus items 6 and 10
12. After tax interest on funds not used for down payment ($30,000 × 5% minus $525 in taxes)	$975		Assumes a 5% return on $30,000 investment

Item	Buy	Rent	Comment
13. Income after housing, taxes, income gain on down payment not made	$27,660	$31,575	Items 11 + 12
14. Difference		$3,915	

Your Own Analysis: Rent or Buy

Item	Buy	Rent	Comment
1. Annual income			
2. Annual rent			
3. Mortgage payments			
4. Real estate taxes			
5. Heat, other extra costs of ownership			
6. Pretax cost of housing			
7. Tax deductions			
8. Tax savings			
9. Taxes due without housing deductions			
10. Taxes due with housing deductions			
11. Income after housing and taxes			

12. After tax interest on funds
not used for down payment

13. Income after housing,
taxes, income gain on
down payment not made

14. Difference

• **If you expect to move in the short run, renting probably makes more financial sense than buying.** Rents reflect the price of housing as *shelter,* but the ownership cost of a house or condominium is a combination of both rent-free accommodation and investment expectation. For this reason you can probably rent an apartment or house for less than the monthly costs of owning it, at least in the early years. In addition, you will save thousands of dollars in closing costs that are part of the home-buying process. If you remain in your new home for many years, the hope is that the house will appreciate in value by more than enough to cover the closing costs. If you move after a couple of years, and your house hasn't appreciated significantly, you may not recoup these costs.

• **The desire not to be tied down to a particular property, not to have to deal with the inevitable nuisances of maintenance, may outweigh the financial incentives to buy.** A well-paid single person or prosperous two-income couple might be better off financially with the tax benefits of homeownership. But for either, the freedom and other lifestyle advantages may simply outweigh the financial logic of ownership. In the book *Unlimited Partners: Our American Story* (Simon & Schuster), Elizabeth Dole recalls that when they married in 1975, she and husband Bob decided to postpone buying a house until they had more time. Two decades later their home base was still a rental apartment in Washington's Watergate complex. If you're on the road a lot, if you rely on someone else to fix the leaky faucet, then maybe you too have the soul of a renter. There's nothing wrong with that.

In the end, the rent-or-buy decision can't be reduced to a dollars-and-cents analysis. For those who want to be home-owners, the desire is strong and deep-rooted. This urge moti-vates them to overcome the perennial difficulties in raising the down payment and persuades them to trade rental payments for a giant note saddling them with mortgage obligations for 30 years to come.

One such believer is Mario Romero, 29, a state attorney in Orlando, Florida, who says he "couldn't stand to throw away money on rent." After two years of patient saving, plus five months of patient searching, he traded his $470 monthly rent bill for a $540 mortgage payment on a three-bedroom stucco house in nearby Altamont Springs. "It cost $74,500 and it's worth every penny," says the proud bachelor homeowner, who hopes to trade up in a couple of years. "All the money I put in will come back to me at resale time."

Is It Time for You to Trade Up?

Maybe you've paired and nested, but your castle feels cramped for space now that the young ones are racing around. And there's a house for sale a few miles down the road that's in a better neighborhood, a better school district. You and your nest mates would get a lot of pleasure from that bigger, more expensive pile of bricks and mortar on that more desirable plot of land.

In truth, the extra cost could be well worth it, if you really want that better house, and the extra space and better neighbor-hood could give you and your family a lot of pleasure.

Before you rush to place your bid, however, think carefully about the total dollars involved as well as the benefits. You've got to move, you've got closing costs, and you're upping your investment in the real estate market. Selling might cost 6% of your old home's value, thanks to the brokerage commission. Then add in home inspection costs, legal fees, title insurance, mortgage application expenses. Put it all together and the round-trip—buying and selling—might run to 10% of your total take.

The ideal strategy, of course, is to buy the right house the first time, to avoid the need to trade up. This is notably tough to do, especially for first-time buyers who are younger and lower paid and frequently unable to afford the sort of house they dream about. These days about two-thirds of home sales are to trade-up buyers.

If you feel you are ready to buy your first, second, or whatever home, a little financial stretching may be in order. Reason: Your income will most likely go up, and your house payments will stay the same if you snag a fixed-rate mortgage. And while annual double-digit increases in value are behind us, houses continue to appreciate at about the rate of inflation. Barring severe economic problems on a national scale, there's no reason to anticipate a broad-based dramatic swoon in real estate values.

That means it's not likely to be any easier to buy in the future. And as soon as you do join the ranks of owners, the tendency of property to appreciate will start working for you, helping you to build equity. In the end, after all, a house remains virtually the only item that you can buy, use, and then sell— generally for more than you paid for it.

So if you have decided you really do want to be an owner, or that you really want to trade up to a fancier house, the primary question is figuring out what you can afford. And that is the subject of the next chapter.

CHECKPOINTS

- If you expect to move in less than five years, renting probably makes more financial sense than buying.
- Consider your lifestyle as well as your finances. If you hate to bother with maintenance, if you resist being tied down to one place, homeownership may not be for you.
- If you're tempted to trade up, recognize that utilities, taxes, and maintenance costs will all increase along with house size.
- If you're a minority, immigrant, or low-income buyer, your chances have rarely been better for getting a mortgage loan. Banks are now taking their community-lending obligations seriously—and it's turning out to be good business for them.

CHAPTER 2

How Much House Can You Afford?

Most people have a gut feeling about what they can spend for a home. But your back-of-the-envelope math may not be accurate, especially if you're a first-time buyer. Perhaps you're relying on the well-worn rule of thumb that states, You can afford a house that costs two and a half times your annual household income. So if you and your partner bring home $120,000, you can safely look for a palace priced at $300,000, right? Nice try—but that kind of calculation is too simple for these complicated times. It doesn't take into account many other key factors that help determine how much house you can afford.

Back up a bit and consider your borrowing power rather than your purchasing power. Just about everyone needs a mortgage loan to buy a home these days. That means your buying ability depends mainly on your borrowing ability—what size mortgage loan a financial institution is willing to grant you. A couple with joint earnings of $120,000 who have three children, a $6,500 car loan, $3,500 in credit card debt, and $2,000 in savings won't stack up the same way with lenders as a child-less couple with the same income, no debts, and a $75,000 portfolio of cash and marketable securities.

Two Key Lending Guidelines

Your income and your debts are the most important factors for determining how large an amount you will be able to borrow. If you are buying a house with someone else (your spouse, a parent, partner, a sibling), you should consider your co-purchaser's earnings and current debts as well your own. If you apply for a mortgage loan with someone else, both of you are legally responsible for repayment of the debt.

Bankers use two guidelines, known as **qualifying ratios,** to determine how much money they are willing to lend.

• **For housing: 28%.** The first guideline says that a house-hold should spend no more than 28% of its **gross income** (income before taxes) on housing costs. These expenses include mortgage principal and interest, property taxes, homeowners insurance, and private mortgage insurance, if applicable. Lenders don't include utility bills in your housing expense ratio. You can calculate the ratio using either monthly or annual figures, but monthly is the most common method. Using this simplified approach, Table 2-1 will give you a fairly accurate estimate of how large a mortgage you might qualify for.

TABLE 2-1

How Large a Mortgage Do You Qualify For?

This chart can help you estimate what size mortgage you might qualify for based on your annual income and the interest rate currently being quoted for 30-year fixed-rate mortgages. Using the normal 28% ratio, this chart assumes that you can pay 25% of your gross income for principal and interest payments and reserve the remaining 3% for property taxes and insurance. Look in the top row and find your before tax income. Then look in the left column for the current interest rate. Locate the point where your income and the current rate meet. If your income is higher than $70,000, add appropriate amounts together. For example, if your income is $100,000 and a 30-year, fixed-rate mortgage goes for 10%, you could qualify for a mortgage of $237,200 ($118,600 + $118,600), or double the amount you could qualify for with a $50,000 income.

Annual Income

Interest Rates	$15,000	$20,000	$25,000	$30,000	$35,000	$40,000	$45,000	$50,000	$55,000	$60,000	$65,000	$70,000
6.5%	$49,400	$65,900	$82,400	$96,800	$115,300	$131,800	$148,300	$164,800	$181,300	$197,700	$214,200	$230,700
7.0%	47,000	62,600	78,300	93,900	109,600	125,300	140,900	156,600	172,300	187,900	203,600	219,200
7.5%	44,600	59,600	74,500	89,400	104,300	119,200	134,100	149,000	163,900	178,800	193,700	208,600
8.0%	45,000	56,700	70,900	85,100	99,300	113,500	127,700	141,900	156,100	170,300	184,500	198,700
8.5%	40,600	54,100	67,700	81,200	94,800	108,300	121,900	135,400	149,000	162,500	176,100	189,600
9.0%	38,800	51,700	64,700	77,700	90,600	103,500	116,500	129,400	142,400	155,300	168,200	181,200
9.5%	37,200	49,500	61,900	74,300	86,700	99,100	111,400	123,800	136,200	148,600	161,000	173,400
10.0%	35,600	47,400	59,300	71,200	83,000	94,900	106,800	118,600	130,500	142,400	154,300	166,100
10.5%	34,200	45,500	56,900	68,300	79,700	91,100	102,400	113,800	125,200	136,600	148,000	159,400

Source: The Fannie Mae Foundation

19

• **Housing plus debt repayments: 36%.** The second guideline states that housing expenses and other long-term debts (usually defined as 10 months or more) combined should total no more than 36% of total income. That means your housing expense previously listed, plus car loans, credit card payments, and similar obligations may not add up to more than 36% of your gross income.

Remember, however, that these ratios are flexible limits, not commandments graven in stone. If you have a consistent record of paying rent that is very close in amount to your proposed monthly mortgage payments, or if you make a large down payment, lenders may stretch the limits and permit somewhat higher ratios. In addition, some lending institutions offer special loan programs for low- and moderate-income home buyers that allow as much as 33% of gross monthly income to be used toward housing expenses and 39% for total debt. Sometimes lenders will permit a very small down payment but reduce the qualifying ratios to 25% and 33%, respectively.

Let's begin conservatively and use the standard ratios of 28% and 36%. Sharpen your No. 2s and put together some simple numbers. Complete Table 2-2 to calculate your gross monthly income.

TABLE 2-2

Calculate Your Monthly Income

The first step in estimating what size mortgage you might qualify for is to add up the total monthly income for you and your co-borrower, if you have one. Be sure you include all money that your household receives on a regular basis.

How Much House Can You Afford?

Item	Borrower	Co-Borrower	Total
Base Employment Income			
Part Time/Second Job Income			
Overtime★			
Bonuses★			
Commissions★			
Dividends/Interest			
Alimony/Child Support			
Unemployment Compensation			
Pension/Social Security Benefits			
Veterans Benefits			
Other Income			
Total Gross Monthly Income $			

★If your overtime, bonuses, or commissions do not fall into 12 equal monthly payments, be sure to divide them so as to spread this income over 12 months. You will need a two-year history of receipts for this income to count.

Source: The Fannie Mae Foundation

After you know your gross monthly income, multiply it by 28% to get your maximum allowable housing expense:

1. Your total monthly income $_____

2. Multiply by 28%   × .28 _____

3. Equals your maximum allowable
   monthly housing expense $_____

The second step is to figure out how much long-term debt you owe. Any installment loans or revolving debts that will take more than 10 months to pay off should be included here. Use Table 2-3 to total your existing monthly payments on long-term household debts for you and your co-borrower.

TABLE 2-3

Long-Term Monthly Household Debts

Total your present monthly payments on long-term credit obligations below. Be sure to include the long-term debts of your co-borrower as well.

ALLOWABLE MONTHLY HOUSING EXPENSE	
1. Fill in Amount You Calculated in Table 2-2	$
LONG-TERM MONTHLY DEBT★ (Please enter the minimum monthly payment required on each of your outstanding debts)	
2. Installment and Revolving Debts (for example, credit card and store accounts)	$

3. Car Loan	
4. Student Loan	
5. Existing Real Estate Loans (if you are not selling the property)	
6. Alimony/Child Support	
7. Other Long-Term Monthly Debts (including loan from relative, loan against insurance policy)	
Add all the debts (1–7) above to calculate your total monthly debt payments.	$
*Note: Ongoing monthly living expenses you pay for in cash such as utility payments; grocery bills; entertainment expenses; and health, life, medical, and car insurance are not considered long-term debts for mortgage loan–qualifying purposes.	

Source: The Fannie Mae Foundation

To find out if your monthly debt payments are more than a lender is comfortable with, complete this calculation:

1. Your gross monthly income $_____

2. Multiply by 36% × .36 _____

3. The result equals your maximum allowable combined housing and monthly debt $_____

Compare that amount to your sum total in Table 2-3. If your long-term debt is greater than the 36% you are allowed, you may have to pay off some debts before applying for a mortgage loan. Double-check your figures by comparing them to Table 2-4, which shows the allowable monthly housing allowance and monthly debt levels for various income levels. For every $50 of monthly debt payments above the guidelines, you can expect about a $5,000 reduction in the amount of money for which you qualify.

TABLE 2-4

Estimating Housing and Debt Allowances

This table gives approximate figures for how high your monthly housing expenses and your long-term monthly debt can be based on your income. "Allowable monthly housing expense" includes your mortgage principal and interest payment, property taxes, homeowners insurance, and, if required by the lender, private mortgage insurance.

ALLOWABLE MONTHLY HOUSING EXPENSE AND
MONTHLY DEBT BASED ON YOUR INCOME

Gross Annual Income	Allowable Monthly Housing Expense	Allowable Long-Term Monthly Debt
$20,000	$467	$600
25,000	583	750
30,000	700	900
35,000	817	1,050
40,000	933	1,200
45,000	1,050	1,350
50,000	1,167	1,500
55,000	1,283	1,650
60,000	1,400	1,800
65,000	1,517	1,950
70,000	1,633	2,010
75,000	1,750	2,250
80,000	1,867	2,400
85,000	1,983	2,550
90,000	2,100	2,700
95,000	2,217	2,850
100,000	2,333	3,000
130,000	3,033	3,900

Source: The Fannie Mae Foundation

Next, take a look at your savings. Use Table 2-5 to prepare a list of all your present financial assets. Use the same table to estimate the upcoming expenses that a new home will bring during the first six months. The next step is to decide how much of the remainder of your savings you are willing to spend on your down payment.

TABLE 2-5

Calculating Your Down Payment

Use this worksheet to prepare a list of your current assets and estimated new-home expenses. Save the result: your mortgage lender will want to see this list when you apply for your loan.

DOWN PAYMENT CALCULATION WORKSHEET

Assets Available for Down Payment		Upcoming New-Home Expenses	
Savings Account		Moving Expenses	
Checking Account		New-Home Repairs	
Cash Value of Life Insurance		Home Decorating	
Proceeds from Sale of Current Home, if Applicable		Major Appliance Purchases	
Gift from Relative*		Estimated Closing Costs at Settlement (usually 3%–6% of your loan amount)	
Other Assets That Can Be Sold to Obtain Funds		Other Major Purchases in Next Six Months Unrelated to New Home (car, etc.)	
A. Total Liquid Assets Available	$	B. Cash Needs for Next Six Months in New Home†	$

A - B = Total Down Payment Available: $

*Some mortgages put a limit on how large a gift you can use for your down payment. Check with your lender to determine exact amounts and appropriate forms to complete.

†Remember, lenders may require you to have two months of mortgage payments in reserve when you go to closing. Be sure to consider this in your cash needs for the next six months.

Source: The Fannie Mae Foundation

Now, the Magic Number . . .

You know how much you can afford to spend on monthly mortgage payments (about 28% of your total monthly income). You also know whether your present debts and projected housing costs are within a range that leaves you and your banker comfortable (36% of gross monthly income). You have looked at your available assets and estimated how much money you will need to put aside for closing, moving, and settling-in costs. You've decided how much you can plunk down as a down payment. Now, consult Table 2-6 to see how large a mortgage loan you can afford. If you know that you can afford a monthly payment of $800, for example, and interest rates are running about 8.5%, then you could borrow about $100,000. (The $769 monthly payment leaves a few dollars over for property taxes and insurance premiums.) Add together your expected down payment and the maximum mortgage amount. *Voilà:* the total should be the maximum amount that you can comfortably afford to pay for a home.

TABLE 2-6

Monthly Loan Payment Table

This table shows how much you'll pay monthly (mortgage principal and interest) for every $1,000 you borrow. Taxes and insurance payments are not included in these amounts. To use the table, find the loan rate on the left side and the term of the loan at the top. At the intersection is the monthly payment for a loan of $1,000 at the given rate and term. Multiply this figure by the number of thousands of dollars you're thinking of borrowing to calculate the monthly payment for your loan. For example, for a 30-year fixed-rate loan of $75,000 with an 8.5% interest rate, multiplying $7.69 times 75 gives you a monthly payment of $576.75.

Monthly Loan Payment Table
Equal Monthly Payments to Amortize $1,000

Interest Rate	15 Years	20 Years	30 Years
5.0%	$ 7.91	$ 6.60	$ 5.37
5.5%	8.18	6.88	5.68
6.0%	8.44	7.17	6.00
6.5%	8.72	7.46	6.33
7.0%	8.99	7.76	6.66
7.5%	9.28	8.06	7.00
8.0%	9.56	8.37	7.34
8.5%	9.85	8.69	7.69
9.0%	10.15	9.00	8.05
9.5%	10.45	9.33	8.41
10.0%	10.75	9.66	8.78
10.5%	11.06	9.99	9.15
11.0%	11.37	10.33	9.53
11.5%	11.69	10.67	9.91

Source: The Fannie Mae Foundation

Maybe the news was good. If so, remember that even if you *can* afford a $500,000 home, there's no law that says you have to spend the maximum. Incomes are growing slowly these days, house appreciation is in single digits, so stretching to buy the best nest you can possibly pay for can be a risky choice. Now consider qualifying for a loan.

Prequalification vs. Preapproval

Many buyers postpone their loan shopping until after they have picked out a house. Be smart and start the process before you start your home search. At the very least, having mortgage money in hand will give you an edge over the competition if you are house hunting in a seller's market. At best, investing the time for a comprehensive mortgage search can save you thousands of dollars and countless hours of aggravation. The goal of your savvy shopping: to ferret out a lender with low rates and a good reputation for customer service. If you call six lenders a day for five days, that's 30 names—and you can be virtually certain that some institution in that group will beat the first deal you were offered.

Start by contacting the financial institution that holds your checking or savings account and ask them about mortgage rates and terms. If you agree to have monthly payments debited automatically from your current account, you may get a small break on the interest rate. Moving on, ask your friends for referrals to banks and loan officers they have found helpful. You can jump-start the process by calling HSH Associates (800-873-2837), a company that publishes interest rate information. For $20 HSH will send you a list of lenders in your area who offer good deals, plus a book on mortgages. For $10 you can download HSH's *PC Mortgage Update* shareware from the Internet (http://www.hsh.com) and search out attractive deals for yourself. (For a full discussion on shopping and applying for loans, see Chapters 8 and 9.)

Besides local lenders, try some of the big national mortgage companies. Countrywide Home Loans (800-570-9888) accepts phone applications supported by faxed copies of your pay stubs and bank statements. And national lenders are popping up on the Internet with increasing frequency, so check their offerings, too.

Ideally your aim in this exercise is to be preapproved by a lender, not just prequalified. **Prequalification** is simply the process of determining how much money a prospective home buyer will be eligible to borrow before he or she formally applies—a calculation of whether income fits the standard debt-to-income ratios. If you have filled out the worksheets in this chapter, you've already figured that out. **Preapproval,** however, means the lender has verified your income and checked your credit and other financial references. You'll get a letter stating that the lender will give you a mortgage up to a specific amount, as long as the home appraisal justifies the price. That's the next best thing to being a cash buyer, so your offer will almost certainly beat an equivalent bid from someone who still must apply for a loan. Rather than wait 45–60 days to find out if the second home shopper also qualifies, the seller will naturally prefer the bidder with a mortgage commitment in hand. (If you can't get through the entire approval process before finding a house, do get a statement of prequalification. It's better than making your sales bid empty-handed.)

The trick to preapproval programs is that you present your documentation at application time, rather than submitting it over several weeks. Once you submit the required material, the lender will probably give you an answer within a few days, after checking your credit history. Then you'll receive a loan commitment that may be good for up to 90 days. In considering preapproval programs, make sure you understand the following points:

- Is the preapproval a firm commitment to lend money or simply an estimate of your ability to borrow?
- If it's a solid commitment, does it cover both interest rates and points, or rates only? Try to lock in both.
- When does the commitment begin and end? Try to obtain a 60-day or 90-day lock-in on terms.

Finally, remember that a quick preapproval deal is no substitute for a mortgage with the best rates and terms available, so don't short-circuit the process. Jiffy financing with a high rate can cost you thousands of extra dollars when you're paying over 30 years.

Beefing up Your Borrowing Power

Maybe, when you did the exercises at the beginning of this chapter, the news wasn't so good. You know you aren't ready to seek prequalification or preapproval for a loan because you're distinctly dissatisfied with the mortgage amount for which you qualify. Maybe you sense that your home-buying possibilities will be relatively limited. Before you abandon the quest, consider four ways to increase your borrowing power:

- Reduce your existing long-term debt
- Wait to apply for a mortgage until your income increases
- Wait for a year or so and increase savings
- Find a guarantor to cosign the mortgage loan

Discuss with your co-borrower ways to change your spending patterns. Can you save more by eating meals at home or taking fewer vacations? Try to clear the financial decks by paying off as many high-interest installment loans as possible. Consider how homeownership might affect your budget. Will the cost of commuting to work rise or fall? Estimate conservatively to leave yourself a margin for error.

If increasing your income and cutting debt aren't realistic options, and no cosigner is in view, you will have to shop for financing options that will result in a lower down payment and smaller monthly mortgage payments. We'll explore these possibilities in detail in Chapter 8. In the meantime, there's one other aspect of loan shopping to which you might attend: your credit history.

Polishing Your Credit Record

Lenders will certainly be looking at your credit report; you should beat them to it. There are three major agencies that gather information on your credit relationships, and they may have very different reports about you. TRW (800-392-1122) will send you one free copy of your report annually. Unless you have been denied credit recently, you'll have to pay up to $8 (some states limit the fee) to get your report from Equifax (800-685-1111) or from Trans Union (312-408-1050). Call first to find out what information to include in your written request.

By getting copies of your credit reports now, you'll have a chance to remedy mistakes or prepare explanations for past misdeeds. Credit bureaus make plenty of errors—from simple name misspellings to more damaging mix-ups, such as wrongly showing that you declared bankruptcy or defaulted on a loan. "I have no middle name," laments attorney Mario Romero, 29, who recently bought a home in Altamont Springs, Florida. "My credit report showed the late payments of every Mario Romero in the country." He straightened out the record before getting his mortgage.

If you find a mistake, write to the agency promptly, documenting your understanding of the facts. The bureau must investigate the dispute within a reasonable time period. The burden of proof lies with them, so the agency must verify that the information in question is correct. If you disagree with the outcome of the inquiry, write a short statement of your position and have the credit agency include it with your report. Most negative information will be deleted after seven years, but if you have filed for bankruptcy, it could take 10 years to get a clean slate. All's not lost till then, however: most lenders concentrate on your behavior in the last three years when evaluating your creditworthiness.

You may know already that your credit history is not as pristine as you would like. If you are currently having problems, you may have to postpone buying a house until they are resolved. To apply for a mortgage now might simply compound your problems. If, on the other hand, your problems are well behind you, your more recent track record may persuade a lender that you are a responsible borrower. Here are the guidelines to which most lenders refer:

- For credit cards and other forms of revolving credit, no payments 60 days or more past due and no more than two payments 30 days past due.
- For auto loans and other types of installment loans, no payments 60 days or more past due and no more than one payment 30 days past due.
- For mortgage or rent, no payments past due. This can be proven through canceled checks for the past 12 months or a loan payment history from the mortgage servicer.

As a final precaution, you should cancel rarely used charge accounts and credit lines. Don't just cut up the cards: call the lenders and close out the accounts. If a tangle of open lines appears in your credit report, lenders get nervous and may count them along with your legitimate debts.

CHECKPOINTS

- Review last year's income and expenses. The maximum loan for which you can qualify will be based on two standard lending ratios: a mortgage payment equal to 28% of your gross income and total debt payments equal to 36% of your gross income. These ratios may fall to 25% and 33%, respectively, if you make a small down payment.
- Look over your savings and other assets. How much are you willing to lock up in a down payment? Mortgage lenders will want you to have a cash cushion of at least two months' worth of payments left after the closing. You may want more, especially if you have kids or your income is variable.
- Talk with several banks and mortgage companies to obtain the best possible deal. Get a preapproval letter that promises the lender will give you a mortgage up to a specific amount, if the home appraisal justifies the price. Do not let the seller or the real estate agent know the amount of the commitment if your opening bid is lower than the maximum dollar limit.
- Check your credit record with the three major bureaus and correct any inaccuracies. Pay off high-rate consumer debt if you can, and close rarely used credit lines.

CHAPTER 3

Defining What You Want in a House

Now that you know *how much* house you can afford, it's time to establish *what kind* of house you want and need. Talk to your partner, and any other members of your household, about the home you all dream of and where you want it located.

This series of conversations may elicit real surprises. Real estate agents never cease to be amazed that a couple may know all about each other's tastes in food, cars, clothing, vacations, and entertainment and yet be clueless about their opinions on what makes a home. Rental living is so often a short-term stopgap that it doesn't offer a good comparison to home shopping with someone. And if you have young children, you probably haven't asked for their two cents' worth before now.

Clare Cooper Marcus, author of *House as a Mirror of Self* (Conari Press, 1995; $24.95) and a retired architecture professor from the University of California at Berkeley, urges families to sit down and explore what home means to each individual member. Start with the neighborhood. "For most of us," Marcus says, "the type of setting we live in is as important as or more important than the type of house." So thrash out whether—

deep down—you're city people, suburbanites, country dwellers, or small-town folks. Then, before you start looking at specific houses, she urges, bring out a box of crayons and let everyone doodle their own sketch of what "home" brings to mind. "Recall the most 'homey' home you ever knew," she says. "Try to articulate what it was that made that house really wonderful."

If house style doesn't matter to you, that might be a good thing, since you will be open to all possibilities. Still, you want to notice if a house meshes gracefully with its natural setting— or doesn't. As you start looking at houses, chances are that you and your family will begin to have opinions about what styles you like in houses. For a primer, take a look at the styles shown in Table 3-4 at the end of this chapter.

The next step is to mesh those individual ideas of home into a cohesive picture, which may involve a lot of talking—and plenty of listening as well. This process can help the family reach a compromise that allows all members to feel they have won at least a portion of their dream. To sidestep these discussions at the beginning, Marcus warns, "is to court late conflict."

After you've had discussions about the kind of place you would be happy living in, gradually ease into the other task: getting a general feel for different locations and an idea of what is being offered at what price. Later on you will search for the house that meets all or most of the specifications on the family shopping list.

Picking the Right Location

You will be buying into a community and a neighborhood, and these will shape your daily life at least as much as the specific home you fasten upon. So before you start touring houses, make some basic decisions about the kind of environment you want to live in.

Be open-minded. A basic mistake that many shoppers make is to conclude too quickly where they are willing to look and what they are willing to consider. Take a fresh look at familiar communities and a first look at towns that are completely new to you. False preconceptions can shut you out of a good opportunity, costing you money and happiness.

Start by considering your commute. If you're committed to driving, take a map and draw a circle with a 40-mile radius around the point where you work. Alternatively, delineate your area in terms of bus, subway, or rail lines. The cities, towns, and neighborhoods that lie within these boundaries define your target market. Within it, decide what your basic choices are and explore each one. You're not trying to see every house in every neighborhood. Rather, make sure you see first-class examples of each one of your basic options. Along the way, keep a free-wheeling discussion going. Be certain all family members will be comfortable with an area's conveniences or—if it is a remote suburb—with its isolation.

Economic vitality is a key ingredient in an attractive area, so find out which towns, suburbs, or parts of cities are growing fastest. One quick measure of how desirable other people think a community is: Look at the difference between the original asking and the final selling prices of the houses. In choice areas the gap is small—houses may sell for just 5% less than their original listing prices. A similar yardstick is how long houses linger on the market: less than 90 days means demand is hot. To get this kind of information, study the real estate section of the local newspaper or call the board of Realtors or the home builders association.

Press for information about recent developments that could erode home values, such as major employers fleeing the area and taking enough jobs with them to flatten the local economy. A huge mall down the road that might cause traffic congestion can also dampen housing appreciation. So can environmental dangers such as hazardous waste dumps and high radon levels.

You want a town with top-flight services, so drive around to satisfy yourself that municipal maintenance is up to snuff. Is garbage picked up at the back door, or do residents lug it to the curb? Are the roads smooth or rutted with axle-breaking potholes? Do residents boast about the local library, the speedy snow removal, the efficient fire department? Do the police have any special programs to combat crime?

Compare property tax bills on homes that interest you with those in nearby towns or neighborhoods. Remember, you're not interested just in what the current owner is paying, but in what you would owe if you move in (an amount that could be considerably higher). The property tax assessor's office can provide that information.

When a particular community piques your interest, find out as much as you can about its school system, whether or not you have children. At resale time you'll discover that superior schools are a top priority among buyers. One favorable sign is local support for the public schools. In places where voters must approve school budgets, ask how referendums have fared in recent years. The school superintendent or the board of education can tell you. At the same time, check on the districting of students. Will your kids go to schools close by, or will they have to ride buses? If one school has a better reputation than another, consider concentrating your house search within its district. For help in your evaluation, you can order a local school report from School Match (800-992-5323). For $19 the Westerville, Ohio, firm will fax you information on local student-teacher ratios, test scores, and property values.

Once you have picked a town, finding the right neighborhood is an easier task. Leafing through the multiple-listing service offerings in brokers' offices will quickly give you an idea of which sections are out of reach financially. Once you start driving around, look for neighborhoods where the houses are approximately equal in value. In areas where there is a wide disparity, the smaller, cheaper dwellings can pull down the prices of their more elaborate neighbors. Keep a keen eye out as you go to see how conscientious the zoning board has been. You don't want to find auto body shops mingling with single-family houses, eroding their property values. Look at the kids on the street: are they playing ball, mowing lawns—or throwing stones at passing cars? Within neighborhoods look for neatly trimmed lawns and hedges, well-tended gardens, and healthy trees. A community that is fastidiously maintained adds value to a house.

A real estate truism is that you lock in your future profit not at resale time, but when you buy your house. If you're neither a remodeler nor a risk taker, your safest bet is probably a traditional house in a well-kept middle- or upper-class neighborhood filled with homes just like yours. If you are willing to gamble, you may be able to find a house that will appreciate at a better than average pace in a section of a city that is out of favor but has the potential for a comeback. The odds improve if you choose an older house with architectural interest. Antiquarian touches, such as stained-glass windows, natural-wood floors, and gingerbread trim, add charm and character—and enhance property values. The risk is that what you thought was an up-and-coming neighborhood is actually down-and-going. That's why you might limit your pioneering to areas where some houses have already been renovated.

The best way to stretch your money is to buy the neighborhood rather than the house—choose the ugly duckling on a street full of swans. That way, even if you don't improve your property, the neighborhood will pull up its value. You might also raise the value-for-money ratio by purchasing a brand-new tract house. Anxious developers sometimes put low asking prices on the first homes built to sell them quickly; they'll raise prices in the second phase if the development proves popular. Early birds can take advantage not only of the low prices, but also of the chance to squeeze extras out of the contractor—better-quality carpeting or appliances, for example.

As you navigate from place to place, let your instincts help guide your investment decision. Ask yourself: "Would I be proud to live here?" If you would be, chances are that future buyers would be also.

Narrowing the Search

If cool reason rules in choosing a town or neighborhood, let the heart have its due in choosing a home. This, after all, will be your sanctuary. Possibly the place where your kids grow into adults. Certainly a spot where memories will weave themselves into the walls.

One way is to start your search with a must-have list and a wish list. (To see what other house shoppers crave these days, see Table 3-1.)

TABLE 3-1

WISH LIST

What do home buyers want? According to a recent survey of 3,800 home shoppers by the National Association of Home Builders, more space is the top priority. Shoppers want 2,200 square feet in their new home, a 29% increase over the 1,700 square feet median size of their existing home. For that bigger house, first-time trade-up buyers expect to pay a median price of $158,000. Other preferences:

- Three-car garages
- Nine-foot ceilings
- Two-story homes with one master bedroom suite plus three standard bedrooms.
- Eat-in kitchens with lots of counter space, a double sink, built-in microwave, and walk-in pantry. Corian counters were rated most desirable, followed by ceramic tile.
- A whirlpool tub; white toilet, tub, and sink, rather than colored bathroom fixtures
- A home office and a den/library were first and second choices; next on the list were a media room and an exercise room.

Some items—a minimum of three bedrooms, two baths, for instance—may be so essential that no compromise is possible.

These features make the needs list. In contrast, you could probably get by without the whirlpool tub, the fireplace, and the glass-walled sunroom. Put them on the wish list. You might start a don't-want list as well. Your personal pet peeves might include windowless kitchens, fake brick siding, too little closet space, a neighborhood dominated by toddlers or retirees. The point is to have a clear sense of your priorities if financial limitations force you to make hard choices about what is essential and what isn't. Once you've settled the central questions, you should be immune to the high-pressure tactics and hype that are too often part of real estate shopping.

The big decision in looking for a single-family house is whether to opt for an older model or something new. (See Tables 3-2 and 3-3 for pros and cons of both.) A Queen Anne charmer may offer winning architectural detail and larger rooms than you'll find in newer homes. On the other hand, those big rooms with high ceilings will cost more to heat. Newer homes are likely to be more energy-efficient, in part because they are better insulated. Recently built houses also offer the promise of having fewer structural problems in the early years. A relatively new roof should be less prone to leaks than one that has been weathering untouched for 20 years.

TABLE 3-2

The Older House

Its Advantages

Location
An older home is often situated near work, downtown shopping, public transportation, schools, libraries, and hospitals.

Space
Many older houses have large rooms with high ceilings, or lots of rooms that can be remodeled, if necessary. The price per square foot is lower than for a new house.

Ambience

The house is likely to be situated in a settled community with mature plantings and a variety of architectural styles. The interior may have lavish, owner-added touches such as stained glass, built-in cabinets and bookcases, and plaster ceiling medallions. It might even have a history (and a ghost) of its own.

Better Construction

This is often, but not always, true of older homes. You should have a professional inspector evaluate on a case-by-case basis. But if you crave slate roofs, hardwood floors, elaborate ceiling moldings, you're more likely to find them in an older house than in a new house in the same price range.

Lower Property Taxes

Property taxes may be less than in a comparable new home. Even if tax bills are roughly equal, they are more likely to remain stable than in a new community or development where streets, sewers, schools, and other infrastructure are still being built.

ITS DISADVANTAGES

Unpredictable Expenses

Old houses can charm your eye and wreck your budget. It is difficult to predict exactly when such items as a roof, furnace, or water heater will need replacing, but when one goes, it's usually a crisis. Renovation or remodeling may be necessary as well, and the work may cost significantly more than the initial estimates. If you need to borrow money for a major remodeling job, the loan will typically carry a higher interest rate than a first mortgage does.

Higher Utility Costs

Lack of insulation, ill-fitting windows and doors, and older systems make middle-aged houses more expensive to heat and cool.

TABLE 3-3

The New House

ITS ADVANTAGES

Predictable Cost and Low Maintenance
Assuming the house passed a professional inspection before you took possession of it, you can expect minimum repair and fix-up expenses. The major mechanical systems and the structural elements, like the roof, should have many years of repair-free life ahead. Your monthly mortgage payment, utilities, and yard expenses (lawn mowing, snow shoveling) should be virtually all the maintenance you pay for in the near future.

Modern Layout
New homes usually boast the latest in floor-plan designs, with leading-edge kitchen and bathroom arrangements, along with ample closets and storage space.

Lower Furnishing Costs
Many new homes come with wall-to-wall carpeting and window coverings, as well as more installed fixtures and appliances.

Energy Efficiency
A new house ought to be well insulated and snugly built, resulting in lower heating and cooling expenses. Storm windows and possibly screens may also be part of the deal.

Recreational Features
Community swimming pools, tennis courts, gymnasiums, and even bridle paths are often found in large, new developments.

ITS DISADVANTAGES

Location
New developments are usually located on the far fringes of suburbia. This means a long commute to downtown, for both work and entertainment.

Shoddy Quality
Flaws can take time to show up, and builders can be slow to correct errors. Also, the craftsmanship and detailing are unlikely to match that found in older homes.

That Raw Look
New developments can look barren, as developers tend to skimp on trees and foundation plantings. If substantial sections are still to be built, graded, and paved, you can expect noise, dust, and mud for months to come.

The Copycat Look
Some developments offer a limited choice of house styles. The sameness may not be apparent if you're seeing only model homes, but when several hundred are lined up together, you may be reminded of the old song deriding little boxes made of ticky-tacky that all look just the same.

On the other hand, a new house is apt to cost more than an older one to begin with—$133,000 and $112,900 were the respective median prices in 1995, for example. With the savings from buying the older model, you might be able to build in the whirlpool and fix the roof. You will have to calculate these kinds of trade-offs in terms of particular houses.

Consider early on whether a home's layout fits the way you really live. Families with small children, for example, often prefer a kitchen that opens onto the family room. That way Mom or Mr. Mom can keep an eye on the kids while preparing meals. Parents should also be mindful of traffic flow—the route you must take to get from room to room. In a toddler-filled household the family room should be well clear of the formal dining room, where you will entertain adult friends. Parents of teenagers often prefer that the master bedroom be placed some distance from their kids' rooms—preferably on the opposite side of the house—to save them from endless hours of Hootie and the Blowfish.

If you're a first-time buyer, you may have to look more diligently, be more creative, and display a greater willingness to compromise than your parents did on their starter house. The home of your dreams may be something to work toward, beyond your reach at the moment. Still, try to incorporate as many of your priorities as you can afford into your first house, then count on price appreciation to carry you to a better-feathered nest next time around. Example: Perhaps you can afford a $110,000 house now, by making a down payment of $10,000 and qualifying for a $100,000 mortgage. Suppose that after a few years the market value of the house rises to $125,000, and you owe the lender just $90,000. If your income and economic circumstances have improved sufficiently to support a larger mortgage loan, you have $25,000 to use as a down payment on a trade-up home—which may have the whirlpool bath and the fireplace you couldn't afford the first time around.

Coming Home: One Who Did It Right

When Mario Romero, 29, an assistant state attorney for Florida's Orange and Osceola counties, set out to look for a house, he was already thinking about resale value. Accordingly, he had clear priorities:

- It had to be a 3/2—that is, three bedrooms, two baths. "This area is very family oriented, and homes smaller than that don't sell well," says Romero, a bachelor.

- It had to be close to his job in Orlando and in a good school district. This narrowed the choice considerably.
- It had to fall within a sharply defined price range: $75,000–$79,000 tops. A local bank had assured the lawyer that they would finance a $60,000 mortgage. As for the down payment, for more than a year Romero had saved like Scrooge, $500 a month squirreled from his annual $25,000 salary. After paying $470 rent and taxes, he had precious little spare change. "I ate a lot of microwaveable burritos from 7-Eleven," Romero recalls. "But I had a big incentive to save because every penny meant a nicer house." His $7,000 savings, supplemented by an $8,000 gift from relatives, gave him a handsome $15,000 down payment.

Romero was short on both spare time and construction skills, so he ruled out buying a fixer-upper. With precious few hours for looking, he drove around evenings to winnow out the losers. "I would eyeball them from the curb and decide 'no way,' " says Romero, who emigrated from Cuba with his parents at age two. "If you have an appointment, you have to spend 20 minutes with the owner just to be polite." After five months of searching he was alerted to a brick-and-stucco model in Altamont Springs: "I hated it at first," he recalls. "It looked like an old folks' home. But I went in and saw it was in tip-top shape." Romero had the wit to realize he could rip out the peach carpet and repaint the mauve walls for very little money. After a little dickering the house was his for $74,500. His leftover cash went for gray-and-white Italian floor tiles, light gray paint, and a new refrigerator. "It's a pleasure to fix it up as I want," says Romero, whose salary has since risen to $36,500. "I figure every penny will come back to me when I sell." He's looking to trade up in a few years when his income reaches $40,000.

Being an owner has changed Romero from carefree single guy to responsible homemaker, however. "When I was at Tulane Law, I didn't care if a friend spilled beer on the carpet," he confesses. "But now that's no longer funny. I get a towel and soak it out."

CHECKPOINTS

- Talk with other household members about the kind of community you want to live in—rural, suburban, or urban. Give each person a chance to say what features would be important to him or her in the new home.
- Consider every option and look at one prime example of each. Then start winnowing your choices.
- For good investment potential and high resale value, pick a home that fits in well with other houses in the immediate area.
- No house is perfect, so develop a sense of which flaws are cosmetic—relatively cheap and easy to fix—and which are deal breakers because they are too costly or too complicated to make right.

A Sampler of American House Styles

1. NEW ENGLAND COLONIAL (1600–1700)

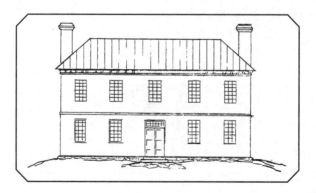

A boxlike appearance relieved by a prominent chimney and small, casement-style windows. The well-known saltbox shape extended the rear roof slope to provide extra rooms. The original one-room house was often expanded, even to adding a second story.

2. GEORGIAN (1700–1800)

The Georgian house is marked by a symmetrical composition enriched with classical detail. The facade often features a projecting, pedimented pavilion with pilasters or columns, and a Palladian or Venetian window.

3. ROMAN CLASSICISM OR PALLADIAN
(1790–1830)

This style, which often features a four-columned portico with a pediment enclosing a lunette, was popularized by Thomas Jefferson. The classical moldings are usually painted white.

4. SHINGLE STYLE (1880–1900)

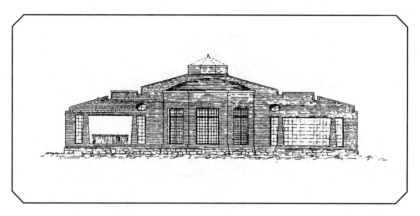

Two or three stories tall, this style is typified by a uniform covering of unpainted wood shingles. Sometimes the shingle siding takes an undulating or wave pattern. The roof is sweeping and sometimes steeply pitched.

5. BUNGALOW STYLE (1890–1940)

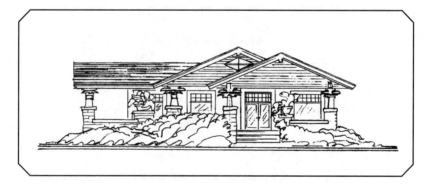

A simple, functional style, this one-story house had many variations but often featured a screened porch and broad, gently pitched gables. Wood shingles are common for the exterior finish, but stucco and brick were used as well. A lower gable often covers a porch, and a larger gable covers the main portion of the house.

6. PRAIRIE STYLE (1900–1920)

A one- or two-story house built with brick or timber and covered with stucco. The central portion rises a little higher than the flanking wings. Usually has a large, low chimney and a low-pitch roof with projecting eaves.

7. PUEBLO STYLE (1905–1940)

Characterized by battered walls, rounded corners, and flat roofs with projecting rounded roof beams (called vigas). Second and third stories are stepped back, resembling the pueblos of New Mexico and Arizona.

8. SPANISH COLONIAL REVIVAL (1915–1940)

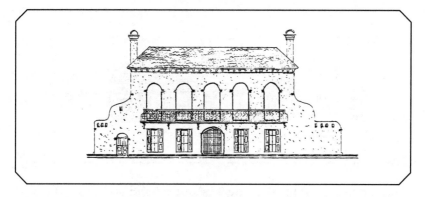

This style is typified by arches, columns, red-tiled hipped roofs, and arcaded porches. Stone or brick exterior walls may be left exposed or finished in plaster or stucco.

9. INTERNATIONAL STYLE
(1920–1945)

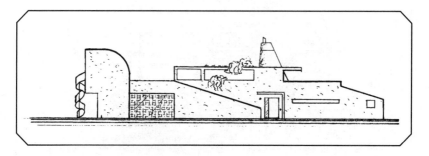

Look for flat rooftops, smooth wall surfaces, large expanses of window, and projecting or cantilevered balconies. The complete absence of ornamentation is the style's defining characteristic. Wood and metal casement windows may be permanently closed or fixed.

10. RANCH (SOUTHERN STYLE; 1950–1965)

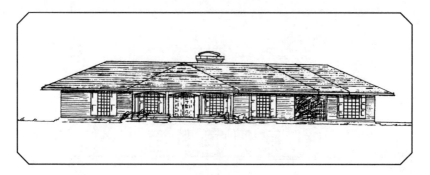

The ranch and split-level are not considered styles so much as building types, and they take any number of variations. Most have fixed blinds, fancy porch posts or wrought-iron supports, and contrasting brick veneer on the front.

11. VICTORIAN MODERN (1980–1990s)

A surge of interest in Queen Anne houses of the late nineteenth century launched a host of imitations. Look for a revival of elaborate spindle work, scrolls, and brackets, all typical of the architecture of the late Victorian era.

Credit: McGilvray Studio, New York, NY

SECTION II

STARTING THE HUNT: THE SEARCH PROCESS

CHAPTER 4

Special Resources for Special Buyers

Buying a house should not be like climbing Mount Everest—and federal, state, and local agencies are finally recognizing the fact. Community-lending plans with a range of special programs are serving to lower the barriers too often faced by first-time buyers, home shoppers with low to moderate incomes, and newcomers to America.

Overall trends are encouraging. Homeownership rates have been on the rise, and more households are achieving this part of the American dream. Even so, many immigrant families find that high housing costs and lack of access to mortgage money and to suitable homes still limit their opportunities.

The chief obstacle for many newcomers, however, is ignorance of how the homeownership process works in this country. They simply don't know how to get started. "Newcomers need a lot of encouragement, especially if English is a second language for them," explains Ana Maria da Hora, housing coordinator for the East Boston Ecumenical Council, which works to help immigrants become homeowners. "These people take it very seriously, but their emotions are mixed. They doubt that they can afford to buy, yet they are filled with excitement at the prospect. For many, it's their dream to have a place that belongs to them."

Da Hora is right about the dream of homeownership. The 1995 Fannie Mae National Housing Survey found that immigrants to the United States are almost three times as likely as all adults to list buying a home as their number one priority. The only milestones that rank higher are getting a college degree and getting involved at their child's school.

If you or someone you care about needs specialized help in entering the housing market, consider these options.

Look to Fannie Mae and Freddie Mac

Despite federal budget cuts, Fannie Mae (the Federal National Mortgage Association) has committed $1 trillion to finance over 10 million homes for needy families and communities before the end of the decade. The agency notes that a particular area of emphasis will be "helping new Americans—those who have taken the step of leaving the country of their birth to come to America in search of opportunity—achieve their goal of owning a home."

Fannie Mae and its close counterpart, Freddie Mac (the Federal Home Loan Mortgage Corporation), are two private companies created by the federal government to help banks and mortgage companies expand their loan offerings to all types of borrowers. Freddie and Fannie serve borrowers of many income levels. "Our mortgage purchases finance housing for borrowers whose annual incomes range from as low as $10,000 to $150,000 or more," says a Freddie spokesman. "However, most cluster closer to $50,000."

To tap into funds from Fannie and Freddie, however, you will have to deal with local lenders. When you shop around lending institutions, ask the loan officer if the institution participates in programs such as FannieNeighbors, available in more than 500 minority and low- to moderate-income communities nationwide, or Freddie's Home Values, which specializes in foreclosed homes that have been fully refurbished. The lenders may give the programs slightly different names, but they'll know what you mean.

Here's one example of the help available: The Fannie 97 mortgage, introduced in 1994, boasts a loan-to-value ratio of 97%—meaning that the buyer makes only a 3% down payment; the lender finances the rest. This is an excellent choice for a home buyer with a good income and credit history who has been unable to accumulate a hefty down payment. (The mortgage is limited to home buyers earning no more than an area's median income, with exceptions for some high-cost areas such as California, Hawaii, New York City, and Boston.) On a 25-year loan, borrowers may use up to 33% of their gross monthly income for housing expenses (principal, interest, taxes, and insurance), more generous than the standard ratio of 28%. Fannie Mae's Community Home Buyer's Program, introduced in 1990, makes it possible for buyers to obtain 95% financing up to a total of $207,000 for single-family homes. Programs change periodically, so ask about current offerings.

You can phone 1-800-7FANNIE for information about affordable loans, home buyer education, lists of lenders in your area, and guides describing the home-buying process. Be prepared however: the operator who answers will probably speak only English. Another resource is your state housing agency (a list of addresses and telephone numbers is provided starting on page 59). A representative should be able to tell you of any special programs that are available in your community.

Search in Your Neighborhood

If you're not sure what you can afford, or where to begin, or even whether you're ready for homeownership, look for one of the community-based housing programs, many of which work with Fannie Mae. They often have connections to state and city housing agencies as well. You'll find notices about such programs posted in local churches and stores, or you might hear neighbors discussing them. Many of the groups offer home maintenance training and guidance as well as counseling on the buying process.

In and around Boston—where, in 1992, the Federal Reserve Bank released a landmark study showing that local lenders discriminated against minority applicants—many groups are offering active guidance and encouragement to minorities and immigrants from many countries. For example, Calling Allston Brighton Home, a project of the local Community Development Corporation, organizes periodic home-buying education classes. To date, the program has graduated 250 would-be buyers; about one-quarter of them went on to purchase a home. Their average income: around $23,000. Classes are given in Spanish, Portuguese, Cantonese, and English. The English-language seminars are populated to overflowing with Irish, Bangladeshi, Indian, and Haitian students. Director Mary Helen Newberger brings in Boston-area lenders, a home inspector, a closing attorney, and real estate brokers to address the students. "When people walk in the first day, they are overwhelmed by doubt," says Newberger, a Peace Corps veteran. "But after five once-a-week classes, people know where to start. They have some contacts in the real estate community and a sense of how the system works. We make sure they are protected."

For many of Newberger's graduates, this has worked out fine. "The course cleared up many of my doubts," says Robson Nascimento, a 39-year-old Brazilian fitness instructor. "I especially liked the information about the home inspection, the sales and purchase agreement, and the tips on how to negotiate with the owner." Nascimento clearly learned the bargaining part well: he recently bought a house for $118,700; the owner had been asking $128,900.

Nothing's perfect, of course. Simon Choi, 60, a property tax assessor who took Newberger's course with his wife (in Cantonese), ultimately bought a condo from Fannie Mae. The class was "excellent," Choi says. The condo price was good. "I paid $55,000, but it's worth $77,000," he says. So what was the problem? "It's very painful dealing with those big organizations," Choi complains. "Too much red tape."

Know Your Rights

"Every American has a right to fair housing," states Henry Cisneros, secretary of housing and urban development. "The right to live where you choose, to raise a family, to own a home—in dignity and without fear of discrimination—is a fundamental right guaranteed to all. It cannot be denied to anyone because of race, color, national origin, religion, sex, familial status, or handicap."

This right is guaranteed by the Fair Housing Act, which covers most housing except (in some circumstances) owner-occupied buildings with no more than four units, single-family housing sold or rented without the use of a broker, and housing operated by organizations and private clubs that limit occupancy to members.

In the sale and rental of housing no one may take any of the following actions based on race, color, national origin, religion, sex, familial status (including having children under the age of 18 living with parents or legal custodians; pregnant women and people securing custody of children under 18), or handicap:

- Refuse to rent or sell housing
- Make housing unavailable
- Deny a dwelling
- Set different terms, conditions, or privileges for sale or rental of a dwelling
- Provide different housing services or facilities
- Falsely deny that housing is available for inspection, sale, or rental
- For profit, persuade owners to sell or rent (block busting)
- Deny anyone access to or membership in a facility or service (such as a multiple listing service) related to the sale or rental of housing

In addition, it is illegal for anyone to do the following:

- Threaten, coerce, intimidate, or interfere with anyone exercising a fair housing right or assisting others who exercise that right
- Advertise or make any statement that indicates a limit or preference based on race, color, national origin, religion, sex, familial status, or handicap (This prohibition against discriminatory advertising applies to single-family and owner-occupied housing that is otherwise exempt from the Fair Housing Act)

If you think your rights have been violated, the Department of Housing and Urban Development (HUD) is ready to help. You may use the toll-free hot line (800-669-9777) or send a Housing Discrimination Complaint Form to the HUD office nearest you. HUD will notify you if it cannot complete an investigation within 100 days of receiving your complaint. (If you think you have been discriminated against in shopping for a mortgage loan, see page 136 in Chapter 9.)

CHECKPOINTS

- Don't let ignorance of the real estate market prevent you from achieving your goal of homeownership. Look around your community for courses that can introduce you to the homeownership process.
- Ask local lenders if they participate in special mortgage loan programs sponsored by Fannie Mae, Freddie Mac, or state and local housing agencies.
- Know your rights to fair housing, and speak up if you feel an owner or broker is violating them.

STATE HOUSING AGENCIES

Alabama Housing Finance Authority
2000 Interstate Park Dr., Suite 408
Montgomery, Ala. 36109
Phone: 334-244-9200

Alaska Housing Finance Corporation
520 East 34th Ave., 2nd fl.
Anchorage, Alaska 99503
Phone: 907-561-1900

Arkansas Development Finance Authority
P.O. Box 8023
Little Rock, Ark. 72203-8023
Phone: 501-682-5900

California Housing Finance Agency
1121 L St., 7th fl.
Sacramento, Calif. 95814
Phone: 916-322-3991

Colorado Housing and Finance Authority
1981 Blake St.
Denver, Col. 80202-1272
Phone: 303-297-2432

Connecticut Housing Finance Authority
999 West St.
Rocky Hill, Conn. 06067-4005
Phone: 203-721-9501

Delaware State Housing Authority
18 The Green
Dover, Del. 19901
Phone: 302-739-4263

Florida Housing Finance Agency
227 North Bronough St., Suite 5000
Tallahassee, Fla. 32301-1329
Phone: 904-488-4197

Georgia Housing and Finance Authority
60 Executive Parkway South, Suite 250
Atlanta, Ga. 30329
Phone: 404-679-4840

Hawaii Housing Finance and Development Corporation
677 Queen St.
Honolulu, Haw. 96813
Phone: 808-587-0640

Idaho Housing and Finance Association
P.O. Box 7899
Boise, Idaho 83707-1899
Phone: 208-331-4882

Illinois Housing Development Authority
401 North Michigan Ave., Suite 900
Chicago, Ill. 60611
Phone: 312-836-5200

Indiana Housing Finance Authority
115 West Washington St.
Merchants Plaza, South Tower, Suite 1350
Indianapolis, Ind. 46204
Phone: 317-232-7777

Iowa Finance Authority
100 East Grand Ave., Suite 250
Des Moines, Iowa 50309
Phone: 515-242-4990

Kansas Department of Commerce & Housing
Division of Housing
700 SW Harrison St., Suite 1300
Topeka, Kans. 66603-3712
Phone: 913-296-5865

Kentucky Housing Corporation
1231 Louisville Rd.
Frankfort, Ky. 40601
Phone: 502-564-7630

Louisiana Housing Finance Agency
200 Lafayette St., Suite 300
Baton Rouge, La. 70801
Phone: 504-342-1320

Maine State Housing Authority
353 Water St.
Augusta, Maine 04330-4633
Phone: 207-626-4600

**Maryland Department of Housing
& Community Development**
100 Community Place
Crownsville, Md. 21032-2023
Phone: 410-514-7800

Massachusetts Housing Finance Agency
One Beacon St.
Boston, Mass. 02108-4805
Phone: 617-854-1000

Michigan State Housing Development Authority
Plaza One Building, 5th fl.
401 South Washington Square
Lansing, Mich. 48933
Phone: 517-373-8370

Minnesota Housing Finance Agency
400 Sibley St., Suite 300
St. Paul, Minn. 55101
Phone: 612-296-7608

Mississippi Home Corporation
840 East River Place, Suite 605
Jackson, Miss. 39202
Phone: 601-354-6062

Missouri Housing Development Commission
3435 Broadway
Kansas City, Mo. 64111
Phone: 816-759-6600

Montana Board of Housing/Housing Division
836 Front St.
Helena, Mont. 59620-0528
Phone: 406-444-3040

Nebraska Investment Finance Authority
1230 "O" St.
Lincoln, Nebr. 68505
Phone: 402-434-3900

Nevada Housing Division
1802 North Carson, Suite 154
Carson City, Nev. 89701
Phone: 702-687-4258

New Hampshire Housing Finance Authority
P.O. Box 5087
Manchester, N.H. 03108
Phone: 603-472-8623

New Jersey Housing and Mortgage Finance Agency
637 South Clinton Ave.
Trenton, N.J. 08650-2085
Phone: 609-278-7400

New Mexico Mortgage Authority
P.O. Box 2047
Albuquerque, N. Mex. 87103
Phone: 505-843-6880

New York City Housing Development Corporation
75 Maiden Lane, 8th fl.
New York, N.Y. 10038
Phone: 212-344-8080

New York State Division of Housing and Community Renewal
Hampton Plaza
38-40 State St.
Albany, N.Y. 12207
Phone: 518-486-3370

New York State Housing Finance Agency/SONYMA
641 Lexington Ave.
New York, N.Y. 10022
Phone: 212-688-4000

North Carolina Housing Finance Agency
P.O. Box 28066
Raleigh, N.C. 27611
Phone: 919-781-6115

North Dakota Housing Finance Agency
P.O. Box 1535
Bismarck, N. Dak. 58502-1535
Phone: 701-328-9800

Ohio Housing Finance Agency
77 South High St., 26th fl.
Columbus, Ohio 43266-0413
Phone: 614-466-7970

Oklahoma Housing Finance Agency
1140 Northwest 63rd, Suite 200
Oklahoma City, Okla. 73116
Phone: 405-848-1144

**Oregon Housing and Community
Services Department**
1600 State St.
Salem, Oreg. 97310-0302
Phone: 503-986-2000

Pennsylvania Housing Finance Agency
P.O. Box 8029
Harrisburg, Pa. 17105-8029
Phone: 717-780-3800

Puerto Rico Housing Finance Corporation
P.O. Box 71361
San Juan, P.R. 00936-1361
Phone: 809-765-7577

**Rhode Island Housing and Mortgage
Finance Corporation**
44 Washington St.
Providence, R.I. 02903
Phone: 401-751-5566

South Carolina State Housing Finance and Development Authority
919 Bluff Rd.
Columbia, S.C. 29201
Phone: 803-734-2000

South Dakota Housing Development Authority
221 South Central
P.O. Box 1237
Pierre, S.D. 57501-1237
Phone: 605-773-3181

Tennessee Housing Development Agency
404 James Robertson Parkway, Suite 1114
Nashville, Tenn. 37243-0900
Phone: 615-741-2400

Texas Department of Housing and Community Affairs
P.O. Box 13941, Suite 300
Austin, Tex. 78711-3941
Phone: 512-475-3800

Utah Housing Finance Agency
554 South 300 East
Salt Lake City, Utah 84111
Phone: 801-521-6950

Vermont Housing Finance Agency
P.O. Box 408, 164 St. Paul St.
Burlington, Vt. 05402-0408
Phone: 802-864-5743

Virginia Housing Development Authority
601 South Belvidere St.
Richmond, Va. 23220-6504
Phone: 804-782-1986

Washington State Housing Finance Commission
1000 Second Ave., Suite 2700
Seattle, Wash. 98104-1046
Phone: 206-464-7139

West Virginia Housing Development Fund
814 Virginia St., East
Charleston, W.Va. 25301
Phone: 304-345-6475

Wisconsin Housing and Economic Development Authority
P.O. Box 1728
Madison, Wis. 53701-1728
Phone: 608-266-7884

Wyoming Community Development Authority
123 South Durbin St.
Casper, Wyo. 82602
Phone: 307-265-0603

Source: National Council of State Housing Agencies

CHAPTER 5

Working with a Real Estate Agent

Real estate agents work hard for their clients, are well paid by their clients, and negotiate to win the best price and terms for their clients.

Trouble is, you aren't the client. The seller is.

Surprised? Many others make the same mistake. To clarify the issue, most states now require the real estate agent to explain who he or she represents to all parties to a transaction. Yet uncertainty still rules in many buyers' minds. Consider this plaintive question recently posed on the World Wide Web to the National Association of Realtors (NAR):

My husband and I were thinking of making an offer on a property when I happened to tell the listing agent that even though we'd start at $80,000, we would consider paying the listed price of $85,500. Was I ever shocked when I heard he passed on this information to the seller. Was this ethical?

67

The action was not only ethical, it was "legally correct," replied the NAR. The listing agent is employed to represent the seller, and anything the agent knows that might affect his client's position must be communicated to him. This obligation filters down to include "brokers and agents from other offices who would show the property as subagents of the listing broker and seller," the NAR says.

This strong pro-seller tilt to most real estate transactions is changing as buyer-brokers and other kinds of agencies enter the field. To protect yourself, however, you need to know what role each one plays and where his or her loyalties lie. Here's a run-down of the real estate sales professionals with whom you might be dealing and a brief description of their responsibilities:

A **real estate agent** or **sales associate** is the person with whom you will spend the most time. He or she (mostly she) must be licensed by the state but works under the supervision of a **real estate broker,** who has attained that status by meeting state licensing standards and working for several years as an agent. A **principal broker** is an owner of a brokerage firm; she may have other brokers working under her supervision. The principal broker is responsible to the public for the activities of the firm's entire sales force. Both brokers and sales associates, however, are properly called agents because they act on behalf of their clients.

The broker and the sales associate may also call themselves **Realtor** and **Realtor associate,** respectively, if they belong to the National Association of Realtors, a trade organization with 750,000 members, as well as to the state association and the local board of Realtors. While the title "Realtor" doesn't guarantee a person's abilities, it does indicate a commitment to the profession and that the member subscribes to the NAR's code of ethics.

In a traditional transaction, an agent may chauffeur you from house to house, but her clients are the sellers, and the goal generally is a quick sale at a high price. These agents are paid a slice off the top of the gross sale price—reflecting the traditional arrangement in which the **listing agent,** who brought the property to the brokerage, and the **selling agent,** who located the buyer, split the sales commission, usually 6% or 7%. The listing agent and the selling agent may work for different brokerages. A **listing agreement** gives brokers the right to market a property at a given price for a given period, often 60 or 90 days. The listing broker may advertise the property, but he or she also cooperates with other brokers through a **multiple listing service,** or **MLS.** All MLS members can look up the property and market it to prospective customers as subagents through the original listing agreement. To help follow the money flows, here's a table showing how the commission you pay when you buy a property might be divided under three different sales scenarios.

COMMISSION FLOWCHART

• Sale price of the house	$200,000
• Commission value at 6%	12,000

• Broker Adams both lists and sells the house; Adams's commission is:	12,000
• Adams lists the house; agent Baker, who works for Adams's firm, sells the house. Adams and Baker each get:	6,000
• Adams lists the house, but agent Carter, who works for broker Davis, sells the house. Brokers Adams and Davis each get:	6,000
• However, broker Davis must split his share with agent Carter, so each winds up with:	3,000

You may also run across different types of agencies, some of them offering greater degrees of loyalty and service to the buyer rather than the seller. Here are the principal types you're likely to encounter:

• **Seller's agencies** work in the traditional manner. Owners recruit them to list a property on the market, and they solicit buyers for the house. You can expect a seller's agent to introduce you to properties in your desired location and price range; list past sales and current listings for a specific vicinity; suggest financing sources; provide you with information on property taxes, utilities, and school districts that serve individual properties. Since the seller pays the commission, however, the seller's broker works for him. For that reason, don't ever tell an agent, "Let's offer the Tutweilers $120,000 for their house, but we'll go to $140,000 if necessary." Wait until the seller refuses your first offer before you volunteer a higher one, and don't disclose the top price you will pay.

• **Single-agency brokers** are a newer alternative to seller's agents. These firms accept property listings but also work as buyer's brokers. They contract to find a home and negotiate price and terms for a buyer who signs on with them. The buyer sometimes pays the agent's fee; more often, the seller's agent splits the commission with the buyer's agent. The single-agency broker is supposed to arrange that the firm never represents both the buyer and seller in the same deal. If you express interest in one of the houses that the agency has listed, the broker should refer you (or the seller) to a colleague outside the agency to avoid a conflict of interest. An agent representing both buyer and seller could pressure you into paying more for the house than it is worth to fatten his commission.

• **Exclusive buyer-brokers** work only with buyers and don't take property listings. Their task is to help you find the best deal at the lowest price. Buyer-brokers can open up the entire local housing market for you. Not only do they have access to the multiple listing service, but they also can assist with the purchase of homes that sellers are trying to market themselves—called **fizbos** (for sale by owner). A traditional agent will have little luck interesting an independent seller in showing you his home. If you buy the house, the seller is obligated to pay the agent a commission. But a buyer-broker has the same entrée to those houses that you do, since you, not the seller, are paying the fee.

Buyer-brokers, a relatively new phenomenon, are still a small slice of the real estate business. Compensation arrangements vary widely, but you may be asked to pay an initial retainer of $200–$500, up to 1% of your expected purchase price, which will be deducted from the final bill. Then the buyer either splits the commission on a home with the selling agent, charges a flat rate ($500–$5,000), or gets paid by the hour (commonly about $200). Remember that compensation is negotiable, so speak with various brokers, compare their offerings, and choose the arrangement that suits you best. A flat fee is often the best arrangement for you because the broker will then have no incentive to guide you toward more expensive properties to increase the compensation.

Since extra cash may be hard for you to come by at closing time, however, you might try for the following deal: When you and the broker submit an offer to an owner, include a provision that the listing broker and the buyer-broker divide the commission equally—usually the most popular arrangement. Alternatively, you and your broker can agree on a fixed fee; then ask the owner to pay 3% to the listing broker and give you, the buyer, a 3% credit at the closing. You pay your broker from the credit—and if you end up owing your broker more than that amount, don't whine. A small credit means you got a reduced price—which is, after all, your chief goal as a buyer. This tactic is unlikely to work in a seller's market, however, where values are rising rapidly and there is intense demand for housing.

Geochemist Susan Gunn used a buyer-broker in her recent

move to the Washington, D.C., area. Instead of receiving the standard 3% commission of $8,550 on Gunn's $285,000 Great Falls, Virginia, house, buyer-broker Stephen Israel got paid $200 an hour. Gunn's total bill: $5,000. Israel, president of Buyer's Edge in Bethesda, Maryland, says he typically saves his clients about 8% of what they would otherwise pay for their houses. Even better, buyer-brokers are more apt to point out flaws in the homes they show. "Sometimes we'd pull up to a house and Stephen wouldn't even let me get out of the car because he could tell there was a structural problem," says Gunn. "I really got the feeling he was working for me."

• **Dual-agency brokers** have the most complicated arrangements of all, but they are becoming common as more buyers insist on a professional representative. Conflicts can easily arise, however. A disclosed dual agent may agree to work for you as a buyer-broker. But the company he works for may have listed the house that you are eventually interested in. What then? The agent tries to stay neutral and act as facilitator. The arrangement appeals to real estate pros because 100% of the commission stays in-house. Critics, however, liken the arrangement to a single lawyer representing both husband and wife in a divorce. Many states, including California, Hawaii, New York, and Pennsylvania, have adopted strong disclosure requirements for dual-agency arrangements, and more states are considering them. No state permits dual agency without disclosure. You are best off avoiding this situation when you can.

Rounding up Agent Candidates

Depending on luck and newspaper ads is probably the worst way to find your real estate agent. Asking friends for recommendations is often the best. In addition, you can call the local board of

Realtors and ask for the names of recent Realtors of the Year or residential sales specialists. You can also ask branches of national chains such as Century 21 or Coldwell Banker for referrals; if you don't like the first agent, don't hesitate to ask for another.

As a customer, you'll get the surest representation from a single-agency broker or an exclusive buyer-broker. While they might be as scarce as 5% mortgages in some areas, particularly the Northeast, their numbers are rising fast. According to the NAR's 1995 survey of real estate firms, 46% said at least one of their sales associates had been involved as a buyer-broker in a residential sale—a sharp increase from the 30% recorded in a 1990 survey. Current estimates, says the NAR, show that buyer-brokerage may account for 10%–20% of all transactions. If you have difficulty locating one, call your local board of Realtors, a title insurance company, or a real estate attorney and ask for names. Or consult one or more of the following referral services:

• **Buyer's Resource** (800-4-BUYERS; http://www.buyers resource.com/brinfo), a franchise agent for exclusive buyer-brokers, has 60 offices nationwide. Consumers seeking information or referrals can call the hot line number.

• **National Association of Exclusive Buyer Agents** (800-986-2322; http://www.naeba.org) is a nonprofit agency for agents who do not take property listings of any kind. Their database lists 325 agents, but they will draw upon outside names if they cannot find a member in your area.

• **National Association of Real Estate Buyer's Brokers** (415-591-5446) has a database of 2,500 agents who are either single-agency or exclusively buyer-brokers. The group will give as many references as are listed in your desired location.

Screening the Contenders

With names in hand, you are ready to conduct interviews. You're looking for an active agent with a track record for closing sales. See if she can explain financing alternatives and provide detailed information on a variety of neighborhoods. Does she have listings in your price range, in communities that interest you?

Watch for obvious personality clashes or basic differences in outlook. You want someone who asks intelligent questions and listens closely to your answers. Avoid any agent who's so aggressive that she could manipulate you into a deal you might not want. Check at least three recent references for each candidate you're seriously considering. Most buyers will stop there, but if you have any lingering doubts, phone the local Better Business Bureau or the local district attorney's office to see if there are past or pending complaints against the agent or the office.

Finally, remember the courtesy that you owe the agent. There is an etiquette to this ritual: you may work with several agents—but only one at a time. If you move on to a second person, be up front about what houses you've seen and the agent who showed them. Before you link up with a stable of agents, be aware that you might be setting yourself up for an unnecessary and confusing duplication of effort. Chances are that all the brokers will be plugged into the same multiple listing service (unless you are searching in communities that are a considerable distance apart) and so will be trying to show you the same properties. Still, if you've been in the passenger seat for weeks with the same broker driving you around, it may be time to find an agent with a broader selection of homes or one who is more keyed in to your needs.

CHECKPOINTS

- Remember that a traditional broker represents the seller's interests, and keep your bidding strategy to yourself. Don't divulge the highest you'll go on an offer or the best terms you'll give the seller.
- Consider using a buyer-broker if there are experienced, reliable candidates available.
- When you have a list of sales agents' names, interview the most promising candidates and check their references. Look for an active agent with a strong track record of making sales. Discuss what the agent can do for you and what compensation he or she expects. Let them compete for your business.
- Play fair with the agents. Let them know what houses you have seen and with whom. Don't try to cut an agent out of a commission by dealing directly with the seller. You're being unethical, and the agent might be entitled to sue for damages.

CHAPTER 6

Inspecting the Candidates

If you have the luxury of time, make multiple visits, at different hours, to any house that you're seriously considering buying. Even if you're tied to a frenzied schedule, plan on at least two visits to all the top-ranked contenders. The first will probably be an informal tour. The final visit should be a full inspection by you before making a purchase offer. (This is no substitute for a formal professional inspection, however, which you arrange before you make an offer, to help you in the bidding process, or after you have signed a sales contract. For details about hiring and using a professional inspector, see Chapter 10.) Here's how to handle both the informal once-over and the formal top-to-bottom scrutiny.

The Initial Walk-Through

You probably know your priorities sufficiently that you won't need a checklist, but do bring a notepad to record your comments and a tape measure. (If you want a missing partner to see the house, bring a videocamera.) Your agent will probably give you an information sheet about the house, and that should spell out the basic data—the square footage of both the lot and house, number of bedrooms and baths, property taxes, and the like. If the house looks like a strong candidate, sketch out the floor plan if one isn't provided.

You can make some preliminary judgments before you enter the house: Do you like the way the building looks in its particular setting? Does it appear well tended? Is there sufficient privacy? Enough lawn—or too much?

If the house meets your basic needs in terms of location, style, size, and price, then consider some nuts-and-bolts items: Do the roof, gutters, and exterior finish appear to be in good repair? Is there crumbling mortar in the masonry? Be wary of worn shingles and foundation cracks. Take a look at the furnace, electrical service, and appliances. Estimate their age and condition. If the floor plan doesn't suit you, decide if you can reconfigure the space or perhaps build an addition. Check ceilings, walls, and under sinks for signs of water damage.

If the house sparks your initial interest, you'll also want to find out as much as possible about the sellers on this first visit. Why are they selling—job transfer, divorce or death of spouse, a need for less (or more) space? Are they scheduled to close on a new house? Find out how long they have lived in the house and what they paid for it; if they won't say, public land records can tell you in many places. Or you can try the *Consumer Reports* magazine service, which will tell you actual sale prices of houses or condominiums in most places. One 10-minute phone call (800-847-7423), costing $10, gives you information on as many as 24 properties sold from six weeks to six years ago. Anything you learn will make you a stronger negotiator, should you decide to make a bid.

Think like a detective: you're here to gather information, not to give it out. It's hard not to be candid in a friendly conversation, but try to muzzle yourself and your mate. Avoid off-the-cuff comments like "Oh, Johnny's trundle bed would just fit along that wall—and the hamster cage could go right in that corner." Once you start placing the furniture, sellers know they've got you.

Returning for a Full Inspection

Whether the home of your dreams is a 100-year-old Queen Anne or so new the windows still have the manufacturer's stickers on them, a thorough inspection is essential before making a bid. It can also help winnow the list when you're trying to evaluate several promising candidates. Call in a professional inspector later if your own investigation reveals serious flaws or if you're puzzled by what you've found. And certainly have a professional take a look before you take possession.

To scope out a house you'll need the owner's permission, plus a basic tool kit that includes

- a flashlight
- a screwdriver
- a pair of binoculars
- a marble
- a circuit tester
- a tape measure

Optional additions are a stepladder (to get to the attic) and an extension ladder (to get to the roof). If climbing around the roof makes you or the owner nervous, as it well might, use the binoculars to check out the shingles and gutters.

Set aside about three hours for purposeful prowling, beginning with a stroll around the grounds. Do driveways and sidewalks slope away from the house? (Good sign.) Has soil near the house settled? (Not so good.) Two of the most serious outdoor problems are improper grading around the foundation of the house and depressions in the lawn within 25 feet of the dwelling. Both result in rainwater collecting around the foundation, which can lead to flooding in the basement or crawl space. In a finished basement, water seeping through the walls damages the wood framing and wall finish materials and will eventually cause mildew problems. If water enters a crawl space, it can evaporate and migrate through the house to the attic. Icy weather will cause this moisture-laden air to cool and change from vapor to droplets. If the weather is cold enough, frost may form on the underside of the roof sheathing and rot it over time. Metal truss plates and nails will rust. Water may condense on uninsulated metal ductwork and run down on the ceiling below. So even if the roof doesn't leak, water can cause problems in the attic.

To remedy the difficulty, a landscape company can build up the slope of the soil to direct water away from the foundation or dig ditches in a swamplike yard and install drainage pipes to carry away the water. But these can be costly fixes, so factor them into your purchase bid.

Examine masonry walls, walks, driveways, and patios for cracks and mortar deterioration. Poke joints with the screwdriver; if mortar crumbles easily, you'll need a mason for repairs. Look for tilting or bulging in the retaining walls, those masonry bulwarks that hold back the earth and form terraces in the yard or along the driveway. If the distortions are obvious at a glance, call in a structural engineer to estimate the cost of repairs.

Use your binoculars to check for rust, holes, or leaks in the gutters and downspouts. Downspouts, which ought to be no more than 20 feet apart, should divert water well away from the house. Look for evidence of holes or rain spilling over the gutters—a small trench directly below them, for instance, or marks of water backsplash on the side of the house.

When you study the roof through the binoculars (or from the ladder, if you're nimble), note any cracked or worn shingles. Curled or buckled asphalt shingles with dark, barren spots should be replaced immediately. If you spy that kind of deterioration on more than half the shingles, the house may need a new roof within a year. While you're up there, examine the flashing—the metal strips between roof slopes and around the tops of dormers and the base of the chimneys. Twisted or broken flashing often results in leaks, so you'll need a roofer to replace and reseal it.

Use your screwdriver—carefully—to check for damage in outside walls. Gentle probing into discolored patches on wood siding and mortar joints between bricks should reveal any rotten or deteriorated spots. A handful of unsound clapboards or deteriorated mortar around bricks can usually be fixed by a carpenter or mason for a few hundred dollars. Stair-step cracks visible on the inside or the outside of the foundation are a sign that it may have settled unevenly. Find out from a pro—an inspector, mason, or structural engineer—if these are serious. Similar cracks may also occur in brick exterior walls. Walls should not buckle outward or appear to have moved sideways off the foundation. Check this by standing at one corner and looking along the length of the wall for bulges in the siding. Porches, attached garages, and additions have engineering problems if there are large gaps between them and the house or if they appear to be falling away from the main structure.

Also inspect outside walls for thin, branchlike mud tubes; these are termite freeways leading from nests in the ground to the appetizing wood beams that support the house. Probe infested areas with the screwdriver to check the extent of the damage. If exterior decay is pronounced—it extends more than about 10 square feet or all along the lowest few feet of an entire wall—call in a professional inspector or a structural engineer no matter how good the condition of the rest of the house.

While you're still outside, take a close look at nearby trees. Diseased or dead trees will have to be cut down; overhanging limbs will have to be trimmed because they might break off and damage the roof during a storm.

Start your indoor inspection at the top and work down

methodically (or the reverse). Even if the attic is only a crawl space under the roof, take a look up there with your flashlight. You should see air vents or some mechanical venting devices that allow moist air to escape and at least six inches of insulation between the attic floor beams to keep heat out or in (more would be better in cold climates).

Next, train your flashlight on the inside of the roof. Look for dark stains and rust trails from nails, both signs of leaks or condensed moisture. A few small leaks are no cause for alarm, especially if the shingles seem fine, but a heavy, damp mark or mildew probably means professional patchwork is needed. If a large leak has been left unattended for some time, expect to find water stains in ceilings and on walls below.

When you come downstairs, check all rooms for cracks and water stains in walls and ceilings. Open windows and doors to make sure they work properly. Place your marble in the center of the floor in every carpetless room. If it rolls swiftly to a wall, you've found a tilted floor. When accompanied by cracks around doorjambs and window frames, doors that don't close easily, and windows that jam halfway, that could be a sign of serious structural problems. In a carpeted room, cracks around door frames and misaligned doors or windows should kindle your suspicion. These problems are usually difficult and expensive to correct.

Count the electrical outlets in every room, and check each one with the circuit tester. Turn on all appliances to make sure they're in working order. In houses that are more than 25 years old, you should check for clogged water pipes by turning on a tap in the uppermost bathroom. Testing first the cold water, next the hot, open the sink taps fully and let them run. Then, with your eye on the sink faucets, open the bathtub taps. If the flow into the sink suddenly drops more than about 25%, it's likely that corrosion inside galvanized pipes is restricting the water flow and you'll probably need major repairs within five years.

In the basement, water marks along the walls suggest

flooding. Be suspicious of a freshly painted basement: the owners may be trying to disguise the evidence. A wet basement's exact cause is notoriously difficult to diagnose. The solution might be as simple—and inexpensive—as correcting a misaligned downspout that has been sluicing water from the gutters into the ground next to the foundation. Or the job could be as drastic as excavating the entire foundation and waterproofing the foundation walls. Don't take chances with a wet basement: call in a professional inspector or an engineer. If the expert is worried, deduct the estimated cost of repair from the selling price or look for another house.

Bulges in the basement walls accompanied by horizontal cracks more than one-quarter of an inch wide suggest that pressure around the foundation may be greater than the walls can stand. Summon an inspector before you buy the house. A few small vertical cracks, especially those filled with dust or the remains of generations of spiders, might only be evidence that the house eased itself into a more comfortable position many years ago. Look for small piles of sawdust near the beams. They are evidence of wood-boring insects, such as carpenter ants. An exterminator can usually rid the house of these and other insects.

The basement is also the best place to judge the condition of the electrical wiring. Look for frayed or loose wires attached to overhead beams. Open the door to the square gray electrical panel, which is usually on the wall in plain sight. Scorch marks around fuses and a burning smell are signs of an electrical overload. Look on the inside of the door for a label stating the house voltage and amperage. As a rule, the house needs 240 volts; the current amperage standard is 100–200. For today's powerhouses, however, 100 amps is probably insufficient service. An electrician can upgrade the power supply.

No matter if it's January, run the air-conditioning for at least 15 minutes. Next, get the furnace running and take a look inside. Heavy oil stains on the floor or a wobbling gas flame are signs of an old and tired heating system. While you're at it, examine the inside of the furnace frame for rust or watermarks.

Wily owners who have spruced up the basement to disguise water damage often forget to clean inside the furnace frame. The water heater—a white cylindrical tank about four feet tall—is usually located near the furnace. Check around the base for rust chips; they indicate deterioration.

If you're giving the once-over to a new house, you probably won't find the same structural ills that beset many older dwellings, but you should be on the lookout for shoddy workmanship and inferior materials.

As you walk around inside a new house, look for such low-quality items as hollow-core wood doors, thin metal sliding doors, and single-thickness window glass instead of double-glazed thermal panes. Take note of the appliances: builders frequently install no-frills models to cut costs. If you don't recognize the brand name on the kitchen or laundry gear, or if a dearth of buttons and chrome suggests a spartan issue, ask for higher-quality stuff. Or at least use the bottom-of-the-line machines as a negotiating point.

Be on the lookout for damage caused by careless workers. Chips in Formica counters, sinks, tubs, and woodwork should be repaired before you move in. The carpeting should fit snugly, with no discernible seams. If joint tape is visible anywhere on walls or ceilings, or if the paint doesn't cover the walls properly, demand that the builder redo the finish work. The entire house should be spotless: sparkling windows, no paint or plaster drops on cabinets and floors, and no dust.

What you don't see in a new house can be just as important as visible flaws. In their haste to move on to the next job, workers have been known to forget to install the baseboards, the insulation in the attic, the caulking around the bathtub. "In new construction, the flaws are wherever a subcontractor was working at four-thirty on his last day on the job," says home inspector Stan Harbuck of Salt Lake City. "They jury-rig it, then pack up and go. Sometimes they cause chips, scratches, or other damage in their wake." But they won't get away with that if you keep a vigilant eye.

CHECKPOINTS

• On your first visit, establish that the house meets your basic needs in terms of size, price, and location. Decide if the architectural style pleases you. But don't be put off by a dowdy interior. Cosmetic changes, like paint, wallpaper, and carpeting, are relatively cheap and easy to do.

• The more you like the house, the more you should hold your tongue. Pretend you're a detective and soak up as much information about the owners and the house as possible, without tipping your hand.

• If the house passes muster on the first walk-through, give it a serious inspection yourself before making a bid. If there appear to be serious flaws, call in a structural engineer or a professional inspector and get a repair estimate. Adjust your bid accordingly, or look for another house.

CHAPTER 7

Condos, Co-ops, and Their Close Cousins

Condominiums and cooperatives have traditionally been the housing equivalent of prom-night wallflowers. Affluent buyers snubbed them, opting instead for the traditional single-family home on a grassy plot. But tastes change, and the wallflowers are starting to waltz these days. The luxury market for condos and co-ops is surging as empty nesters and others move in, attracted by urban and recreational amenities, round-the-clock security, and hassle-free living. Two examples:

• **In Atlanta's fashionable Buckhead area rises the Wakefield,** a luxury cooperative that sold 16 of its 22 apartments before it was even completed. "Our average buyer was coming out of a $3 million house into a $1.5 million co-op unit," says architect-developer George Heery. The attraction: large, high-ceiling rooms in a building with lavish services, ample security, and an elegant lobby. "My owners want discreet, not flashy," Heery says. According to Herbert Levy, executive director of the National Association of Housing Cooperatives, the Wakefield is the first new, market-rate co-op to be built anywhere in the nation in the past 10 years.

• **On Chicago's most exclusive street,** two historic buildings have recently been through the conversion process. The Mayfair, at 181 East Lake Shore Drive, was transformed from a hotel to a condominium; the rental building next door became a luxury co-op. Both new projects sold briskly, at prices ranging from $1.25 million to $5 million.

Such high-end homes remain the exception, of course. But the middle- and low-price parts of the condo and co-op market are also experiencing a reinvigoration. In Manhattan, where rentals are scarce and pricey, co-op sales rose 13% in 1995, spurred by a significant increase in the purchase of studio and one-bedroom apartments. Nationwide there are more than 200,000 condo communities and about 8,500 cooperative buildings, says Kathleen Luzik, vice president of the Washington-based National Cooperative Bank, which specializes in loans to all sorts of cooperative organizations. These buildings house about 32 million residents.

More than 6,000 residential co-op buildings are situated in and around New York City, with 42% of them in Manhattan. Most of the others are clustered in neighborhoods of Washington, D.C., Chicago, San Francisco, and parts of Florida. These are primarily conversions from rental housing (including, in a few cases in Florida, houseboats).

As for condominiums, they pop up almost everywhere, in every imaginable form. There are commercial lofts and office buildings in urban centers, luxury apartments carved from gilded mansions, snug nests fitted into former churches, schools, and even farm silos. Finally, of course, there are the virtually self-contained villages of freestanding houses, complete with pools, golf courses, tennis courts, and community activity buildings, and giant planned communities such as Reston, Virginia, with 19,000 units.

A broad range of financial and legal subtleties distinguish co-ops from condos—and from their subculture of near relations such as planned-unit developments (PUDs), common-interest communities, and reciprocal-easement communities. (Note that the architectural form of the building gives you no clue whatsoever to the ownership form of the property. Many people wrongly assume, for instance, that all town houses are condos. Not true.)

Since the form of ownership has serious legal implications, your jumping-off point is to be sure you know what type of dwelling you are considering. Here are some basic descriptions:

1. *Cooperative living.* In a co-op, you buy shares of stock in a corporation or association that owns the entire building and serves as landlord. You are its tenant, and a **proprietary lease** gives you the exclusive right of occupancy of a specific unit. The lease sets the terms and conditions for occupancy, subleasing, and maintenance of your unit. **Stock, shares,** or **membership certificates** serve as your proof of ownership in the corporation. You pay a monthly fee, usually called a **maintenance charge,** which the association uses to cover your proportionate share of the bills for mortgage payments, repairs, operations, and taxes. In a well-run co-op, part of your maintenance will be stashed in a reserve fund for eventual replacement or renovation of major systems. The portion of your maintenance used to pay municipal taxes and interest on the building's loan or mortgage will be tax-deductible to you.

Besides the documents just mentioned, you and your lawyer will want to read the **articles of incorporation,** which lay out the corporation's purpose, powers, and obligations. The articles delegate to the board of directors the power to make, alter, and repeal reasonable **bylaws.** Study the bylaws carefully, since they contain ground rules critical to settling any future disputes. And they impose regulations that may shape your daily domestic life to a remarkable degree. Hamlet, your Great Dane, won't be welcome if the bylaws forbid dogs weighing more than 15 pounds. Your shopping cart might be unwelcome if you drag it through the formal lobby. Junior may have to restrict bike rides to limited areas.

Finally, study the **minutes,** or official records, for at least one year's worth of board meetings. These will alert you to any serious financial or operational problems the building may be suffering and reveal any friction within the board on what changes should or should not be made.

2. *Condominum life.* In a condo you have exclusive title to the block of air within your own unit, and you share ownership of common spaces (like corridors, elevators, and tennis courts) with other owners as tenants in common. As in a cooperative, all unit owners must pay their share of the monthly assessment for operations, repairs, and reserves. The **master deed** legally establishes the project as a condominium. Among other items, the deed authorizes residents to form an **operating association,** which you as an owner are required to join, and describes individual units and common areas. The operating association enforces the rules and maintains the common spaces but doesn't actually own anything. You're free to mortgage, sublet, or sell your unit as you please. **Bylaws** spell out the association's powers and responsibilities and may set forth insurance requirements. **House rules,** which may be part of the bylaws or a separate document, further limit what owners can do. Restrictions on pets, children, decorations, and use of the common facilities are usually part of the deal, though terms may be less strict than in the typical co-op.

3. *Planned community living.* In a planned development, you have individual ownership of your unit and a corporation has title to the common areas. Planned communities take several forms. The **planned-unit development (PUD)** combines the co-op and condo structures. In these communities the homeowner holds title to the unit—often a single-family detached house—and may own the air above and land beneath it as well. The common spaces, like parks and playgrounds, belong to the incorporated association, which all owners must join. In a **reciprocal easement community,** a shared easement crosses the individually owned parcels so that common driveways, party

walls, and even shopping centers are maintained jointly by the owners through assessments. To understand the legal setup and management structures of these types of communities, take a look at the articles of incorporation and the bylaws. The **declaration of covenants, conditions,** and **restrictions** will cover the physical arrangements of the community as well as the operational details.

Which Is Better?

When they have a choice, many buyers choose condos and related variations over co-ops because they give individual owners more freedom. (As a practical matter, however, you often don't have a choice. Different regions may have a preponderance of either co-ops or condos but rarely offer a wide selection of both.) With a condo you buy a tangible unit of housing, and you can sell it when you want to whomever you choose without the hassle of seeking approval from a board of directors.

With a co-op a new owner is technically buying shares in a corporation. The shareholder is a tenant, while the corporation acts as landlord. The "cooperators" have the power to guide the building's financial operations and the ability to prescreen applicants who would like to buy in, since a co-op is basically a private club. Prospective members are scrutinized by a board of directors, which often requires a complete baring of the applicants' financial souls, not to mention recommendation letters from pillars of the community.

In certain top-drawer buildings, the board sets arbitrary restrictions on how much of the purchase you can finance. Some co-op boards require that you buy with 50% or even 100% cash. In practice, the most common reason people are turned away is that co-op boards fear that certain prospective owners may not be able to carry the monthly maintenance fees. Since a default by one owner affects all shareholders, boards are understandably exhaustive in delving into applicants' finances. A less common reason, though the more publicized one, is that co-op boards fear certain people might throw noisy parties or damage the reputation of their building.

Actually, the board is free to arbitrarily reject anyone it wants, as long as no one can prove it has broken laws barring discrimination for reasons like race, gender, age, disability, lawful occupation, sexual orientation, or religion. But boards do not have to give reasons for their decisions, so illegal discrimination is almost impossible to prove.

In Manhattan, high-end real estate brokers make a fine art of tracking who's in and who's not in exclusive co-ops. In legendary cases, former president Nixon and Barbra Streisand were both rejected on the exclusive Upper East Side; he retreated to New Jersey, while she was welcomed across town in a West Side co-op building more tolerant of celebrities.

Cooperatives are sometimes cheaper to live in than similarly situated condominiums. If the Wakefield were a condo, says George Heery, it would have been assessed based on the purchase price of each unit. As a co-op, the assessment is set according to the overall land and construction costs. The result, according to Heery, is property taxes that are 30%–40% less than they would be in a comparable condominium project.

Maintenance fees in co-ops are often set higher than those for a comparable condo, however, in part because they usually include most utilities and real estate tax. Many condo owners pay utilities individually, and all of them pay their tax bills individually. To offset the higher maintenance fees, asking prices for co-ops are typically somewhat lower than for comparable condos.

In addition, co-ops offer lower closing costs. The closing costs on a **share loan,** the term used to define a cooperative mortgage, average between 1% and 2%, according to the National Cooperative Bank. Closing costs on condominiums average around 5%. And because of their corporate structure, cooperatives have the ability to borrow funds for repairs and capital improvements. Condominiums, on the other hand, are often forced to assess each individual owner when the building needs unexpected repairs. The interest paid on each cooperative member's pro rata share of the corporation's mortgage or loan is tax-deductible; special assessments are not. Table 7-1 enables you to run a quick comparison of the financial benefits of a condo versus a co-op.

TABLE 7-1

Financial Scorecard: Comparing a Co-op to a Condo

	Condo	Co-op
Sales price	$_____	$_____
Down payment needed	$_____	$_____
Mortgage rate	_____%	_____%
Points	_____	_____
Estimated closing costs	$_____	$_____
Annual maintenance fees	$_____	$_____
Percent deductible	N/A	_____%
Utilities	$_____	$_____
Property taxes	$_____	N/A
Board approval of me likely	(automatic)	yes/no
Added assessments within two years are likely	yes/no	yes/no

N/A: not applicable

Be warned, however, that federal law offers only limited protection if you buy into some form of shared ownership housing. The Fair Housing Act forbids discrimination against families with children, unless the organization meets the strict qualifications for senior citizen communities. The Fair Housing Amendments Act requires community associations to permit construction of facilities for disabled residents, which those residents may be required to remove when they leave. If the community has over 25 parcels, sales are governed by the Interstate Land Sales Full Disclosure Act, which requires the delivery of an offering plan and provides for a seven-day cooling-off period if you change your mind about the deal.

Beyond those statutes, however, owners' associations of all sorts are governed by a crazy quilt of state regulations. Some states barely deal with condominiums—others actively micromanage them. In Florida, for example, where about three million people live in condos, the legislature passed 161 amendments to its condominium statute in 1991, including four separate laws regulating bingo. Several were changed the following year—before they even took effect, according to the American Bar Association (ABA).

Because some states have stricter regulation of condos than of cooperatives and planned-unit developments, developers in those states sometimes choose a legal form that you wouldn't expect from looking at the buildings, according to the ABA. In Connecticut, for example, you can find PUD town houses, single-family detached cooperatives, and reciprocal-easement high-rises.

In practice, however, residents mostly feel the heavy hand of the board of directors. Rules-violation letters to offending owners are extremely common, says the Community Associations Institute (CAI), a national nonprofit organization created to help officers in condo and co-op associations. In a 1991 survey of more than 2,000 CAI member organizations, 91% reported writing at least one letter to a member about rule violations; 26% reported that they had to resort to mediation or arbitration at least once; and 18% reported filing at least one lawsuit. (Only a tiny fraction of the cases ended up in court, however.) Complaints are mainly about mundane matters—late payments, architectural control, pets, noise. Mr. Dudding insists on storing an old refrigerator on his balcony; Mrs. Warren keeps parking in Ms. Gladstone's space. The board steps in to keep up appearances or to keep the peace.

The Joys of Shared Ownership . . .

For many people, happiness is owning their own home without having to mow the lawn. Saturday morning is time for tennis, not tending the green stuff. Or for museum going and lunch with friends. Community ownership at its best provides homes that are comparatively hassle free. Here are some of its other charms:

BUILDING EQUITY

Condos and co-ops are a great way for dedicated urbanites to build profit from homeownership. In the center of many older cities, such as Boston, Chicago, and New York, where there simply are no single-family homes beneath the million-dollar range, shared ownership provides the answer. Nonmillionaires can own a piece of a house—and it may even be a nineteenth-century architectural showpiece.

RECREATIONAL OPPORTUNITIES

A five-star selling point in many suburban complexes is the chance for fun. Some condo communities provide the illusion that you're living in a country club. Playgrounds, rec rooms, pools, golf course with clubhouse, tennis courts, health club—all these can be yours, plus a ready-made circle of playmates for your offspring. Even in urban areas, newly constructed condominiums routinely include health clubs. The newest twist, however, is to install sports facilities in urban co-ops situated in older buildings, which often have lavish basement areas. New York City's Gym Source, which sells and services exercise equipment, expected to outfit at least 50 private gyms in older apartment buildings in 1996. And a couple of seasoned Manhattan co-ops with cavernous subterranean spaces have even installed basketball minicourts.

And the Potential Drawbacks . . .

LESS PRIVACY

If you want a home where the buffalo roam, a condo is clearly not for you. Shared ownership is a form of group living. Even if you enjoy living in an environment filled with people to talk to and have fun with, one obnoxious spoiler can destroy that camaraderie.

POSSIBLY HIGHER UPKEEP COSTS

If you are coming from a rented home, expect to spend more on routine maintenance. A developer may give you a paint job when you move in. After that you own the place, and the privilege of paying for repairs and maintenance within your walls is entirely yours. For example, if a main waterline breaks and stains your carpet, the community association will repair the pipes and plaster damaged because workmen had to go through your wall to fix it. But you are responsible for replacing the carpet and touching up the peach paint on the wall. Look for a home-owners insurance policy that will provide coverage for such events.

RISING ASSESSMENTS

Many condo and co-op owners complain of being forced to pay these. The cost of maintaining amenities, such as a swimming pool or tennis courts, will almost certainly increase at least as fast as the inflation rate. In addition, the association may start to charge for features that once were free, such as use of a health club. In older buildings, the roof or the plumbing systems may be nearing the end of their useful life and need to be replaced. Your best protection is to ask the manager and neighbors about past or future problems—and study the minutes of the board meetings for further clues.

RESTRICTIONS ON REMODELING

These may be more or less onerous, but all condos and co-ops will impose some. You virtually always need permission to move any supporting walls in your unit, for instance. Probably you need an official go-ahead before you can paint the exterior of your unit a shimmering chartreuse. If you want to screen in a porch or enclose your balcony, you might find that the owners association considers these to be "limited common areas," subject to their control. Other actions that might prove contentious include parking campers or motorcycles in your driveway, installing an aboveground pool, installing *any* pool, mounting a satellite-dish antenna, leaving garbage in the wrong place, and building a flagpole and flying Old Glory. To avoid future disputes, read the covenants and bylaws carefully before you buy. You want to be a bylaw-abiding citizen.

Sizing up a Prospective Condo

If you determine that a condo fits both your budget and your lifestyle, then begin touring. On your first visit inspect the community closely to get an overall impression of how well it's maintained. Your scrutiny begins as you park your car: Are the walkways clean and free of debris? Is the shrubbery well kept? the lawn tended? Is the security as protective as you would like? Do the doorman and other service people seem attentive and polite?

As you head toward your prospective unit, check out the hallways, the elevators. Try to talk to at least five owners, particularly the occupants of the units adjacent to the one you are contemplating. How long have they lived there? Would they recommend this as a home for a person of your age and interests? Have monthly fees risen substantially during their tenure? Do they like their neighbors? How about the manager and the owners association?

Once inside, inspect an existing unit just as closely as you would a resale house (see Chapter 6). Before you seal the deal, a professional inspector should go over not only your unit, but the common areas as well. Since you will have a financial interest in the whole community, you need to know about its physical condition. Obtain access to the roof and the boiler room so your inspector can take a look.

If you're buying in a project that's still being built, realize that you're taking a gamble. If the builder promises a move-in date of June 1, you can hope for that, but be prepared for September 1. New construction rarely comes in on deadline. Expect some inconvenience, too, since muddy roads and dawn serenades from arriving workmen are likely to be part of your daily existence until the entire project is completed.

On the financial side, recognize that you may not know how much the upkeep fees will be when the maintenance is finally turned over to the condo association. The developer will give you an estimate, but it's not binding, so leave yourself some financial breathing room. If you're a bargain hunter, though, reward yourself with a pat on the back: you get the cheapest deal if you buy a condo before it's built. Prices start very low to attract buyers, raise money, and give some momentum to the project. You can be the beneficiary, provided you shop carefully.

Before signing on the dotted line, however, take time to check the builder's reputation. Has the developer ever declared bankruptcy? Visit another condo built by the same outfit, and talk to the owners there. Was the construction sound? Did the builder take care of problems after they moved in? How much are fees now in the finished buildings? If yours is a similar unit and quoted fees are much lower than in the condo that's up and running, find out why there is such a discrepancy.

The best way to nail down value in a condo is to concentrate on developments where most units serve as the primary residence for the owners rather than as rental real estate investments. Live-in owners have a bigger stake in the upkeep and appreciation of their properties. Also, be wary about buying if the condo development is near an area where a number of new complexes are being constructed. Overbuilding means that supply could outstrip demand, and that will make it extremely tough for your unit to rise in value.

Because condos have become so common, getting a mortgage is scarcely different from getting financing for a single-family house. Review Chapter 2 and do the math to compare the down payment, mortgage costs, and closing costs, on competing condo units.

Prepare for homeowners insurance to be somewhat more complicated in a condo than in a conventional home, however. Determining where the owners association's liability ends and yours begins can be tricky, so it often pays to use the same insurer that covers the overall project. If you go with a different company, have a good agent compare the association's coverage with your own to be sure there are no glaring holes in your safety net.

Scoping out a Prospective Co-op

The main difference in shopping for a co-op, as opposed to any other residence, is that you may be investigated by the co-op board just as extensively as you investigate the co-op. To avoid embarrassment, ask your real estate agent early on about the size of down payments required by the building and the type of buyer the board is apt to approve. Of course, you'll also want to perform the usual due diligence in investigating the neighborhood, examining the building for signs of good housekeeping, and talking to people who live in the building about their experiences. Try to meet the manager or superintendent in charge of routine care.

Satisfy yourself completely that the building is well run, as well as physically and financially sound, since your fortunes are tied to those of your fellow cooperators more than in any other form of shared ownership. Make sure you, your lawyer, and perhaps an accountant scour the co-op board's minutes and financial statements to uncover immediate problems, but also to spot signs of trouble down the pike. As with a condo, your inspector should check out the common areas of the building as well as your prospective home.

The criteria for qualifying for a co-op share loan are the same as those used for single-family mortgages and condo financing. Your total cost of housing, which includes the monthly payment on the share loan plus the monthly cooperative maintenance fee, should not exceed more than 28% of your gross monthly income. The amount you can borrow will be limited by three factors:

- the amount of debt that your income can support
- the unit's appraised value, which must exceed the amount of your share loan plus the share of any building loans attributable to your unit
- any financing restrictions the cooperative imposes on how much you can finance

Co-op loans have become more widely available in the past decade, as banks become more familiar and comfortable with this form of debt. If you have trouble obtaining local financing, however, phone the National Cooperative Bank (800-322-1251) and they will quote you current co-op financing rates and supply you with the name of the NCB loan representative in your area.

CHECKPOINTS

- Read the bylaws, the financial statements, and the minutes of board meetings to satisfy yourself that the project is financially sound.
- Talk to people who are living in the project to confirm that they are pleased with the way it's run. Try to get a sense if a person of your age, interests, and financial circumstances would be compatible with other owners.
- When the professional inspector checks out your unit, make sure he or she also takes a look at the boiler room, the roof, and other common areas to identify potential problem spots.

SECTION III

FINDING A LENDER, GETTING A LOAN: THE FINANCE PROCESS

CHAPTER 8

Shopping for Your Mortgage Loan

In your grandparents' day a phone was black with a rotary dial, the phone company was Ma Bell, and a mortgage lasted 30 years, with a fixed rate that scarcely varied from one financial institution to another.

Now, just as competing phone companies woo you with ever more complicated options, so do mortgage lenders. Recently a Michigan mortgage broker was offering prospective customers free trips to Orlando or Las Vegas. American Airlines offered free miles, one mile for every dollar of mortgage interest. Lenders nationwide were slashing fees, lending 100% of a home's value, swallowing up-front costs—and offering a dizzying array of mortgages to boot.

The tenor of the market can change dramatically. Whether money is cheap or costly to come by, however, the contemporary mortgage market is a wide-open bazaar with an infinite variety of wares. You can get loans that are fixed-rate, graduated, variable, or convertible, loans that balloon, a final payment that's 15 or 30 years away or somewhere in the middle. With the arrival of nationwide mortgage companies, and new lenders popping up daily on the World Wide Web, you can get a deal custom-tailored to your circumstances. Trying to pick the perfect model is no easier than choosing among 200 differently patterned rugs for your living room.

The difference, of course, is that such confusion can be risky business. Chances are that your mortgage is your largest single debt, and it's a lien on your house, which is probably your largest single investment. Unlike the wrong rug, the wrong mortgage choice can have serious consequences not only for your short-term cash flow, but for your long-term financial health.

With a few guidelines, however, you can cut through the static from competing lenders. If you're wondering whether it's worth paying more cash up front to get a lower rate or if you'll truly save money with an adjustable-rate mortgage instead of a fixed-rate, the following pages will guide you to some clear answers. You'll discover the primary money sources to tap, the major loans that are available, and who might benefit from each kind.

We can't offer a substitute for shopping around, however. You have to arm yourself with a general idea of the rates in your area—and you'll almost certainly find that they vary widely. Consult your local newspaper first. Many offer shopper's guides to mortgage credit. Work the telephone, and if you've got Internet access, try surfing the Web, where there are dozens of lenders, some of whom accept on-line loan applications. Make all your inquiries in a relatively short period, since rates and terms change daily. If you obtain quotes spaced over several weeks, you will end up with no basis for meaningful evaluation.

A necessary tool in your comparison shopping is the **APR, or annual percentage rate.** That's the number you find in the mortgage loan ads, next to the mortgage rate. It's usually slightly higher than the loan's stated rate because it factors in an array of other charges you may have to pay to get the loan, such as points and application fees. The APR should make your analysis a complete no-brainer—but, unfortunately, it's not that simple, since one APR may omit an item that another includes. For instance, an application fee that will be refunded if a borrower is rejected must be included in the APR, but a nonrefundable fee is not part of the calculation. On adjustable-rate mortgages, lenders usually figure the APR only for the initial rate, so you can't compare a fixed-rate loan with any type of adjustable loan. To sidestep this difficulty, ask each lender to list the loan fees it charges, note if they are refundable or not, then compare rates and fees directly. Tables 8-1 and 8-2 contain questions and explanations that will help clarify your loan shopping.

TABLE 8-1

Fixed–Rate Mortgage Comparison Shopping Chart			
	Lender 1	Lender 2	Lender 3
1. Company name/phone number: Loan officer name?			
2. Mortgage type:			
3. Interest rate and points: Interest rate quoted on __ / __ / __ is ? (day) (month) (year) How many points quoted? Annual percentage rate?			
4. Interest rate lock-ins: Upon application? At approval? Lock-in costs? Effective how long? Lower lock-in if rates drop?			

	Lender 1	Lender 2	Lender 3

5. Minimum down payment required:
Without mortgage insurance
With mortgage insurance
If mortgage insurance is required:
  Up-front costs?
  Monthly premiums?
  Can it be financed?			

6. Prepayment of principal: Is there a penalty? Duration of penalty? Extra principal payments allowed?			

7. Loan processing time:
How many days estimated from
  application to approval?
  Approval to closing?			

8. Closing costs: Application/origination fee Credit report fee Lender's attorney fee Document preparation fee Transfer taxes Appraisal fee Survey fee Title search/title insurance Any other closing costs quoted?			

Source: The Fannie Mae Foundation

Checklist of Fixed-Rate Mortgage Shopping Terms

Note: Each item in this checklist is numerically coded to the Mortgage Comparison Shopping Chart on the previous page. So if you don't understand an item there, this list of terms will help you when asking questions of various mortgage lenders.

1. Company name/phone number: Write down the name of the loan officer with whom you speak, so you can get back in touch if you decide to apply for a loan at that institution.

2. Mortgage type: Your task will be simpler if you've narrowed your search to the type of mortgage loan you prefer. When comparing mortgages among lenders, compare the same loan among the lenders you call—in other words, a 30-year fixed-rate to a 30-year fixed-rate, a one-year Treasury ARM to a one-year Treasury ARM, etc.

3. Interest rate and points: Interest rates change often, even daily. Make sure you record the date of your rate quote. Try to call all lenders on the same day, so you have an accurate comparison. Another way to evaluate rates is by examining the annual percentage rate (APR). It indicates the "effective rate of interest paid" per year. The figure includes points and other closing costs and spreads them over the life of the loan. While the APR provides you with a common point for comparison, it's important to look at the whole product before deciding which mortgage to get. For a fuller discussion of points, see page 117.

4. Interest rate lock-ins: When a lender agrees to hold the quoted rate for you, this is called a "lock-in." Ask when the rate can be locked in, at the time of application or only upon approval. Will the lender lock in both the interest rate and points? Can you get a written lock-in agreement? How long does the lock-in remain in effect? Is there a charge for locking in a rate? If the rate drops before closing, must you close at your locked-in rate or can you get the lower rate?

5. Minimum down payment required: Ask the loan officer what the lowest allowable down payment is—with and without private mortgage insurance. If private mortgage insurance (PMI) is required, ask how much it will cost. Find out how much is due up front at closing and the amount included as monthly premiums. Ask if you can finance the closing cost of mortgage insurance. Also ask how long PMI will be required. In some cases you may be able to cancel the PMI when your loan balance drops below 80% of the original value of the property or when a new appraisal establishes that your mortgage is 80% or less of the new appraised value.

6. Prepayment of principal: Some lenders charge borrowers a prepayment penalty if they pay off the loan early. If you think you may sell your home before the loan is paid off (most mortgages are repaid early) or plan to make principal payments before they are actually due, you need to know if there will be a penalty and for how long it will remain in effect. Some penalties are in effect only for the early years of the loan.

7. Loan processing time: Loan approvals can take 30–60 days or more. Peak business periods, particularly when rates are dropping and many homeowners are refinancing, can affect a lender's response time. Ask each lending institution for its estimate and see which can promise very short approval times. If interest rates are rising or you have an urgent need to get moved in, these "express" services may be the answer.

8. Closing costs: Closing costs are fees required by the lender at closing and can vary considerably from one financial institution to another. Ask specifically about the application fee, origination fee, points, credit report fee, appraisal fee, survey fee (if required), lender's attorney fee, cost of title search and title insurance, transfer taxes, and document preparation fee.

TABLE 8-2

Adjustable–Rate Mortgage Comparison Shopping Chart			
	Lender 1	Lender 2	Lender 3
1. Financial index and margin: Treasury, cost of funds, certificate of deposit, or other? What is the margin over the index used by the lender to calculate the fully indexed rate?			
2. Initial interest rate:			
3. Adjustment interval: What is the interest adjustment interval (six months, one year, three years, etc.)?			
4. Rate caps: Lifetime interest cap? Periodic interest cap?			
5. Payment caps:			
6. Conversion to fixed-rate loan: When can the loan convert? How is the new converted rate determined? Are there any conditions under which a conversion option will not be offered to me? Is there a conversion fee?			

Source: The Fannie Mae Foundation

Checklist of Adjustable-Rate Mortgage Shopping Terms

If you're shopping for an adjustable-rate mortgage (ARM), ask about the additional items that follow. The most important thing to discover is the maximum amount your payments might increase.

1. Financial index and margin: The interest rate on an ARM is determined by adding a margin or spread to a specified financial index. This is called the fully indexed rate. Find out both the financial index used (Treasury, certificate of deposit, cost of funds, etc.) and the margin (that is, how much higher is the ARM rate than the index rate?).

2. Initial interest rate: Is the initial rate quoted the fully indexed rate or a lower introductory rate, sometimes called a teaser or discount rate? A teaser rate may sound like a bargain today, but it may turn out to cost you more in the long run. This low rate lasts only until the first adjustment. After that you will be charged the fully indexed rate, at which point your payments may become unmanageable.

3. Adjustment interval: How often can the interest rate be adjusted—every six months, one year, three years, five years? A loan that adjusts its interest rate after six months is called a six-month ARM; after one year, a one-year ARM; etc.

4. Rate caps: Rate caps limit how much your interest rate can move, either up or down. Periodic caps limit the change per adjustment period, and a lifetime cap governs the maximum amount the interest rate can increase or decrease over the life of the loan. For example, you may find a one-year ARM with a 2% periodic cap and a 6% lifetime cap. If this one-year ARM is originated at 8%, after the one-year adjustment period it could be adjusted upward to as much as 10%, or downward to as low as 6%, depending on the movement of the index. Remember to consider the adjustment interval when comparing rate caps. The one-year ARM just described could reach its lifetime cap of 14% (original interest rate of 8% plus lifetime interest rate cap of 6%) in three years if interest rates rose steadily. A three-year ARM would just be making its first adjustment after such a three-year period.

5. Payment caps: Payment caps may appear similar to rate caps, but don't be misled. While they can limit how much your monthly payment increases, they don't restrict the interest rate from going up. Many ARMs with payment caps have no corresponding interest rate caps. As a result, you may end up paying the lender less than the amount of interest you owe each month. If this happens, this unpaid interest is added to your loan balance, and the principal amount you owe increases rather than decreases with each payment. This is called negative amortization—and generally should be avoided.

6. Conversion to fixed-rate loan: Some ARMs let you convert to a fixed-rate mortgage at specified times, typically during the first five years of the loan. Because the convertibility feature is often an added expense (some lenders charge an extra point, for example), find out the exact conversion terms and how much it would cost you to convert your ARM to a fixed-rate loan. You'll want to compare this cost with the costs incurred and the interest rate savings you might gain by refinancing your mortgage to a fixed-rate loan. This will help you decide the relative advantages of each option to determine which is most cost-effective for you.

Ideally you're reading this chapter before you have signed a sales contract. If so, you have plenty of time to look around for a lender that offers the loan best tailored to your needs. Check with six to 12 sources to compare terms, including the interest rate, points, and closing costs. If you stumble on a good deal, find out if the lender will agree to preapprove your application.

With a **preapproval,** the lender commits to offering you a mortgage before you find the home you want to buy. The preapproval letter will **lock in,** or hold, a quoted rate for you. If the loan rate drops before you find a house and go to closing, find out if you must stay with your locked-in rate or if you can get the lower number. Some lenders let you lock in at no charge; others impose a fee equal to 1% of the loan amount. Don't confuse preapproval with **prequalification,** which is usually a quickie process of determining the maximum amount of money a home shopper will be eligible to borrow before he or she formally applies. If you completed the exercises in Chapter 2, you've already done that for yourself.

Once you cut a deal on a house, even if you have a preapproval arrangement with one lender, make one last check. Satisfy yourself that the rates and loan terms offered by that institution still meet or beat whatever the competition is offering.

Tapping the Primary Sources

Start your search for a mortgage with a **commercial** or **savings bank** with which you already have a consumer loan, savings, or checking account. Ask whether they offer home mortgages and if they grant favorable terms to their good customers. You have the advantage of being a known risk if you already have a loan. If you have in-house checking or savings, many banks will cut your borrowing rate by one-eighth of a percentage point if you authorize them to collect your monthly payment directly from the account. Some large **federal credit unions** provide home financing on favorable terms, although you must be a member to borrow. If you're eligible, the deal could be unbeatable, especially if you are a first-time borrower.

Moving further afield, consider using a **mortgage banker,** such as Countrywide, to name the nation's largest. Though ARMs are usually on their menu, many mortgage bankers specialize in fixed-rate loans at highly competitive rates. And they are known for processing applications quickly, which can be useful when rates are low and shoppers are rushing to buy or refinance.

Don't confuse mortgage bankers with **mortgage brokers,** who don't lend dollars directly; they are intermediaries between you and the money source. Mortgage brokers, who are paid a commission by the lender, are supposed to know the market so well that they can ferret out deals that you would never find on your own. If your situation is complicated—you just changed jobs, for instance, or your credit history is spotty—a broker may know a deal that's custom-tailored for your situation. As middlemen they can save you time, do much of the tiresome paperwork, and provide a degree of handholding.

Mortgage brokers have in the past been criticized for being untrustworthy and expensive, the lenders of last resort to borrowers with shaky credit. Times have changed, however, and the bad rap is now largely undeserved. Mortgage brokers arrange about half of all mortgages issued. To make best use of one, get a complete rundown of rates, points, and closing fees from at least six competing lenders, then take your best offer to one or more mortgage brokers to see whether they can beat it. For a list of members in your area, contact the National Association of Mortgage Brokers (703-524-0664).

How can a mortgage broker get you a cheaper loan than you can line up yourself? They scan the offerings of numerous lenders, including some who work only with brokers, and they may find low-rate deals you missed. Even if you find a great offering on your own, a broker might be able to arrange a better one, partly by shaving his fee. Usually mortgage brokers earn a commission from the lender of 1.5%–2% of the loan amount. "But a broker may choose to take a reduced commission because he's dealing with an informed shopper," says Robert Walker, national sales director of Foster Ousley Conley, a consulting firm for mortgage lenders.

You should check the broker's references thoroughly, since

there are still a few shady operators who take hefty application fees and never produce a loan. You're best off picking a broker who has been recommended by someone you know or who has made the effort (and spent the money) to join a professional association. Keep a keen eye on prices, and don't fork over a deposit or pay up-front charges apart from fees for an appraisal and a credit check. The rates, points, and fees of a broker's deal should be better than what you can get directly from a financial institution. If terms are essentially equal, go with the direct lender.

If you don't need the kind of help a broker offers, comb the newspapers, Yellow Pages, and the Web, and you may locate a first-rate offering on your own. A few services can help with your shopping, including HSH Associates, which collects mortgage data nationwide. Call 800-873-2837 and for $20 you'll get current information on lenders in your area plus a booklet on mortgages.

Loan offerings by computer, a growing market, may take into account your specific needs and circumstances and offer in-house financial counselors who can help you calculate which deal is most advantageous to you. "Technology is making tailor-made mortgages easier to implement," says Harry Tomlinson, executive vice president with PNC Mortgage in Chicago, which has teamed up with Coldwell Banker to form the Home Mortgage Network on-line.

For basic mortgage market information on-line, check out the HSH Associates home page (http://www.hsh.com), which offers daily and weekly updates of mortgage rates around the country. Money Personal Finance Center (http://moneymag.com), offered by **MONEY** magazine, lists the best deals in mortgage loans for 100 large metro areas. For information about innovative mortgage programs, consult the Web site of Fannie Mae (http://www.fanniemae.com), the quasi-government company that buys mortgages from primary lenders and resells them to large investors. On-Line Mortgage Calculator, run by Fair Oaks Financial Services, a California mortgage broker (http://fofs.com/FairOaksHomePage.html), can compute whether an adjustable-rate mortgage beats a fixed-rate deal.

If, in the course of comparison shopping, you hear that new loans and refinancings are touching all-time highs, take that as a warning signal. It probably means that you don't have much room to negotiate rates and terms on your mortgage package. Conversely, if you learn that lenders are offering free toasters and trips to Vegas, that's your cue that a buyer's market prevails and you have lots of maneuvering room.

Answering the Primary Questions

CONFORMING OR NONCONFORMING?

No, this is not a test of your political correctness. Many banks and savings institutions, as well as the national mortgage companies, originate **conforming mortgages,** so called because they meet the underwriting guidelines of Fannie Mae (the Federal National Mortgage Association) and Freddie Mac (the Federal Home Loan Mortgage Corporation). Fannie and Freddie generally require that total housing costs not exceed 28% of pretax income and monthly credit obligations, including housing, should not exceed 36%. Packages of conforming loans are sold in the **secondary market** to Fannie, Freddie, and Ginnie Mae (the Government National Mortgage Association), as well as to insurance companies and pension funds.

Conforming lenders generally impose the most restrictive criteria on prospective borrowers. The underwriter sets the parameters of the loans—the maximum size, the necessary down payment, and other terms and qualifications required, as well minimum standards for the house. But—and this is a big but—a conforming loan is nearly always the best financial deal on the market at any given time. If you qualify, and if the terms meet your needs, you probably can stop your search at this point. (A number of specialized programs for low- to moderate-income home shoppers offer more relaxed requirements. For more on these, see Chapter 4.)

A **nonconforming loan** is one that can't be resold to Fannie or Freddie and is the special province of midsize banks and savings and loan associations, which typically hold in their own portfolios the loans they make. (For this reason they are sometimes called **portfolio loans.**) These midsize institutions are characteristically the most nimble and aggressive players in the adjustable-rate market. If you can snag a decision maker with some authority, typically a branch manager, you might be able to haggle your way to an attractive, custom-cut deal—but it will probably cost more than a conforming loan.

If you need to borrow a large amount, you may be forced to shop for a portfolio loan. Recently, conforming loans were limited to $207,000, though amounts are adjusted upward periodically. A larger-size loan is known to the trade as a **jumbo,** and its rate may be one-half of a percentage point higher than that for a conforming mortgage, since it can't be resold as easily as a smaller loan (although some lenders have been aggressively chasing the jumbo market, because of rising home prices and relatively stable interest rates). Large banks have traditionally been the leaders in jumbo loans.

Brokerage firms such as Merrill Lynch also have jumbo mortgage loan programs for valued clients. Merrill's Mortgage 100 plan lets qualified home buyers mortgage the entire purchase price of their house by transferring securities to a Merrill Lynch account, then agreeing to maintain the account at specified levels. For those who aren't so flush, but whose parents are, Merrill offers Parent Power—a 100% mortgage program that allows parents to provide help to their children in purchasing a first home without actually parting with any cash. Under the Parent Power plan, a parent or close relative pledges to a Merrill account securities worth 39% of the mortgage amount. The owner retains the right to trade the stocks, but the market value of the portfolio cannot drop below 33% of the loan amount. If it does, the securities can be sold by Merrill and held as cash collateral.

POINTS OR NO POINTS?

There are two basic ways that mortgage lenders charge you for the use of their money: through the interest you pay over the life of the loan and through **discount points,** a onetime prepayment of interest, which lenders charge to increase their yield on the loan. One point equals 1% of the loan amount, so one point on a $100,000 loan would equal $1,000; on a $50,000 loan it would amount to $500. You usually don't write a check to cover this sum; instead the points discount the value of the loan. If you pay two discount points, or $1,000, to borrow $50,000, you've really borrowed only $49,000. But you will pay back the full $50,000 face value of the loan, plus interest on that amount.

The more points you can swallow up front, however, the lower interest rate you pay. For instance, you may be offered an 8% rate with no points, 7.7% with one point, and 7.6% with two points. So how do you decide which is the best deal? The longer you plan to stay in your house, the more reason to pay points. You'll have time to recover the cost and then even longer to reap the benefits of a low rate.

To calculate the precise break-even point, divide the cost of the points by the dollars you save on the payments each month. The result is the number of months required for you to come out ahead. For instance, let's assume you can get a $100,000 fixed-rate 30-year mortgage at the terms just described. The monthly payment on the no-point loan would be $734; on the two-point loan it would be $706. Saving $28 a month, you would need 72 months to recoup the $2,000 in points. Thus, paying points to get the lower rate would make sense if you plan to stay in the home for at least 72 months.

If you're simply trying to make a rough comparison of competing offerings, consider one discount point to be equivalent to one-eighth of a percentage point, or .125%, on the loan rate. Thus a loan at 7% with two discount points would be roughly equivalent to a loan at 7.25%.

Bear in mind, however, that the cost of points on a buyer's loan is a negotiable item, often shared between buyer and seller. So if you can offload one or more of the points onto the seller, adjust your calculations accordingly. For the tax implications of points, see Chapter 13.

AN ADJUSTABLE- OR FIXED-RATE MORTGAGE?

Stripped of all bells and whistles, almost all mortgage loans fall into one of those two categories. A **fixed-rate mortgage,** as the name suggests, has an interest rate that stays the same for the life of the loan, usually 15–30 years. Predictability is its primary attraction. If in 1998 you get a 30-year loan of $60,000 at 8%, your monthly principal and interest payments will be $448 until 2028, when the loan is discharged—unless you sell the house or initiate some kind of change. (Higher taxes and homeowners insurance premiums may increase your monthly payment, however.) This could be ideal for a young couple who are anticipating starting a family. They need to know what their monthly mortgage bill is going to be, especially if one spouse's income might disappear when the baby arrives. A retired couple on a fixed income might also welcome the reliability and relatively low payments that a 30-year fixed-rate loan offers.

A 15-year fixed-rate mortgage might make sense for a prosperous two-income couple. For one thing, the interest rates are usually one-quarter to one-half percentage point lower than those on comparable 30-year loans. And because they are paying off their loan more quickly, the pair would cut interest costs almost in half. As a result, this imaginary couple would build up equity in their home faster and wind up with more money for the next down payment if they want to move to a trade-up house. A $100,000 30-year loan at 8% costs $164,155 in interest over its term. A 15-year loan at the same rate has a total interest cost of $72,017—fully 56% less.

If you are tempted by the 15-year term but fear you can't afford the high payments on a regular basis, consider this strategy: Sign on for the full 30-year term, then make additional principal payments in months when you're able. Most loans permit at least some prepayment without penalty.

An **adjustable-rate mortgage (ARM),** sometimes called a **variable-rate mortgage,** permits the lender to raise or lower its interest rate periodically on the basis of changes in a specified index. ARMs are especially attractive to first-time buyers since they usually carry initial interest rates that are about two percentage points lower than for fixed loans, which makes for lower initial monthly payments. In addition, if a lender follows the common guideline that a household should spend no more than 28% of its pretax monthly income on monthly housing expenses, the lower ARM payments permit the buyer to stretch for a larger loan. A couple would require an annual income of $44,039 to qualify for a 30-year fixed-rate mortgage at 10%, but only $35,302 to qualify for a one-year adjustable-rate loan priced at 7.125%.

If you plan to stay in your new home for less than five years, an ARM will almost certainly be the better deal. The interest rate on most ARMs cannot increase (or decrease) more than two percentage points a year and six points over the life of the loan. So a 6% ARM that maxes out, jumping to 8% in year two, 10% in year three, and 12% in year four, would cost you a four-year average rate of 9%, which would beat a 30-year fixed-rate average of 9.2%. And if rates remain steady or drop, your ARM could be far less expensive over a long period than a fixed-rate mortgage.

Against these advantages, however, you have to weigh the risk that an increase in rates would lead to unaffordable monthly payments in the future. In return for the ARM's low initial rate, you are shouldering more risk. Consider the following questions:

• **Is my income likely to rise enough to cover bigger mortgage payments if interest rates go up?** Find out what limits or caps have been placed on the adjustments. Discuss with your lender the maximum amount that your mortgage can increase in any single adjustment period and over the life of the loan.

• **Will I be taking on other substantial obligations, such as a car loan or school tuition, in the near future?** This could make rising mortgage payments difficult to meet.

• **How long do I plan to remain in this home?** If you expect to sell in a few years, rising rates may not pose the problem they do if you plan to own the house for a long time.

If you feel confident about proceeding with a variable-rate loan, make sure that you understand the ARM's basic features. First, the interest rate changes are nearly always tied to a financial index. According to Fannie Mae, the three most popular ARMs are these:

1. *Treasury-indexed ARMs,* which are tied to six-month, one-year, or three-year Treasury securities. An ARM tied to the six-month T-bill rate would be adjusted on the six-month anniversary of your loan and every six months thereafter, in line with the T-bill rate prevailing at that time. A loan linked to the one-year rate would change once a year, and so on. The longer the adjustment period, the better you will be able to plan your future household expenses.

2. *CD-indexed ARMs,* which adjust according to a certificate of deposit (CD) index. Adjustments typically occur every six months, with a per adjustment cap of one percentage point and a lifetime cap of six percentage points.

3. *Cost of funds–indexed ARMs,* which are linked to the actual money costs of a particular group of lending institutions. Lenders using this index can choose to adjust mortgages

monthly, every six months, or annually. The most popular index of this type is the cost of funds index for the Eleventh Federal Home Loan Bank District of San Francisco. (Insiders call it the COFI.)

Know the benchmark to which your prospective loan is tied, and ask the lender to show you how that index has performed over the previous 10 or 15 years. The pattern will give you an idea of how your mortgage payments could change. At the same time, find out how to follow its future performance. Lenders are required to provide you with information on how to track the index they use.

In addition to exploring the benchmark index, you should ask about the lender's **margin.** This is the amount the lender tacks on to the index rate to determine what your adjusted mortgage rate will be at each periodic review. Say you get an ARM with an index rate of 6%. If the lender's margin is 3%, which is fairly common, the rate you pay will be 9%. Even borrowers who comparison shop assiduously for the lowest interest rate often forget to inquire about the margin. It's a negotiable item that generally falls between 2.5% and 3%, and knowledgeable bargaining might get you a break of a fraction of a point.

Ask about the initial mortgage rate. Is it a **"teaser" rate** that includes a special discount? If so, you could have a large increase in your monthly payments when your rate is adjusted for the first time. Be absolutely clear about what limits or caps have been placed on the adjustments. Find out the "worst case" situation in the event of a sharp increase in your index rate.

You'll need to know also if **negative amortization** can occur. If your ARM has a cap that prevents your payment from rising to the level dictated by the index, your monthly payment may not cover the full amount of principal and interest due. In that case the interest shortage is added to your debt, and the amount of principal that you owe increases. Imagine your shock if you sell your home, only to discover you owe the bank more than you borrowed initially. Some mortgages contain a cap on negative amortization, limiting the total amount you can owe to 125% of the original loan amount—but even that could be a large pill to swallow. Ask your lender about negative amortization to understand how it will apply (if at all) to your loan.

Both fixed and adjustable mortgages may be styled as **convertibles,** meaning that they convert from a fixed to a variable rate, or the reverse, after a specified number of years. A delayed-adjustable, for example, carries a fixed rate for its first three, five, seven, or 10 years and then converts to a one-year ARM that adjusts annually. This kind of loan can be a winner for homeowners who plan to sell shortly before the adjustable rate kicks in. (These mortgages are known as **3–1s, 5–1s,** and so on, depending on the term of the fixed-rate portion of the loan.) Lenders style other convertibles in the opposite fashion, permitting you to switch from an adjustable- to a fixed-rate loan after a specified time period.

A CONVENTIONAL LOAN OR AN ASSISTED LOAN?

The fixed-rate and adjustable-rate mortgages previously discussed, whether conforming or nonconforming, are the most common types of **conventional mortgages,** meaning a mortgage loan that is not insured or subsidized by the government. Lenders commonly require a down payment of at least 20% on conventional loans but offer them with lower down payments if the homeowner buys **private mortgage insurance (PMI),** which protects the lender if the homeowner defaults on the loan. You will pay for PMI in two ways. There is an up-front premium (usually 0.5% of the loan amount) paid when the loan is originated. And there's a recurring annual premium (often 0.35% of the declining loan balance), one-twelfth of which is paid monthly. It's a myth that PMI will be removed automatically from the loan at some predetermined time. You must make the request to the lender, who usually will require that your equity in the property has reached at least 20%, either by paying down the mortgage or profiting from a rising real estate market, and that you have a history of timely payments. Sometimes, however, you have to wait until the loan is five years old. A few lenders make you keep the coverage forever.

A handful of tax-smart buyers have convinced lenders to eliminate the requirement for PMI by agreeing to an increase in the mortgage rate of one-quarter of a percentage point. (This increases the monthly payment by roughly the amount of the monthly insurance premium.) The advantage is that mortgage interest payments are tax-deductible, while private mortgage insurance payments are not.

There are other types of conventional mortgages that you may come across. A **balloon mortgage** is a nonamortizing loan—which means that the monthly principal and interest payments don't pay off the loan, so you owe a humongous final payment. A common version of the balloon mortgage loan may have a principal and interest payment that is calculated as if it would pay off the loan in 30 years, but the loan, in fact, comes due in five or seven years—when you either have to come up with an elephantine amount or refinance. People sometimes opt for balloon loans when they anticipate a substantial chunk of cash—perhaps a major bonus or inheritance—before the loan comes due, but that's a risky course. If the money doesn't appear on schedule to cover the balloon payment, you could be forced to refinance at unacceptably high rates. And that could put you in seriously hot water.

Some loans, called **balloon-reset** or **two-step mortgages,** from the outset contain provisions for renewal, or for rewriting, if certain conditions, such as a history of timely payments, are met. The monthly payments stay at the same level for the early years, then are reset for the duration of the loan. The initial rate on a two-step is often one-half to three-quarters of a percentage point less than that of a 30-year fixed-rate deal. If you plan to sell before the reset comes due, this loan could be the right call.

The **biweekly mortgage** lets you pay off your debt more

quickly, since you make half the regular monthly payment every two weeks. Because there are 26 two-week periods in a year, the borrower makes the equivalent of 13 monthly payments annually—which allows him or her to complete payment on a 30-year mortgage in about 22 years. To reduce the paperwork, most lenders require that payments be deducted automatically from the borrower's checking account. If a lender insists on a fee to arrange the accelerated payments, that's an unnecessary charge, so don't bite. You can make the extra payments yourself with a little self-discipline, avoiding both the extra payment and the legal obligations that come with the formal program.

Sometimes a home builder or a cooperative relative may provide funds to lower the borrower's interest rate over the first two or three years of the loan. This practice is known as an **interest rate buy-down,** and it's most common when rates are especially high. A buy-down can cut your payments by 15%–25% during the early years of the loan. Gary Eldred, executive director of the National Initiative for Homeownership, a nonprofit group dedicated to helping renters become owners, offers this example of how a buy-down works: At an interest rate of 9%, your payment for a 30-year fixed-rate mortgage of $125,000 would equal $1,006 per month. A 3-2-1 buy-down would cut your interest rate to 6%, 7%, and 8% for years one, two, and three, respectively. Thus your respective monthly loan payments would equal $794, $831, and $917. The payment difference would be supplied by the buy-down cash—in this case more than $5,000—coming from the home builder, seller, parents, or some other donor. Eldred rightly points out that a 3-2-1 buy-down for $5,000 will add far more to affordability for cash-strapped buyers than will a $5,000 price reduction on the house. The buy-down can be used with either fixed- or variable-rate loans.

Shared equity mortgages treat the purchase of a home as an investment that can be shared between a resident owner and an investment owner. The latter contributes a share of the down payment or the monthly payment (or both) and shares proportionately in the ownership of the property. At resale, the borrower and the investor split the proceeds accordingly after repayment of the balance of the loan. Many lenders limit this type of mortgage to immediate family members.

Besides the array of conventional loans just discussed, there is a universe of **assisted loans,** meaning transactions in which the buyer receives financial aid from an individual or institution that has no stake in the future appreciation of the property. Besides government agencies, family and friends may help make the home purchase possible.

1. *Public agencies.* These make below market rate financing available to eligible low-income and moderate-income buyers. At the national level you may get help through the **Federal Housing Administration (FHA)** or the **Department of Veterans Affairs (VA).** Most banks and mortgage companies offer FHA-insured or VA-guaranteed loans and can provide you with details on current offerings.

FHA loans require a very small down payment—between 3% and 5%, depending on how much you borrow—and carry below market interest rates, which makes them excellent for first-time buyers. In addition, you may add your closing costs to your mortgage and borrow the entire amount. You will be charged points, however, and have to pay an additional 0.5% interest to cover mortgage insurance that protects the lender.

One encouraging note: The FHA has recently revised and relaxed its lending guidelines to eliminate some requirements and to make the process easier for creditworthy minority and nontraditional buyers. The agency is more willing now to give credit for overtime income, bonus income, and part-time income, for example. Qualifying debt-to-income ratios are less rigid than in the past and can be exceeded where compensating factors exist.

There are no maximum income limits for FHA borrowers, but there are maximum loan limits, which vary around the country. In high-cost cities like New York and San Francisco, the maximum mortgage limit for FHA-insured loans was recently $155,250 for a one-family house. In most other places the limit ranged from $78,660 for a one-family up to $151,150 for a four-family property. (Alaska, Guam, Hawaii, and the Virgin Islands are exceptions.) Amounts are adjusted periodically. If local banks and mortgage companies can't give you complete information, including current loan limits, contact your local Housing and Urban Development (HUD) office.

VA loans are the second major avenue of federal mortgage help. The VA offers partially guaranteed mortgages to qualified veterans and their surviving spouses. These loans generally don't require a down payment (although lenders, mostly mortgage companies, may require one) and carry below market interest rates. Aside from the veteran's certificate of eligibility and the VA-assigned appraisal, the application process is similar to that of a conventional loan. Borrowers may choose a traditional fixed-payment loan or from a variety of adjustable-rate mortgages, which may allow qualification for a higher loan amount. There are no maximum income limits for applicants; the top loan amount is generally $203,000. For further information, or to find out if you qualify, call 800-827-1000. If you need a certificate, make an application on VA Form 26-1880, Request for Determination of Eligibility and Available Loan Guaranty Entitlement, to the local VA office.

Finally, if you live in a rural area, you may be entitled to a **Farmer's Home Administration (FmHA) loan.** If your local bank turns you down for an FmHA-guaranteed loan, you may apply directly to the FmHA district office, for the agency acts as a lender of last resort. These loans are restricted to low-income buyers, and if your income rises, the FmHA may require you to refinance.

2. *State and local housing agencies* have scores of programs to help eligible low- and moderate-income buyers. Many of these last for only a limited time—or have limited funds available—so the trick is to get plugged in to what's available. You will have to use your

initiative to keep up-to-date by contacting state housing agencies and local lenders. For the name, address, and telephone number of your state housing agency, see the list on page 59.

Here is one widely praised example of state largesse: Massachusetts's American Dream Program in 1996 offered $125 million in home financing to provide affordable homeowner-ship opportunities for up to 1,200 families who needed assis-tance qualifying for conventional mortgage loans. Over the preceding four years, 3,200 Massachusetts families have become homeowners under the program. Borrowers who have incomes of up to 135% of the median income in their area—in Boston, that would be $76,000—may make down payments as low as 5%. For some borrowers, 2% of the down payment could come from a gift or grant.

3. *Private aid from families and friends* can help strapped bor-rowers with both their debt—ensuring that it doesn't exceed allowable limits—and their down payment. The first and most obvious possibility is for a prosperous well-wisher to **cosign the loan.** Lenders are cautious these days, however, and the mere fact that Dad's name is also on the promissory note doesn't mean that you can borrow $1 million on your $30,000 salary. But they are likely to accept more generous debt-to-income ratios when a cosigner is backing you up. If you take a hike, however, your guarantor will have to make good on the loan or face foreclosure and a splotched credit record.

Another possibility is for your benefactor to offer **down payment assistance,** either through a gift, a loan, or the interest rate buy-down described earlier in this chapter. Your first choice, of course, is a **gift** that need not be repaid, but lenders may add certain restrictions. If you put down 20%, a gift for the entire amount is usually perfectly fine. You don't have to contribute a cent from your own funds, but you probably will have to prove that the funds are a gift and not a loan. Ask the mortgagor what kind of documentation the institution requires.

If you put down less than 20%, however, most lenders want

you to pay at least 5% of the down payment amount from your own verified savings. The rest may be gift money.

You will have to repay a **loan** from any source, so your lender will add the loan's fair market interest rate to your total debt-to-income ratio. In addition, the debt will have to be secured by an asset—often the house you are hoping to buy. The mortgage lender won't be happy to see another loan levied against the property, of course. As a result of these practical complications, loans from family members are rarely part of the package when buyers are making a mortgage application.

A family member could, however, purchase an ownership interest in the property through an **equity-sharing investment.** This arrangement is likely to appeal to parents who wish to keep continuing control over their investment. Usually their money is used to provide a very large down payment. When you decide to sell the house, your parents will have to sign off on the deed. In return for their investment, they get a portion of the sales proceeds, based on their percentage of ownership. If you come to such an arrangement, be sure to have a lawyer draw up the agreement, to avoid legal and familial hassles when it's time to sell.

CHECKPOINTS

- Determine first what kind of mortgage makes the most sense for you. This will depend chiefly on how long you plan to remain in the home and what size payments you can afford.
- Shop at least a half a dozen lenders, using the annual percentage rate (APR) to compare their loan offerings. Take the best deal to a mortgage broker and see if he can do better.
- Get a letter of preapproval for your loan, if possible, before you start house hunting. You'll know what you can afford and be able to move quickly when you are ready to bid on a home. If you can't obtain a preapproval, ask for a prequalification, which tells you and the seller the approximate amount you might be able to borrow.

CHAPTER 9

Applying for Your Loan

Once you have scouted out the lender that offers the best terms on the mortgage you want, you're ready to set up that crucial appointment with the loan officer. When you phone, ask the officer to mail you a loan application form, and find out what documentation to bring to the interview. Most lenders use a basic form developed by Fannie Mae and Freddie Mac that seeks information about the house you intend to buy, as well as your income, assets, and debts.

Required Documentation

Lenders vary in their specific requirements, but this list covers the paperwork basics. Bring originals, not photocopies, of the following:

- The purchase contract for the house, if one has been drawn up.
- The three most recent statements for all bank accounts, brokerage or cash-management accounts, and similar documents. Include all account numbers and the address of your bank branch.
- Proof of employment and salary, such as W-2 forms for the last two years and recent pay stubs. If you are self-employed, bring balance sheets, tax returns for the past two years, and a year-to-date profit-and-loss statement.
- Information about debts, including loan and credit card numbers, and names and addresses of your creditors.
- Evidence of your mortgage or rental payments, such as canceled checks, money order receipts, or mortgage statements.

In special circumstances, other documentation may be required:

• If your current primary residence has just been sold, the lender will want to see a settlement statement from the sale before closing your new loan. If your present home is on the market but hasn't been sold, the lender will want a copy of the listing agreement with a broker to show that you're making a good faith effort to market the property. **If your old residence has not been sold by the settlement date of your new home purchase,** the old mortgage, taxes, and insurance will be counted as debt and current expenses by many underwriters. These obligations will limit, if not wipe out, your ability to borrow for the new residence. The thinking is that if the old home hasn't been sold by closing, it may never be sold.

• If you're receiving alimony, child support, or maintenance funds, you need not declare this income to the lender. You may choose to report the income, however, in order to qualify for the largest possible loan amount. Conversely, alimony, child support, and maintenance that you pay are considered debts and must be reported.

• **If you're relying on a cash gift from a relative for part of your down payment,** the lender will probably require a letter detailing who's giving how much to whom and for what purpose and stating that repayment is not expected. The lender will also want proof of the donor's ability to provide the funds. Ask the loan officer in advance exactly what documentation is required.

Home buyers with complex finances, including self-employed people and those with scarred credit histories, sometimes arrange for **low-documentation loans,** which are usually speedier and require less paperwork than conventional mortgage loans. For example, you might not have to furnish copies of tax returns for a "low-doc" loan. You won't need to furnish the scrupulous proof of income and outgo that a "full-doc" loan requires. (Some lenders advertise no-documentation loans, but these are really low-docs in disguise. Everyone wants some financial information before lending you tens or hundreds of thousands of dollars.) Be prepared for higher costs with a low-doc deal. Because lenders are taking more risk, you'll need a larger down payment—often 25% or 30% instead of 5%–10%. And you'll pay a higher interest rate: one-half of one percentage point is common.

Processing Your Application

To get the deal going, the lender will arrange for a property appraisal, call for a credit report on you and any co-borrowers, and seek verification of the information you provided on the loan application. He or she may also request the approval of a mortgage insurer, if that is a requirement of the loan. If you are obtaining an FHA or VA loan, the loan must also meet the agency's standards. Let's consider each of these steps in turn:

1. *The appraisal.* The lender will arrange for this service, for which you may be charged. (If you ordered an appraisal of the house before making your bid, this may satisfy the lender's requirement. For more details, see Chapter 10.) A professional appraiser will estimate the market value of the house, a necessary part of establishing what lenders call a **loan-to-value ratio (LTV).** Lenders will not lend you more than a given percentage (often 90% or 95%) of the value of the property. You can calculate the LTV by dividing the requested loan amount by the appraised value of the property.

If the appraised value turns out to be less than the agreed-on purchase price, the maximum amount of the mortgage may be smaller than you anticipated, and you may have to come up with a larger down payment. Let's assume that you have agreed to pay $180,000 for a property, and you have applied for a 90% loan of $162,000. If the appraisal comes in for $175,000, you've got a problem. The lender may be willing to lend only 90% of the appraised value, or $157,500, which is $4,500 less than you requested. To go ahead with the purchase, either you'll have to scrape up the additional cash or the seller will have to accept a lower price (or a combination of the two measures). If your purchase agreement included a provision that the property must appraise for the sales price, you would have a legitimate way to get out of the contract.

Of course, you might prefer to save the deal. In that case, get a copy of the appraisal. You have the right to see it if you have paid for it. You and your sales agent should study it together. If you both are convinced that the low appraisal is off-base, ask the lender to review the finding. Your agent can help by providing comparable sales figures to show the lender that the property is worth the original sales price. As a last resort, try a different lender. Discuss the low appraisal early on, provide comparable sales figures, and get assurance from the new loan officer that the low appraisal is not a deal breaker before you apply.

2. The credit report. The lender will seek a credit history of you and any co-purchaser or cosigner. The report will reveal how you have handled past debt and credit accounts, such as car loans, store charge accounts, and credit card balances. If you have checked your credit profile in advance, as you should, you can rest assured of no surprises (see Chapter 2). Be forthcoming about past credit mishaps. Even one late payment on just one account may require a written explanation from you. Respond truthfully about whatever circumstances caused the lateness, but try to show that the problems are behind you. If you need to rebuild a seriously flawed history, it might be a good idea to consult a nonprofit credit counseling agency first and to postpone talking to the bank. If you get your spending under control and can demonstrate even one year of timely payments, lenders will look more favorably on your application.

3. Verification. Any information you provide about income, employment history, and assets such as checking and savings accounts, the lender will check out. Don't yield to any temptation to prettify the picture. Remember that the lender isn't doing you a favor: he wants to approve you, because making loans is how the institution makes money. But if the loan officer catches you trying to inflate your assets artificially, or trying to pull some financial wool over his eyes, that will almost certainly queer the deal.

4. Approval by the mortgage insurer. If mortgage insurance is part of the loan requirement, then the insurer will have to approve your agreement. If you are getting an FHA or VA loan, the loan must also meet the standards of those agencies. This can add a week or more to the time it takes for final approval.

In the final analysis, lenders are weighing what they call the **"four C's"**—capacity, credit history, capital, and collateral—in deciding whether to extend you credit. **Capacity** means your ability to repay the debt. Lenders will look at what you earn, how long you have worked, and what your expenses are, including how many dependents you support. **Credit history** is more than just a record of how much you owe and how often you borrow. Lenders also weigh character—whether you live within your means and show willingness to pay your debts. Stability is another consideration: how long you have lived at your current address and worked at your present job or in that occupational field. **Capital** includes whether you have enough cash for the down payment and closing costs, or whether you need a gift from a relative. Lenders want to be certain you have enough money to hold on to the house. **Collateral** refers to the house itself, which secures the mortgage. Lenders must be sure that the property you are buying has sufficient value to back up your loan.

Speeding up the Process

Do more than keep your fingers crossed. Phone the loan officer about once a week to see how your application is progressing. If it has hit a snag—your employer hasn't bothered to verify your employment history, for instance—you can contact the personnel office or others who need to provide documents and nudge them along. Be polite but assertive to stay on top of the situation.

When You a Get Thumbs-Up . . .

Bingo, it's yours! Your application is approved and the lender sends you a **letter of commitment,** a formal loan offer that outlines conditions of the mortgage and gives the go-ahead for the purchase of your future home. Once you have the letter you are locked in to the loan rate and terms described there, so read it carefully. It will state the loan amount (the purchase price minus the down payment), the term of the loan (the number of years you have to repay the debt), the loan origination fee (a percentage of the loan amount), the points charged, the annual percentage rate, or APR (the total finance charge, taking into account the interest rate, origination fees, and mortgage insurance fees), and the monthly charges (including principal and interest, taxes, and insurance—or PITI, as it's sometimes called). You will be given a fixed amount of time to accept the offer and to close the loan. If all these are satisfactory, sign the papers and deliver them. Shake your loan officer's hand.

You're almost a homeowner now, but there's one more step to negotiate—the closing, discussed in Chapter 12. Don't pop the champagne cork just yet—but treat yourself to a new key ring. You'll be needing it in about 60 days to hold the new set of keys.

If You Get a Thumbs-Down . . .

This situation is tough but not terminal. Federal law requires the lender to tell you, in writing, the specific reasons for the denial. Go back and talk to the loan officer in detail about the institution's objections. Perhaps you can present new information that might cause your request to be reconsidered. If not, ask for suggestions on how you can improve your ability to get a mortgage. Make sure you understand the advice given. It may improve your chances with the next lender you visit. Different institutions have different standards, so don't give up after only one try.

Here are three common obstacles that may affect the loan decision, with suggestions on getting around them:

• **If your proposed down payment is insufficient,** ask if the lender offers other types of mortgages with lower down payment requirements, or try a different institution. You may be able to lower the down payment. In that case, however, you will need to increase the size of your loan, which means you'll need more income to qualify. Maybe relatives can pitch in with a gift.

• **If you have too much debt,** you may be able to persuade the lender to reconsider, especially if you are very close to qualifying and have an excellent credit history. If you regularly have been spending 43% of your pretax income on total debt, for example, the lender may stretch a point on the qualifying ratio (which usually calls for a 36% maximum). Otherwise, wait a few months and pay off some of your obligations—or choose a less expensive house.

• **If the lender is doubtful because of your credit history,** ask for a chance to explain. Perhaps there were special circumstances surrounding your past credit problems. Come clean and volunteer a good explanation: you lost your job or had unexpected medical bills, for example. Lenders today tend to be more sympathetic to such problems than they were in the past. If your plea falls on deaf ears, you may want to turn to a mortgage broker, some of whom specialize in helping bad credit risks.

Finally, if the way you were treated suggests the possibility of unlawful discrimination, understand your rights. The **Fair Housing Act** prohibits discrimination in housing loans (or sales) on the basis of race, religion, color, national origin, gender, handicap, or familial status (having children under the age of 18). The **Equal Credit Opportunity Act** forbids discrimination in any aspect of a credit transaction on the basis of most of the same factors (but not handicap and familial status), plus receipt of public assistance funds, age, or the exercise of any right under the Consumer Credit Protection Act.

If you think your rights have been violated, first talk to **private fair housing groups**. They can walk you through the mortgage process to help you understand why your application came up short. They can also help you decide whether your experience suggests that the lender is discriminating unlawfully and discuss whether to file a complaint with one of the **human rights agencies.** These are government organizations set up by a city, county, or state to deal with discrimination. Federal or state enforcement agencies can check mortgage lenders to ensure they complied with the laws against lending discrimination. If you choose to write, include your name and address; the name and address of the lending institution you are complaining about; the address of the house involved; and a brief description of the alleged violation and the date it occurred.

Attorneys can also advise you whether the lender's treatment gives you grounds for bringing a lawsuit against the lender and tell you about monetary damages and the other types of relief available if you can prove that illegal discrimination took place.

CHECKPOINTS

- When you find the mortgage you want, make a date with the lender and ask in advance about the required documentation.
- Come clean about any credit problems and offer a good explanation. If your history is seriously flawed, consider waiting a year until you have a record of timely payments.
- Remember that institutions vary in their lending standards. If one turns you down, find out the exact reasons why—then try another loan source.

SECTION IV

CUTTING THE BEST DEAL: THE BUYING PROCESS

CHAPTER 10

Assembling a Professional Team

The pathway to homeownership is marked with predictable headaches. Professional help is like aspirin: it can dissolve much of the pain—especially if you're a first-timer. Before you even start looking at houses, begin scouting for a real estate lawyer, an appraiser, and a home inspector. Get recommendations from friends, mortgage lenders, and title and escrow companies. Be cautious about accepting recommendations from a real estate agent, though. He wants the sale to go through, so the professionals he recommends may be disinclined to uncover problems—structural, legal, or financial—that could turn out to be deal breakers.

You'll need the pros at different points in the buying process, but there's an advantage to lining them up early. When you spot your perfect jewel of a house, you'll be able to swoop in fast—giving you a decided advantage over unprepared buyers who must have the sales contract reviewed by a not-yet-selected attorney and the premises checked and evaluated by a still-to-be-chosen inspector and appraiser.

Putting a Lawyer on Your Case

You may be wondering if you need legal advice. The answer is that you'll never know for sure until it's too late. Real estate transactions are full of pitfalls, and many of those traps can be costly. A real estate attorney is vital when you don't fully understand every document that you're required to sign. If a phrase or term puzzles you in a contract, a lawyer can translate and warn you if it's a potential time bomb.

In some states, notably California and Florida, buyers rarely use attorneys to help them through the settlement process. A title company, an escrow firm, or even the lender will ordinarily handle the closing. If you feel comfortable with local custom and your own expertise, then go it alone. If you have any doubts, however, put an attorney on your team, since he or she may be the only professional player who is wholly devoted to your interests during the wheeling, dealing, and closing.

Shop early for your attorney so you have plenty of time to ask questions. Some suggestions: Will you charge by the hour, or can you offer a flat fee for all the work related to this purchase? How much would the fixed rate be? Do you have an attorney-client relationship with either the banker or the seller? Can you give me a few references among your clients?

When you've picked your counselor, request a letter that spells out both the expected costs and the services to be performed. You want a practitioner who does a lot of real estate work so he or she won't have to spend hours researching basic topics at your expense. It won't take long for an experienced attorney to review a simple transaction. If there's a problem detected in the early stages, it could save you serious money in the long run.

If you're a novice negotiator, confer with your attorney before submitting your opening bid on the prospective house. If the seller makes a counteroffer you can live with, then make your final acceptance subject to your counsel's review of the new terms. Also look to your lawyer to add buyer-protection clauses to your contract. If you want to ensure you can get back your deposit if you can't find an acceptable mortgage, for instance, or if you aren't sure that you can scrape together the down payment in time for the closing, your attorney can insert some so-called escape clauses, giving you extra time to find the funds or the right to back out of the deal.

Adding an Appraiser

Chances are that if you want a mortgage on your property, your lender will require you to pay for a professional home appraisal to make sure the house is worth the amount the bank is lending you. Even though financial institutions have the legal right to waive appraisals on property transactions under $250,000, most still order an evaluation. "I don't think many lenders among our membership would make a mortgage loan without using a licensed or certified appraiser and a full appraisal," says Sam Pincich, program manager for the real estate market at America's Community Bankers, a Washington, D.C.–based trade organization.

This can work in your favor. If you and your lender agree in advance on choosing an appraiser, you can use the appraisal not only for obtaining a mortgage, but also for setting a price. Appraisers working for lending institutions tend to be conservative, so chances are good that the appraised value will be lower than the seller's asking price. (Many real estate agents acknowledge that the initial offering price on a home typically runs 10%–20% higher than its true value.) Having the appraisal in hand gives you a strong stance in the bargaining game. Just remember that if you don't buy the property, you're still liable for the cost of the appraisal.

If you're not willing to spring for a full appraisal of a house you aren't sure you want to buy, you may opt for a "limited scope" appraisal that typically will cost $75–$150 and be done in several hours. That's substantially cheaper and faster than a traditional report, which might cost $250–$500 and take several days. Your banker probably won't accept it, but a quick evaluation can serve as a sharp reality check if you're concerned about overpaying and the seller won't budge on the price.

Since these "drive-by" appraisals are often based on a quick curbside evaluation, plus price data on comparable properties culled from databases, they can come in wide of the mark. To protect yourself from inaccuracies, choose an experienced practitioner—preferably one who belongs to a professional organization. All appraisers must be licensed or certified by the state in which they operate. Those who belong to a trade group such as the Appraisal Institute or the American Society of Professional Appraisers have also met certain education and experience requirements and shown a commitment to the profession.

Finding a Qualified Home Inspector

Of the whole cast of characters involved in a typical real estate transaction—the agent, lawyer, lender, and the rest—most all are accountable to a licensing board or regulatory agencies. But the home inspector, who can make or break the deal, needs no license or credentials to do business in most states. (Texas is an exception.) So how to separate the ones who know what they're doing from the ones who hope you don't?

One way is to look for membership in a trade association, such as the American Society of Home Inspectors (ASHI), which requires applicants to pass standard tests and conduct numerous inspections before they are accepted into the group. Phone ASHI (800-743-2744) and it will supply a list of qualified inspectors in your area, mailed (in about a week) or faxed (in seconds) to your home or office.

Ask any candidate you're considering how long he or she has been in the home inspection business. A good bet is a former home builder or a structural engineer who has been checking houses for a decade. A sales agent who has hit slow times and taken up inspecting as a sideline probably isn't.

Get referral names from a friend or your attorney. If your sales agent suggests a practitioner, try to get a second reference. Agents are nearly always working for the seller (see Chapter 5) and may send a not-so-subtle message to the inspector to go easy. You want a tough, straightforward construction cop who will give you a detailed explanation of any problem, along with an estimate of the cost to fix it. He should not offer to make the repairs himself, nor should he suggest potential contractors. (If you feel confident there is no conflict of interest, however, you may ask for recommendations.)

Finally, ask your inspector if he is bonded or carries liability insurance. If so, you'll have some hope of being compensated if the inspector fails to note a flaw that becomes a financial headache after you buy the home.

The cost of the inspection will vary with the size of the house—a 40-room mansion obviously takes longer to inspect than a two-bedroom bungalow—and the region of the country. Whatever the price, it should be a flat fee (never a percentage of the valuation) and agreed upon before inspection day. A rock-bottom amount is $150, says the Council of Better Business Bureaus, and prices move up from there to $500 or more.

Once you've made the initial appointment with the inspector, lace up your sneakers and tag along for the few hours that the process takes. You'll be amazed at all you can learn about your new habitation—the condition of the wiring and the gutters, the quality of the construction materials, whether the workmanship was meticulous or sloppy. Follow the inspector down into the crawl space and learn about your annual maintenance chores. Do not ask the inspector to give you a flat "buy" or "don't buy" opinion. That decision is yours, and rightfully so. The defects that emerge, however, can give you valuable leverage in negotiating the final sales price of the house.

As a rule, you can expect the inspector to examine

- the **structure** of the house, including the foundation, walls, ceilings, stairs, and attic;
- the **exterior,** including chimneys, caulking and weather stripping, roof, grading, drainage, driveways, and patios;
- the **interior,** including visible insulation and ventilation, steps, counters, railings, cabinetry, sinks, and showers;
- the **interior plumbing,** such as fixtures, faucets, drains, and the water heater;
- the **electrical system,** including wiring, fixtures, and overload protection;
- the **heating and air-conditioning systems,** including both the basic equipment and the distribution system.

There are limits to the examination, however. The inspector should not move furniture or boxes that block access to any part of the house or do anything in the course of the inspection to damage the property in any way. This means, for example, that he won't disassemble walls or systems, but only examine visible and accessible parts of a property. He also won't inspect for termites or other pests, forecast how long appliances will last, or estimate the value of the home. (That last item is the appraiser's job.)

If the inspector uncovers a major problem—the roof is collapsing, the house is sinking because it is on unstable ground—have your lawyer take up the matter with the seller. You'll want the present owner to fix the problem or deduct the cost of the repair from the final sales price. If the owner is paying for the repairs, however, he has a financial incentive to cut costs and perhaps settle for a shoddy job. For your own protection, insist on the right to say exactly how you want the work to be done. This could include specifying the materials the workmen will use, even the type of professional who performs the job—a cabinetry specialist, for example, or a master electrician. Retain the right to sign off on the completed work prior to closing.

For added security you could require as part of the purchase agreement that funds equal to 150% of the highest estimate for the repair be withheld from the seller's proceeds until you—or your inspector—approve the finished job. For minor defects you and the seller may opt to split the expense, but you should still keep a critical eye on the quality of the workmanship.

A few penny-wise, pound-foolish buyers decide they can skip the professional inspection, especially if they are buying a never-lived-in house. Don't join their ranks. True, you might save a few hundred dollars—but you could also wind up paying thousands of dollars if structural problems show up at your new address. A California survey of 200 home buyers found that inspections saved the new owners an average of $1,573 each in prepurchase repairs or reduced sales prices. The greatest gains, however, were in "peace of mind" and "absence of surprises." So you might consider the inspector's fee as a premium for emotional insurance, bought to save you from a paralyzing case of buyer's remorse.

CHECKPOINTS

- If there's any part of the sale documents that you don't fully understand, enlist a lawyer to help. Make sure that he or she is a real estate specialist.
- Understand that an appraiser will estimate fair market value—but won't tell you the condition of the house. Consider getting at least a limited appraisal before making your opening bid on a property. A professional valuation may save you money on the ultimate sales price.
- Check house inspectors' credentials thoroughly, since most states don't license them. Don't omit the inspection process, even if you're buying a brand-new house. And tag along with the inspector, to learn all you can about the upkeep on your new castle.

CHAPTER 11

Making Your Bid

You and your partner have laughed, cried, fought, hugged, lost sleep, and done all else necessary to reach your decision. At last you agree on a home that you love, the price is about what you expected to pay, and you're ready to—well, home in. Now what?

Before making that opening sales bid, be confident you know about any major problem areas in the house. You should have inspected the property to the best of your ability (and perhaps ordered a professional inspection as well) and questioned the real estate agent and the owner about the structural soundness and condition of the basic systems. (Both sellers and sales agents can be held liable if they fail to tell the buyer of any defects they are aware of in the house.) Have a clear idea of what it will cost to fix any major problems.

Get a feel for the sales climate in your area, if you haven't already. What is the average selling time for a house? Anything over four months indicates a slow market. Are owners making price cuts or playing competing buyers against each other? Would you describe the market as stone cold with nothing moving, starting to blaze—or simply temperate?

To assess values, ask the seller's broker (or your own) for **comparables,** or **"comps,"** an analysis showing the recent sale prices for comparable houses nearby, as well as the asking prices of comparable properties presently listed for sale. By adding or subtracting the dollar value of the positive and negative attributes of the house you've picked, you will get a good idea of its true market value. If local real estate is depressed, and houses linger on the market, consider offering 10% below the past half year's sales price for a comparable property.

Finally, nose around to determine how anxious the owners of your intended dream house are to sell. If the owners have lowered the listing price by at least 3%, they may be ripe for a lowball offer. You also stand an excellent chance of negotiating price cuts with sellers who have lived in their houses more than 15 years or so. They could be sitting on a thick equity cushion, large enough to let them accept a lower price and still post a sizable profit.

If you have the stomach for it, you can adopt vulture tactics—pressing an owner who is already experiencing financial difficulties. Likely candidates: couples in mid-divorce who want a fast resolution, heirs who must raise cash to pay estate taxes, and sellers who have already bought another home or are forced to move quickly for a company transfer.

Conversely, recognize that you will have the least negotiating room if the market is hot, the property is in excellent condition and new to the market, the location is a winner, and the seller has the patience to wait you out. In this case a low bid is unlikely to succeed.

Whether the market is hot or cold, try to have your financing in hand. A preapproved buyer is in a far stronger position to obtain seller concessions than a bidder with no financial backing. In choosing between competing bids, the seller will virtually always go with the buyer who has cash in hand. The reason: More deals go down the tubes over the buyer's inability to get financing than any other factor.

There's one final point to weigh. You and your partner must

come to a private decision about how much you want the house. If you and/or your mate conclude that you absolutely must have that eighteenth-century shepherd's cottage with the Dutch entrance door and the brick oven—or life as you know it will lose its meaning—then be prepared to offer something close to what the owner is asking. This may leave others gasping in disbelief, but never mind. A lifetime of regret or a sourpussed spouse is not worth a few thousand dollars. Still, you needn't confess your passion to the seller. Keep your cool to keep the upper hand.

Now, into the fray. You and the owner have three financial arenas in which to wrestle: the sales price, the closing costs, and financing terms. Don't expect to pin the seller on each point, however. Instead, determine *your* primary objective. Do you want the best possible price—or is your major goal to obtain a commitment from the seller? If the house is hard to come by—that eighteenth-century cottage, for example, or the only three-bedroom in tony Yuppie Heights priced under $350,000—obtaining the seller's agreement to the deal may be primary. Then make an offer 5%–10% below the asking price, but always leave yourself some bargaining room.

If price is paramount, don't be afraid to make a lowball bid. Never let a broker intimidate you with that harrumphing line: "I wouldn't insult my client [the seller] with an offer that low." This is simply a ploy to get you to raise your dollar amount. If a broker refuses to pass along your first submission—and in a soft market anything within 20% of the market value should be seriously considered—make tracks for another agent. (Note that the bargaining rules are different when you are buying a newly constructed home from the builder. For advice on this point, consult Chapter 15.)

Depending on your choice and local custom, the negotiating process may begin with an aggressive opening bid made verbally through your agent. More formally, it may start with the buyer's submission of a written "offer to purchase" the property for a particular price, subject to specified conditions or contingencies that you think are important.

In many places the offer to purchase is a binding legal document, so don't proffer it casually. It commits the buyer to sign a more complete piece of paper known as a **purchase and sale agreement,** sometimes called a **sales contract.** Whatever the custom in your area, remember that any written offer will have legal implications, so ask your attorney to review it. Trying to save a few dollars by bringing the lawyer on board at a later stage is truly a false economy. It's easier to get the terms right at this stage than for an attorney to have to extract you later from an ill-advised commitment.

The initial offer is usually accompanied by **earnest money,** a good faith payment you submit to show the seller you are serious. What is customary differs by location, but plan on at least $500–$1,000, with the check made out to the brokerage firm of the sales agent. The firm should deposit the funds in an escrow account to be returned to you if the seller doesn't accept your offer within a specified time period. You usually forfeit the money if the seller accepts the contract and then you back out of the deal.

If the seller agrees to your first written offer by signing it, this document becomes the basis for the legally binding sales contract. That's why it is so important that you understand everything in the offer to purchase and that it be a comprehensive work. Fannie Mae suggests that an offer to purchase should include at least the following items:

- A complete legal description of the property.
- The amount of earnest money accompanying the offer.
- The price you are offering.
- The size of your down payment and how the remainder of the purchase will be financed (including the maximum interest rate you are willing to pay if you still must seek a mortgage loan).
- Any items of personal property the owner has said will stay with the house or that you want to have included. Articles that are often contested include washing machines, air con-

ditioners, and other appliances, lighting fixtures, window draperies, and fireplace screens. (Later in the bidding, if you are responding to a counteroffer, you might ask the seller to toss in some of your "would like's," such as a custom-made room divider or the potted palm on the patio.)

- A proposed closing date and occupancy date.
- The length of time the offer is valid (often three to five days).
- The stipulation that your obligation to buy is dependent on the negotiation of a satisfactory formal sales contract.

In a typical scenario, the sales agent presents your offer to the owners and relays their response back to you. The seller may accept your deal, reject it, or make an alternate proposal, known as a counteroffer. It's generally not worth haggling further if the seller comes back with a figure within 3% or so of the price you want. But if you still consider the price too high, let the counter expire. Then make a new bid for an amount between your first offer and the seller's counteroffer.

When you're negotiating, don't overlook financing terms. If the seller is willing to take on some or even all of your closing costs, then you may not want to quibble over the last fistful of dollars on price. Closing costs can easily total 5% of the purchase figure—that's $7,500 on a $150,000 house—so try to lay on the seller all or part of the loan-processing fees, the points, or the cost of the inspection. Other items that could go up for grabs: the cost of the title search; title insurance; appraiser fees. Many owners find it easier to yield on terms than on price, and this could prove valuable at a time when you're almost sure to be cash short.

Another cost-shaving tactic that's worth considering is asking the seller to lower your mortgage rate for the first few years through what's known as a **buy-down.** This is an especially sound move if you're worried about affording the monthly mortgage payments on the house in the early years. Terms vary, but in a buy-down on a 10%, 30-year fixed-rate $100,000 mortgage, for example, the seller might pay your lender an up-front fee of about $5,100, lowering your interest rate to 7% in the loan's first year and cutting the monthly payment to $665 from $878. The rate would then climb one percentage point each year until it locks in at 10% in year four.

When the offer-counteroffer contest comes to a satisfactory close, and each side has tweaked the deal to suit, the game ends. Typically you'll go to closing 30–60 days later. Now, let's look at some ways to rein in those closing costs.

CHECKPOINTS

- Investigate financing before you enter a bid. A buyer who is prequalified or, even better, preapproved by a lender is in a far stronger position with the seller.
- Decide whether your primary objective is to obtain the best price or the best terms—or simply the owner's commitment to sell. Adjust your strategy accordingly.
- Have a lawyer review any written bid. It's cheaper and easier to have the attorney make changes now than to extricate you from a document you agreed to earlier.

CHAPTER 12

Keeping a Lid on Closing Costs

You have a sales contract and you have the financing. Now it's on to the closing, a landmark event involving many serious people in suits. You will sit around a large table, where you'll turn over a cashier's check for the down payment and sign on for mammoth future mortgage payments. In return you'll walk out with the house keys, the garage door opener, and a thick folder of hammered-out agreements and reports. Most owners remember the experience as a blur—a blizzard of paper, signing documents and checks one after the other. But knowing what to expect, what kinds of papers you'll sign, can make the closing a less overwhelming experience—and may help you to rein in some of those obstreperous costs.

The closing process begins weeks (even months) earlier and follows an outline set largely by your original offer. That proposal, when it's been adjusted to suit both parties, becomes the sales contract once the seller signs it. So consider closing fees before you make your opening bid and throughout the negotiations. Customs vary nationwide about who pays for what, but you and the seller are free to dicker over most of the charges.

You can shift some bills completely to the seller, which will lower your total cash outlay. In most states you can also cut costs by shopping among providers of the settlement services.

Three days after you apply for a mortgage, your lender must send you a detailed estimate of the costs you will face at closing. Federal law also requires your lender to give you closing documents at least one day before the close if you request them, so make sure you do. If the final fees listed are much different from the ones in the preliminary estimate, don't be shy about challenging them and asking for reasons. Here are three basic categories of charges that you will meet in your settlement or closing transactions:

• **Charges for establishing and transferring ownership:** title search, title insurance, related legal fees, and fees for conducting the closing.
• **Amounts paid to state and local governments:** city, county, and state transfer taxes, recording fees, and prepaid property taxes.
• **Costs of obtaining your mortgage:** surveys, appraisals, credit checks, loan documentation fees, notary charges, loan origination, commitment and processing fees, homeowners insurance, interest prepayments, and lender's inspection fees.

Let's take a closer look at each of the three categories to see what they contain and how you can deflate some of the costs:

1. *Who owns what.* If you're buying or selling a car, proving ownership is relatively simple. The state in which the car is registered issues a certificate of title to the owner. When it comes to houses, proving title is more murky. Your lender won't give you a mortgage loan on a house unless you can prove that the seller owns it. That's why a **title search** is essential, and the lender usually bills you for its cost. A growing number of localities have computerized property records so the searcher can accomplish the job with relative dispatch. Low-tech still prevails

in many areas, however, and then the investigator must search public records by hand, a time-consuming task. Documents affecting the title may be spread among several government offices, complicating the job.

In addition to a formal title search, your lender is likely to require a **title insurance** policy to protect against an error by the searcher. Let's say, for example, that the seller's long-lost cousin Iris returns from Patagonia with indisputable evidence that she holds legal title to the house you intend to buy. Although the searcher should have found this in the public records, he or she missed the claim somehow. The omission creates a contretemps in which the lender finds that it has loaned you, the home buyer, tens or hundreds of thousands of dollars to purchase a house from someone who doesn't own it. To prevent this fiasco, the lender will insist on title insurance prior to the settlement. The cost of the policy (a onetime premium) is usually based on the loan amount and is customarily paid by you, the purchaser. During the sales negotiations, however, a wily buyer could lay off all or part of the cost on the seller.

That title insurance protects only the lender, however, and you should take out an owner's title insurance policy as well. The additional premium cost is commonly only a small fraction of the price for a lender's policy. If the seller owned the house you are buying for only a few years, check with his title company to see if you can get a **reissue rate.** If no claims have been made against the title since the previous search, the insurer may consider the house to be a low-risk property, and your premium is likely to be significantly lower than the regular rate for a new policy. Finally, check what coverage a proposed policy offers. Generally the best policies are those with the fewest exclusions on coverage.

Last and by no means least, budget a sum for **legal fees,** including an attorney to represent you and possibly one for your lender as well.

2. The government's cut. Transfer, recording, and property taxes, collected by local and state governments, may be among the heftiest fees you pay at your closing. You can't duck the taxes, but you may be able to trim your share of the bill—again, by offloading some of these costs to the seller of the house.

3. Mortgage-related costs. You paid some of these along the way, starting when you applied for the mortgage loan. The **application fee,** charged by the lender, covers the initial costs of processing your loan request and checking your credit history. The **appraisal fee** covers the independent assessment of the fair market value of the house. The lender usually requires a **property survey** as well, to ensure that no adjoining structures have encroached on your lot since the last survey and that the house and other buildings legally are situated where you and the seller say they are.

The **loan origination fee** is charged for the lending institution's work in evaluating and preparing your loan. **Points,** as you know, are prepaid finance charges that the lender imposes at closing to increase his loan yield beyond the stated interest rate on the mortgage note. One point equals 1% of the loan amount. Sometimes the points are financed, not paid, by adding them to the amount of money you borrow. A **private mortgage insurance** premium will most likely be charged if you make a down payment of less than 20% of the value of the house. The policy covers the lender's risk in case you fail to make the monthly loan payments. If your mortgage is insured by the FHA, or guaranteed by the VA, you will have to pay FHA mortgage insurance premiums or VA guarantee fees. And, of course, your lender will expect you to have a **homeowners insurance** policy in effect at closing, to protect against physical damage. (For more about choosing this policy, see Chapter 14.)

Just when you think you have paid every conceivable tithe, tariff, and tax, a few more bills may crop up to annoy you. There might be an **assumption fee** if you're taking over or assuming an existing mortgage on the house. You might be hit with an unexpected **home inspection fee** for an analysis of the structural condition of the property and for a **termite**

inspection, though the seller often antes up for this one. And there are inevitably **adjustments,** for various types of expenses prorated between you and the seller. Local property taxes, annual condo fees, and other service charges, for instance, may be split between you and the seller to cover your respective periods of ownership for the tax period or calendar year. The seller might also charge you for heating oil left in the tank—unless you haggle your way out of that one.

You've heard the worst now, but there's a bit more to chew over. You might, in the worst-case scenario, encounter a slew of lender-imposed charges for courier service, document processing, and similar fuzzy items. "For 99% of the residential real estate loans that I review, one or more of the fees is inflated or downright fake," advises David Allman, an Atlanta real estate attorney whose clients include title companies nationwide. Adding insult to this injury, recent amendments to the federal **Truth-in-Lending Act** limit your right to challenge overcharges after the closing. On a new mortgage, your only recourse is to sue the lender.

The best defense is a good offense. When shopping for a lender, ask what closing fees you're likely to owe. If they seem inflated, request that the lender reduce or eliminate them. Many lenders will deal to get your business, acknowledges Robert O'Toole, senior staff vice president of the Mortgage Bankers Association. In particular, cast a cold eye on administrative charges for drawing up, reviewing, and evaluating your loan. These are often tagged as "document preparation," "general processing," or "underwriting" fees, and they usually range from $150 to $250 each. But such fees should already be built into the basic loan application fee, points, and interest rate, according to Allman.

Customs vary significantly from region to region, so no one estimate for closing costs will fit all cases. A helpful rule of thumb is to estimate that settlement expenses will add at least an additional 3% to the price of your home in low-tax parts of the country. In high-tax places figure on 5%–6%. Table 12-1 gives a sample range of closing cost charges for specific services on a $75,000 home purchased with either a 10% or 20% down payment.

TABLE 12-1

Sample Closing Costs on a $75,000 House

Because costs may vary significantly from area to area and from lender to lender, the following are estimates only. Your actual costs may be higher or lower than the figures indicated below.

	Down Payment, 10%	Down Payment, 20%
Mortgage Amount	$67,500	$60,000
Application Fee	$75–$300	$75–$300
Loan Origination Fee (1%)	$675	$600
Points (1%–3%)	$675–$2,025	$600–$1,800
Mortgage Insurance	$338–$675	—
Title Search and Insurance Fees	$450–$600	$450–$600
Lender's Attorney's Review Fees	$75–$200	$75–$200
Appraisal Fee	$150–$400	$150–$400
Adjustments	—	—
Homeowners Hazard Insurance	$300–$600	$300–$600
Home Inspection Fee	$175–$350	$175–$350
Survey Costs	$125–$300	$125–$300
Notary Fees	$10–$25	$10–$25
Recording Fees	$40–$60	$40–$60
State/Local Transfer Fees	$75–$1,125	$75–$1,125

Source: The Federal Reserve

Table 12-2 is a worksheet to aid you in comparing settlement costs required by different lenders.

TABLE 12-2

Settlement Costs Worksheet

	Provider 1	Provider 2
Items Payable in Connection with Loan		
Loan Origination Fee	_____	_____
Loan Discount	_____	_____
Appraisal Fee	_____	_____
Credit Report	_____	_____
Lender's Inspection Fee	_____	_____
Mortgage Insurance Application Fee	_____	_____
Assumption Fee	_____	_____
Items Required by Lender to Be Paid in Advance		
Interest from to @$ per day	_____	_____
Mortgage Insurance Premium for months	_____	_____
Hazard Insurance Premium for years	_____	_____
Reserves Deposited with Lender		
Hazard Insurance months @$ per month	_____	_____
Mortgage Insurance months @$ per month	_____	_____
City Property Taxes months @$ per month	_____	_____
County Property Taxes months @$ per month	_____	_____
Annual Assessments months @$ per month	_____	_____

Title Charges

Settlement or Closing Fee	_____	_____
Abstract or Title Search	_____	_____
Title Examination	_____	_____
Title Insurance Binder	_____	_____
Document Preparation	_____	_____
Notary Fees	_____	_____
Attorney's Fees	_____	_____
Title Insurance	_____	_____

Government Recording and Transfer Charges

Recording Fees:
  Deed $ Mortgage $ Release $ _____   _____
City/County Tax/Stamps:
  Deed $ Mortgage $ _____   _____
State Tax/Stamps:
  Deed $ Mortgage $ _____   _____

Additional Settlement Charges

Survey	_____	_____
Pest Inspection	_____	_____

Total Settlement Charges   _____   _____

Source: The Federal Reserve

One last caution: Real estate agents say that the house keys are the one item that sellers most commonly forget to bring to the settlement. Make sure you get keys for all the doors—basement, garage, shed, and the whole shebang. Thread them on your new key ring, inspect your new home, and rejoice in your new role.

CHECKPOINTS

- Think about settlement fees before you submit your sales offer. Consider asking the seller to shoulder some of the costs.
- Shop around for competitive prices for as many services as possible.
- Don't hesitate to negotiate the costs either with the seller or with the service provider.

SECTION V

ENHANCING VALUE: THE OWNERSHIP PROCESS

CHAPTER 13

Capitalizing on Tax Breaks

Your new house, condominium, or cooperative apartment provides a major shelter from taxes as well as from the elements. It provides deductions when you buy it, while you live in it, and when you sell it. If you have always taken the standard deduction rather than itemizing write-offs on your federal income tax return, now is the time to reconsider that decision.

While the following rundown is no substitute for professional tax advice, it will give a general idea of the tax advantages available to you as a homeowner and anticipate some of the questions that may arise when you tackle your next 1040 form.

The tax breaks begin even before you lasso a mortgage. The IRS allows you to deduct **moving expenses** that arise from a change in your employment. You may write off, without limitation, the cost of moving your household goods and personal belongings, including your car and pets, from your former residence to a new location. In addition, you may deduct transportation and lodging costs for you and your family en route to your new abode. (You may not, however, deduct the cost of meals in transit.) For you to qualify for moving expense deductions, the distance between your new job and your old home must be at least 50 miles greater than the distance from your old job and your old home, and you must stay in your new post full-time for 39 weeks in the year after the move. Self-employed people must follow similar but somewhat more stringent guidelines.

Points, the additional amount of interest you pay when a loan is closed, are deductible in the year you buy your primary residence and pay the points, with a few limitations. The payment of points must be an established practice in your area, and the number of points you pay must not exceed the norm for your community. If you pay, for instance, six points in a locality where two are the average, only two points can be written off that year. The IRS rarely demands proof of typical fees, but if points where you live are extraordinarily high, get a statement from the lender saying so, in case you're audited.

One further warning: You may not be able to deduct points currently if you pay them with money you borrowed from the same bank that holds your mortgage. To make clear that you're using your own cash, write a separate check to your lender for points attributable to your mortgage loan. When you tackle your tax return, make sure you pick up the amount of points you paid from the Form 1098 the bank sends you in January. The allowable amount (shown in Box 2 of the form) may also include the loan origination fee, which is considered a point carrying a fancy name. (In a relatively recent change, FHA and VA loan origination fees are also allowed as deductible points.)

Even if points are paid by the seller, you are entitled to take them as a deduction—though you must reduce the purchase price of your home by the amount of seller-paid points. (This will come into play when you eventually sell your home and are calculating your taxable gain or loss.)

Points paid for a vacation home, or that don't meet the IRS test for a deduction in the current tax year, may be deducted proportionately over the life of the loan. So if you have a 30-

year mortgage, you can deduct one-thirtieth of the total amount each year until the loan is repaid. If you sell or refinance before the mortgage loan expires, you may deduct any remaining points in that year.

Any state or local **property taxes** are fully deductible on your federal return. (A few states also permit the deduction.) Condo owners may write off both the real estate taxes on their units and a proportionate share of the taxes paid on the common areas of their buildings. Co-op owners can deduct their allocated portion of the association's property tax bill. Low- and moderate-income homeowners may qualify for a full or partial property tax abatement in some localities.

The biggest annual tax windfall, however, is the **home-mortgage interest deduction,** which costs the U.S. Treasury about $50 billion each year. If you finance your home or condo purchase with a 30-year, $80,000 mortgage at 10%, you will pay the lender $7,944 in deductible interest the first year—and only $480 in nondeductible principal. (As time goes on, the balance shifts and you pay progressively less interest and more principal.) If you are paying off both a first and second mortgage on your house, the interest you pay on the second mortgage is also deductible up to $1 million. (You may also deduct interest on a home equity line of up to $100,000.) And co-op owners, who own stock in a corporation that entitles them to occupy their residence, get the same tax break. The IRS lets them deduct the interest on debt secured by their stock just as if the loan were secured by their residence. In addition, co-op owners can deduct their proportionate share of the interest payments on the underlying mortgage on the building.

If you've started a home-based business, you may qualify for a **home office write-off,** though in recent years the IRS has cracked down on them with a vengeance. But don't be cowed. Martin Kaplan, a New York City accountant, estimates that if "your business grosses $25,000 to $50,000 a year, the deduction can save you about $1,000 in taxes annually." Just be scrupulous in making sure you qualify. The basic rules are strict:

- The space that you set aside as an office or workshop must be used regularly and exclusively for business. It can't double as your child's playroom.
- A tougher standard requires that the activity at the heart of your work—meeting with patients or clients, for instance—be done at home. Keep meticulous records to back up the fact that even if you travel for off-site meetings, the bulk of your work is done at home. If that's impossible, skip the deduction.

If you believe you meet these tests, consult an experienced accountant to advise you on your best moves. You may be able to depreciate your work space, write off ordinary business expenses, and even deduct certain indirect expenses, such as a portion of your home alarm costs.

If your house is robbed or damaged, you may be able to claim a deduction for the uninsured portion of your **casualty losses.** After you have figured your total loss and subtracted any reimbursements, you must calculate how much of that amount you can deduct. First, you must reduce each loss by $100; then you must further reduce the result by 10% of your adjusted gross income. In addition, the loss must be sudden, unusual, or unexpected. What counts as a qualified casualty? Floods, earthquakes, bursting boilers, and shipwrecks seem to satisfy the IRS, but damage from termites, beetles, or droughts doesn't necessarily meet the test. These are murky waters, and you had best ask your tax adviser to help you navigate them if you have suffered a major loss.

You may be surprised (or dismayed) to learn that you can't deduct the cost of **improving or repairing** your new residence—though there are some valuable write-offs you may capture further down the line. The initial point to grasp is that improvements and repairs are different actions in the eyes of Uncle Sam. A repair is anything you do to keep your property in good condition, such as mending its fences, replacing broken windows, or patching leaks. Admirable tasks all, but none of them will cut your tax bill.

An improvement, however, adds to the value of your property or prolongs its life—and garners more favorable tax treatment: putting up a new fence, adding a new wing, even planting a new sugar maple tree—these are worthy improvements that will return money to your pocket in the future. While you can't deduct their cost, you can add the amount to your home's **basis**—that is, its value, which will be the financial starting point for calculating your capital gain when you ultimately sell the property. If you buy your home for $100,000, add $20,000 in improvements, then sell for $150,000, your taxable gain is $30,000—not the $50,000 that you would be taxed on without the $20,000 of enhancements. As a practical matter, you don't need to distinguish between nondeductible repairs and capital improvements at the time you do the work—simply save the receipts for both. Your tax adviser can help you make the distinction between improvements (which add to your basis) and repairs (which don't) at the time you sell your home.

Over the years your ownership stake in your house will be growing steadily, and the day may come when you want to **tap into the equity** for some ready cash. You have three choices:

- Refinance your house
- Take out a second mortgage loan
- Apply for a home-equity line of credit

The interest you pay for any of the three kinds of loans is ordinarily tax-deductible. In other respects the deals diverge. When you **refinance,** you apply for an entirely new mortgage loan, typically at a lower rate or for better terms. **Second mortgages** and **home-equity lines** both allow you to borrow against a portion of the difference between the balance due on your existing mortgage and the current value of your home.

All three equity-tapping methods can be risky. First, you may incur costly fees up front. A worse hazard is rising interest rates. If you have a floating-rate loan (as most home-equity lines and many mortgages do), rising rates could inflate your monthly payments to an uncomfortably large amount. Suppose that you fall behind on your bill. Even though you may have used the borrowed money to buy a boat or a car, it's your house that secured the loan and it's your house the bank will come after. So proceed with extreme caution.

When you eventually sell your house, you can take advantage of two important tax breaks:

- The **home-sale rollover,** which permits you to postpone payment of tax on your capital gain.
- The **over-55 exclusion,** a once-in-a-lifetime benefit that permits up to $125,000 of capital gain to escape income tax entirely if the seller meets certain conditions.

To qualify for the tax rollover on the sale of your principal residence, you must reinvest the entire adjusted sales price of the old home within a limited period of time, usually two years before or after the sale of the property. You can reduce your capital gain by adding to your original purchase price the cost of any lasting improvements you've made—the fencing, the sugar maple, the new wing mentioned earlier—and such selling expenses as the real estate agent's commission and advertising. If you buy a cheaper house and fix it up, the renovation costs may be added to your basis and let you defer all or part of your gain.

Chances are you'll be able to defer most or all capital-gains taxes permanently. There's no limit to the number of times you may use the tax-free rollover, though generally you may not use it more than once during any two-year period. (The IRS waives this limitation if you sell your home to begin work at a new principal location and you qualify for the moving expense deduction.) If you die before taxes are due on your successive house sales, the accrued gains will never be taxed as income, since the tax basis for the new owner, your heir, will be the property's market value at the time of your death.

If you want to scale down to a smaller, less expensive home—or decide to rent—try to wait until you or your spouse hit age 55 at least. Then, if you have lived in the same house for a minimum of three of the past five years, you may be able to exclude up to $125,000 of your capital gain from the sale of your home. A married couple who own the house jointly can claim this tax break so long as one spouse meets both the age and the residency tests. The exclusion is a once-in-a-lifetime gift, so before taking it, consider if you will have a larger gain from another home sale in the future.

All this information—some of which may not apply to you until April, some not for decades—could be more than you care to digest in your first happy daze as a homeowner. Never mind. You can always refer back for the details.

The primary action you must take now is a simple one: Start a file and label it "House." Keep it beside the big one named "House Closing Documents" and not far from where you keep old tax returns. Into the "House" file stuff receipts for any improvements or repairs you make over the years, along with papers related to casualty or theft losses, should you be so unlucky. It may seem like a nuisance now, but the resulting savings will amply compensate you for your effort and make homeownership a far less taxing experience.

CHECKPOINTS

- The major deductions you can claim are for points paid to get a mortgage, the interest on your mortgage, and property taxes.
- To make the most of future tax breaks, hang on to papers that relate to any improvements or repairs. At sales time you'll relish every receipt that helps increase the cost basis of your home.
- When you sell you can defer capital-gains taxes if, within two years before or after the sale, you buy another home costing at least as much as the first one.
- If you are 55 or older, you may be able to exclude from capital-gains taxes up to $125,000 of profit from the sale of your primary residence.

CHAPTER 14

Protecting Your Home's Value

Let's hope that money *has* bought you happiness. Certainly it has bought you a choice place to live. As a new buyer, however, you have new obligations to match the tax advantages and emotional satisfactions that come with your changed status. You must protect your haven, guarding it against both physical and financial perils. The following list will refresh your knowledge of what the ownership process entails, counting the ways you can protect and enhance your home's value.

Homeowners Insurance

When you got your mortgage, the lender almost certainly required you to buy sufficient insurance to guarantee that the institution would get its money back if your house burned down or was otherwise destroyed. That's fine for the lender, but it's inadequate to protect your investment. You need full-value coverage, probably enhanced by an inflation-adjustment clause that keeps your policy's face amount rising with home prices. As many as two-thirds of U.S. homes are underinsured, by 35% on average, according to Marshall & Swift, a Bridgewater, New Jersey, firm that supplies building-cost data to insurers. And underinsurance is the last thing you want for your new acquisition.

Broadly speaking, an acceptable homeowners policy should pay for the repair or replacement of your house and belongings after a catastrophe, plus money for extra living expenses if you and your family have to live in a hotel while your home is being rebuilt. Coverage should also extend to claims and legal judgments against you for injuries people suffer in your home or for damage you cause. How much the insurer pays depends on your policy limits.

There's a whole raft of homeowners policies on the market, including variants for co-op and condo owners. The one you want to get is a **guaranteed replacement-cost policy,** which promises that the insurer will pay to rebuild your house at today's prices—even if that costs more than the dollar limit set in your policy. (Despite the policy name, only a handful of companies will commit to paying unlimited replacement costs. Expect a ceiling of around 120%–150% of the policy amount.) The insurer won't deduct for depreciation—the decrease in value due to age, wear and tear, and other factors—and will use materials of similar kind and quality. The ceiling for contents coverage is generally set at 75% of the home's replacement cost, significantly higher than the 50% limit that is standard on other policies. Even better is a variant, known as **law-and-ordinance coverage,** which will pay to rebuild your house to meet current building codes if they are more stringent than standards in force when the place was originally built.

While guaranteed replacement cost is the model policy to aim for, unfortunately there's no guarantee you will be able to get it. Some insurers won't offer it for period homes with plaster walls, elaborate ceiling moldings, and other details that are costly to duplicate today. Others withhold guaranteed coverage for relatively expensive homes or for older homes in deteriorating neighborhoods, where the property's market value may be significantly less than the cost of rebuilding. Some companies will reject even a 25-year-old house as "too old" for guaranteed replacement cost coverage.

As an alternative, you may be offered **replacement-cost coverage,** which pays you the cost of rebuilding your home but stops at the policy limit. Or an insurer may suggest **modified replacement-cost coverage.** This means that instead of repairing or replacing features that are characteristic of period homes—plaster walls, hardwood floors, slate roofs—with similar materials, the policy will pay for repairs using the standard building materials and construction techniques in use today. Or the insurer might offer **cash-value coverage,** which will cover the cost of replacing what's damaged, minus depreciation. If your new house has a kitchen that was built 20 years ago and it is destroyed, however, that "cash value" won't get you very far in rebuilding.

When you're comparison shopping—and you must, because prices and coverage vary widely—be sure to ask explicitly what limitations the contract sets. If you're running a business out of your home, be sure to mention it. Most policies cover business equipment in the home, but only up to $2,500. A more serious gap: Most policies offer no business liability insurance unless you request a supplementary package linking homeowners and business coverage.

The amount of homeowners insurance you should carry depends on the replacement cost of your house—what you would have to spend to rebuild your dwelling exactly as it stands now. Don't confuse this notion with market value or you could wind up seriously over- or underinsuring your property. The replacement cost of an ornate Victorian period piece situated in a deteriorating inner-city neighborhood could be far higher than its current selling price.

You can get a back-of-an-envelope estimate of the replacement cost of a standard house by multiplying the square footage by local building costs per square foot for that type of dwelling. For example, if a house is 2,000 square feet and local building costs are $110 per square foot, the cost to replace the house would be about $220,000.

Most insurers figure out the replacement cost by using printed estimating forms. They consider such factors as the soundness of construction, the number of rooms, and the quality of finishes, fixtures, and appliances. This method is fine for the typical house, but if you own a custom-designed or period home, you should get a written estimate of its replacement cost from a seasoned appraiser—perhaps the same one who estimated your home's market value for the mortgagor.

If possible, get a policy that indexes the replacement costs to inflation, which can rise or fall independent of a home's market value. If you make a substantial improvement or addition to your house, raise your coverage to reflect the new replacement cost.

In the same vein, add a replacement-cost endorsement to your policy for personal possessions to make sure that you'll be adequately reimbursed when you have a claim. Standard policies pay you for a destroyed item's actual cash value—that is, replacement cost minus depreciation. So that five-year-old TV that went up in smoke might fetch only $100 instead of the $700 you paid for it or the $600 cost to replace it today. In addition to adding the replacement-cost endorsement, raise the claim limit to 75% if your policy provides the standard 50% of the amount of coverage on the house itself. Thus, if your home is insured for $90,000, you could collect up to $63,000 instead of $45,000 on your personal contents.

A replacement-cost endorsement for personal contents is especially important for condominium owners. The condo association insures the structural elements of the buildings, so an owner is in effect buying mainly the personal contents portion of a homeowners policy. Bear in mind, if you're a condo owner, that the association's insurance doesn't cover interior structural improvements. So if you renovate the kitchen or redo the bathroom, be sure to add replacement-value coverage under the additions and alterations section of the policy.

By the time you've shaped your policy to your particular circumstances, you may find that the premiums add up. One way to cap the costs is to take advantage of special discounts offered by most insurers. You can usually get at least 5% shaved off your premium for installing a smoke detector, dead-bolt locks, and fire extinguishers. Retirees, who stay at home more than working people, may qualify for a 10% discount. If you have your house and car insured by the same company, it will pare 5%–10% from your premium.

The number one way to limit the cost, however, is to increase your deductible. Agree to absorb the first $500 of any loss instead of the standard $250 and you lop an average 12% off your annual bill. If your budget can handle a $1,000 loss, you can pocket savings of up to 24%. It's often a good idea to pay for small claims yourself, anyway, because insurers can raise your rates or refuse to renew your policy if you make too many claims. And if one insurer drops you, competitors probably won't rush for your business.

Don't let the quest for savings lead you into the common trap of choosing a low deductible *and* scrimping on overall coverage to hold down the premium. Countless homeowners, concerned about recompense for minor losses, have given in to this temptation, leaving themselves dangerously underinsured against major risks. "Insurance is really there for the catastrophic situation," says Jeanne Salvatore, director of consumer affairs at the Insurance Information Institute, an industry-funded group. "If you need to keep your premium cost down, do it with a high deductible, not by reducing your coverage." For consumer brochures, or answers to specific questions, call the National Insurance Consumer Helpline at 800-942-4242.

Flood Insurance

Your homeowners agent can tell you whether your community participates in the federal flood insurance program. If it does, get the coverage, which is provided by Uncle Sam but sold by private companies. Your homeowners policy covers damage from windstorms, including wind-driven rain, but you must buy separate insurance to cover flooding damage. To qualify, property must be located in one of the 18,000 communities participating in the federal flood control program. Coverage doesn't kick in until 30 days after you buy the policy, so don't wait to sign up until Hurricane Humbert is heading your way. If you need further information, call the federal government's National Flood Insurance Program at 800-638-6620.

Credit Life, Life, and Disability Insurance

Once you're on record as a homeowner, you may be deluged with solicitors trying to sell you **credit life insurance,** which would pay off the mortgage if you die. The offering is usually for a decreasing-term policy, in which the premium stays the same but the amount of coverage declines each year, in tandem with the declining balance owed on your mortgage.

Sellers tout mortgage life insurance as a surefire shield to keep your family from losing the house in the event of your death. Yes, it does do that—but there are cheaper and better ways to provide the same protection. One problem with mortgage life insurance is that the beneficiary is the lender, so the home loan is paid off automatically. But your spouse *may not want* to pay off the mortgage and possibly shouldn't if it's a low-rate loan. In any event, there may be sufficient income from other sources to make the mortgage payments, and he or she may have better uses for the insurance money, such as investing for your children's college tuition.

Chances are, however, that you do need to boost **life insurance** and **disability coverage** so your family will be able to meet the mortgage payments and other basic costs of living if the primary breadwinner dies or becomes incapacitated. Review your needs with an accountant, financial planner, attorney, or trusted insurance agent. If you are relatively young and cash is in short supply, some form of term insurance, with your spouse or estate as beneficiary, is likely to be the optimum choice. If invested prudently, the proceeds would produce enough annual income to keep your family afloat in case of the breadwinner's death. Statistically, however, disability is far more of a threat than death at an early age, so investigate what coverage is available at a decent price if your employer doesn't provide sufficient protection.

Refinancing

Having recently obtained a mortgage, this may be the topic furthest from your mind. But interest rates jump around constantly, like bullfrogs in a bucket. In a couple of years you may find that refinancing makes sense. With a no-closing-costs or no-points deal, it can be worth considering if you can get a loan for even one point below your current rate and plan to stay in your home at least two years. To see if you could save money by refinancing, divide the estimated closing costs on the new loan by the amount you'll save each month on your mortgage payment. The result will be the number of months you would need to stay in your home to break even.

Refinancing can also slash your long-term mortgage interest costs. In 1996 North Carolinians George and Theresa Tilton traded their 30-year adjustable with an 11.56% cap for a 15-

year fixed mortgage. Their monthly payment remains the same at $1,400, but their house will be paid off in half the time, saving them at least $60,000 in interest. "Now I think we're here forever," says Theresa Tilton.

Furnishing, Repairing, and Renovating

You've just moved in and most of your belongings are still in boxes. But you notice that your worn sofa and chairs look a shade shabby in their fresh surroundings. Maybe your head is dancing with plans to redo and reconfigure—to add homey charm to a standard room, perhaps, or revamp that avocado-applianced kitchen.

Stop right here. Paint the closets, certainly, even the walls, but don't do major restructuring right away. Having acquired a home, you and yours are entering a period of adjustment. Your mortgage payments and related housing costs are probably significantly higher than your former outlay for rent. You may need time to adjust to a more spartan regime. Many first-time buyers realize in anguish a year later that they had no idea how much it costs to run a house. You may regretfully (but rightfully) decide that buying flood insurance is a more pressing priority than redoing your teenage daughter's bedroom. Taking your time will give you a more realistic view of what you can cope with financially.

In addition, a time-out will give you a chance to modify your off-the-cuff impulses before indulging in costly, irreversible renovations or big-ticket purchases. After living in your new home for six months, you may find that installing a second bathroom has zoomed to the top of your must-do list, far ahead of the new living room furniture you thought you had to have or the deck that would be great for summer. The message is simple common sense: You're probably going to be living here for years. There's no need to do everything overnight, even if you can afford it.

One thing you should do right away, however, is establish two **reserve funds**—one for regular maintenance and repair, the other for more elaborate renovations and decorating in the future. For maintenance, depending on the age and condition of your house, you should allocate about 1% of the purchase price annually. If this turns out to be high, consider yourself lucky—it may work out differently the following year.

The size of the refurbishing allowance necessary to turn house into home is a matter of personal choice. But even if you are laboring under the most punishing budget, try to allot some dollars for special trimmings. Your goal: to avoid what designers call the "naked-lady syndrome." Every new home calls for a few special furnishings to accommodate its idiosyncracies—pictures to fill a conspicuously bare wall, perhaps, or custom window treatments. "Most rooms look better dressed," observes Los Angeles designer Sharon Landa. "Without these accoutrements, even the best design falls flat."

CHECKPOINTS

- Don't skimp on homeowners insurance. Go for the best coverage you can get, preferably a guaranteed replacement-cost policy. To keep a lid on the premium, ask for a $1,000 deductible, which can save you up to 24%.
- Resist sales pitches for credit life insurance, which would pay off the mortgage if the primary breadwinner dies. The surviving spouse may not want to pay off a low-rate loan, and may have better uses for the money.
- Review your life and disability coverage to ensure your family will be able to meet the mortgage payments and other basic living costs if the chief earner dies or becomes incapacitated. Beef up coverage if necessary.
- Establish two reserve funds—one for regular maintenance and repair, one for more elaborate renovations and future decorating. Routine maintenance, depending on the age of your house, will run about 1% of the purchase price annually.

CHAPTER 15

Three Special Cases:

The Fixer-Upper;
the Not-Yet-Built House;
the Custom-Designed Home

Investing in a Fixer-Upper

One consistently smart strategy for crafty buyers, especially in robust housing markets, is to shop for a "handyman's special." That's what Jerry Lyons, 42, and his wife, Heide, 25, did in fast-growing Salt Lake City in 1995. They selected a $131,000, four-bedroom ranch surrounded by newly constructed half-million-dollar homes in the desirable Cottonwood Heights neighborhood.

"If you're not a fixer-upper by nature, this wouldn't have been a good deal," says Heide, who teaches English part-time at Salt Lake City Community College (SLCCC). "It would have overwhelmed most people." The couple have spent about $12,000 to overhaul the electrical system, add a garage, replace

windows, rip out wallpaper, and add a bathroom, doing most of
the work themselves. Jerry, an associate professor in the health
sciences department at SLCCC, used free scrap lumber,
Sheetrock, and oak veneer taken (with permission) from a
nearby construction site. He hauled 18 truckloads of rocks from
a local canyon to augment the landscaping. He replanted the
lawn with seed ($15) and compost from the dump (free).
"You've got to be a real scavenger to do this," says Jerry,
explaining his rehabbing philosophy. "If you're too proud to
take somebody's leftovers, you'll have to pay." The couple have
seen a very sweet return on their sweat equity investment: their
house was recently appraised for $160,000.

Not everyone welcomes this kind of challenge. "The
market's soft for ramshackle structures because most people
don't have the time to work on them," says Boyd Smith, 38, a
Pasadena florist. But smart rehabbers, like Smith, know how to
enhance a property's commercial appeal. After buying his two-
bedroom house for $208,000 in 1989, he invested $150,000 in
new pipes and wiring, as well as the addition of a den and extra
bathroom. Smith sold the house in 1995 for $452,000, despite
the region's anemic housing market. Says Smith: "I remodeled
for my own comfort, but I never forgot that someday my home
would belong to someone else." After that success, he bought a
$170,000 condo and invested approximately $80,000 in renovations, including double-glazed thermal pane windows to keep
out the noise on his busy street. His Realtor has since called
him with two offers for $335,000, but Smith intends to stay put
this time.

Do you have the soul of a rehabber? Evaluate your tolerance
for the unbridled chaos that results from a major makeover. Are
you allergic to sawdust? Are you prepared to use the bathroom
at the local fast-food restaurant, cook on a hot plate in what
will "someday" be the kitchen? The promise of affordability
may be far outweighed by the grim prospect of endless
evenings and weekends devoted to making an old house livable.

Joan Motyka of Larchmont, New York, recalls when she and

husband, Gregory Miller, were hopelessly mired in the renovation of a nineteenth-century brick town house in Brooklyn, New York. After two years, with energy and funds exhausted, they put the half-finished project—they called it Bleak House—on the market, where it languished for a year. "My mother, godmother, and grandmother burned candles and prayed novenas that we could sell that house," she says. The whole clan danced a jig when a solid offer finally came on St. Valentine's Day. Shortly after, Motyka and Miller moved into a co-op apartment needing minimal work. "My first child would have been born two years earlier if it weren't for Bleak House," says Motyka.

Even if you have the will and the energy for such a project, do a coolly realistic analysis before buying a "fixer," as such houses are called in the trade. Don't even consider one in a neighborhood where real estate values are stagnant or, worse yet, slipping. When you find a wreck you love in a promising community, hire a builder or contractor to come and estimate how much time and money it will take to make your dream house a reality.

You may be able to get financing help from a little-known program of the Federal Housing Administration. The 203(k) loan was created especially to encourage people who want to buy and restore houses. It combines purchase and fix-up funds in one convenient loan bundle. Most homes are eligible, as are most improvements costing more than $5,000 (barring luxuries like new tennis courts). Most potential buyers qualify since there are no income limitations; closing costs can be built into the loan. But fixed-rate, 30-year 203(k) loans usually cost 1.5 percentage points more than conventional loans, and there are regional limits on the amount you can borrow. The main hitch: Your banker may be unfamiliar with the program. If so, phone the nearest office of the U.S. Department of Housing and Urban Development.

Once you own your dream wreck, you'll need to sort out when it does and doesn't pay to do it yourself. If you're nervous about your skills, research what's involved in a given project, then walk it through mentally. If you can imagine yourself coping with each task, you'll do fine.

Certainly you can save thousands of dollars by taking on the labor-intensive jobs. Most people can paint and wallpaper, and you can probably refinish a wood floor. Hooking up new fixtures to existing plumbing and wiring is doable, too, if you pay attention to where everything was originally. Installing completely new plumbing or wiring is more difficult and time-consuming. In addition, local building ordinances may require such projects to be done by a licensed tradesman. If a project seems too complicated to try on your own, you may be able to contribute money-saving labor by working with the professional.

Some projects are usually *not* worth trying alone, notably those that involve expensive materials that you can either waste or spoil. For example, laying carpet or installing granite countertops takes proper tools and an expert to know how to cut and fit economically. And experienced hands warn that plastering a ceiling is a miserable job for an amateur, since goop falls in your face constantly. "I don't know how Michelangelo painted the Sistine Chapel, especially if he had to plaster it himself," says JoAnne Liebeler, a host of *Homeline,* a PBS home-improvement show.

No matter how handy you are, you will probably need professional help for making structural changes, like framing an additional room or adding windows and doors. A straightforward interior improvement—a new kitchen or a room addition that doesn't change the structure of your house—can most easily be handled by a contractor who does both design work and construction. The contractor will then subcontract carpenters, plumbers, and other workers, buy materials, organize work schedules, and supervise the job's day-to-day progress.

If you plan to dramatically change the design of your home—opening up the kitchen to include a family area and a greenhouse, for instance—you will probably need to hire two types of professionals: first either an architect or an interior designer to plan and oversee the project; then a contractor to build it. Architects are best (and may be required) for jobs involving structural changes such as moving walls. Designers generally specialize in making existing rooms more livable. They can devise a more appropriate lighting scheme, for instance, order to-the-trade furniture and accessories, and coordinate colors. Expect to pay either one about 10%–15% of anticipated construction costs.

Investigate contractors by asking local architects, designers, and friends for referrals. In addition, call your local builders association for names of contractors who are among the National Association of Home Builders' certified graduate remodelers, since these people have at least five years' experience in owning or managing a remodeling company. Interview at least three candidates and ask them for price estimates for your project. Don't jump at the minimum offer. "The guy with the low bid may take his profit out of the job by using shoddy materials or taking shortcuts," advises Frank Spivey Jr., president of an Indianapolis design/build firm.

When you've identified a promising contractor, find out answers to these three key questions:

• **Is he solvent?** "The biggest disaster is watching your contractor go out of business in the middle of a job," warns Todd A. Russell, president of a construction company in Glendora, California. In addition to the delay, expense, and inconvenience of finding someone to finish the job, you may face claims from subcontractors who have not been paid for their work on other projects. For a clue to a contractor's financial stability, ask for names and phone numbers of his regular subcontractors and suppliers. Then call them to see whether he typically pays promptly. If he has been slow lately, that could be a sign of money trouble. Be especially wary of newcomers, since an estimated 90% of new contractors go out of business within five years.

• **Is he reliable?** Contractors rarely say no to a job. You'll get your best gauge of reliability by visiting at least one of the contractor's clients who recently lived through a rehab project like yours. Any experienced, reputable contractor will gladly provide such references. Find out how well the contractor met deadlines and budget constraints. Inquire too whether the work and materials matched the standards originally agreed upon by the owner and contractor. Finally, be sure the contractor will be using his regular team for your job, not the second-string pickups he might employ when he's juggling a number of projects. If he tells you the crew he will assign have worked with him for less than six months and most of the subcontractors have never worked for him, find another person for the job.

• **Is he honest?** The Better Business Bureau can tell you if any complaints have been filed against a contractor. You should also check his probity by asking local architects, suppliers, and customers.

When you've found your master builder, you will need to bear down hard on his contract because of the minutiae involved. Even a modest job might call for several pages of specifications. Show the contract to your lawyer and to the architect or designer if you're using one. For $9.95 including shipping, the American Homeowners Foundation, a private group, will provide a six-page model agreement that you can compare with yours (800-489-7776). If anything is missing from your contract, such as deadlines, brand names, or descriptions of materials, write it in before signing.

There are two types of contracts: fixed-price and time-and-materials. A **fixed-price contract,** as the name suggests, limits your costs and for that reason is the safer of the two payment methods. If anything comes up during the job that will change the project, you and the contractor must sign an official change order noting and agreeing to any related expenditures. In a **time-and-materials contract** you will get only a rough estimate of the job's cost. Your actual cost will depend on the hours of labor and expenses ultimately incurred.

With either type, stipulate the payment schedule. On a fixed-price contract a typical arrangement is 30% to start, 30% midway through the job, and 30% at or near completion. Hold back the final 10% until all remaining details are finished to your satisfaction. Make payments for a time-and-materials contract every two weeks or so to cover ongoing costs.

When you're finally "out of rehab," but before you write that last check, review the work with your contractor to be sure all the specs were met. Test the toilets, sinks, and tubs for plumbing leaks; look for paint that needs touching up; open and close the doors and windows to be sure they don't stick. If something needs fixing, have the contractor do it. Then sit back and enjoy the fruits of your laborers.

Buying a Home Before It's Built

If you're buying a house that's only a dot on a developer's map, faith, hope, and charity are often essential parts of the deal. It's an act of faith to plunk down an initial deposit for the fifteenth house in a final field of 250. You hope the builder won't make mistakes, take shortcuts, or even—heaven forfend—declare bankruptcy. If weather, labor problems, or materials shortages delay construction and your closing—and they often do—you try to be charitable. Meanwhile you pray that mortgage rates won't shoot up.

Face it: you're betting on an unknown quantity. If there are structural problems or other hidden flaws, you won't discover them until you've moved in—and your disappointment is likely to be more acute because you were expecting perfection.

Your best protection is to arm yourself with a shot of healthy skepticism before you enter the deal. Recognize that professional builders are tougher negotiators than individual sellers, who are generally eager to close the deal and move on to their next house. You can bolster your faith—and have a happier moving day—by following this seven-step strategy:

1. *Investigate the builder's past.* You're best off buying from a developer with a history of satisfied customers. But don't rely solely on references that he provides. Instead ask him for the location of his last project, then go knock on doors. If home-owners are unhappy, they'll tell you.

A recent survey by the Better Business Bureau suggests that builders resemble the little girl with the curl in the middle of her forehead: when they are good, they are very good, and when they're bad, watch out. Eighty-one percent of those sur-veyed said they were satisfied overall with their builder. Of the 10% who complained, however, an overwhelming majority (84%) stated that the builder did not resolve their problems to their satisfaction. The biggest gaps were in follow-up and cus-tomer service.

If you're contemplating buying in an existing development, consider paying a professional inspector $200 or so to check completed houses and ones under construction for their quality of workmanship. You want to see, for example, that the builder hasn't used a flimsy grade of lumber in the framing. If you dis-cover a recurring problem, such as leaks around skylights, be sure the developer will guarantee in writing to fix any such leaks in your house. Some buyers regard the inspection process as so crucial that they schedule three checkups during the con-struction of their homes: once when the foundation is poured; second when the frame is up but not covered by drywall; and a final walk-through before closing. This may cost $500 or more, but the process is also likely to resolve skirmishes between you and the builder before they escalate to pitched battles.

2. *Study the land plans.* It's possible that the adjacent piney woods you love will be razed in six months for an apartment

complex. The dairy farmer down the road may be selling out to a used-car dealer. Ask at the local zoning office about any plans that have been submitted to develop nearby land or whether any developers have asked for a zoning variance, which would permit them to do something not currently allowed in the zoning plan.

3. *Check out the homeowners association.* In large metro areas at least half of new-home sales include membership in a home-owners association. If you're seriously interested in buying in, ask how much the association fee is (it's not tax-deductible) and get a copy of the group's rules. Study them with an eye for onerous restrictions—maybe you're stuck forever with one paint color, or you can't park your beloved motorcycle on the premises or mount a basketball hoop. This is a club you can't quit, so it's best to know the rules before you join.

4. *Argue for upgrades, options, or a buy-down.* Subdivision developers like to keep home prices high. Lowering the selling price for you automatically reduces the builder's asking price for subsequent sales. In addition, your new neighbors would be enraged to learn you paid $8,000 less than they did for a similar model house. As a practical matter, the builder doesn't have much wiggle room on the house price. Profit margins are as slim as 6% on the basic structure—but they typically run about 50% on the frills.

For all these reasons your negotiations are most likely to succeed if you press for hidden discounts rather than a visible price cut. Instead of lowering the cost of the house, the builder offers a more valuable package by tossing in upgrades and options such as better appliances or kitchen cabinets, lusher landscaping, fencing, or even completion of an unfinished basement.

You can also argue for indirect financial concessions. If you go to the developer on your own, without a real estate agent, you can negotiate with him over the 6% fee he would otherwise pay an agent. Try asking for an interest rate buy-down, in which the builder prepays some mortgage interest, resulting in a decline of your monthly costs. For example, the builder could agree to buy down the initial interest rate for a temporary period—taking a 10% rate to 9% for three years or so. Even better, he might take it down for the life of the loan. Either way, this is done at the closing with the builder paying discount points to offset the difference.

You'll be in the strongest position to negotiate a buy-down, upgrades, or even a price cut of 5% or more if the house is finished and sitting unsold. Loan interest, insurance, and other expenses accrue alarmingly. As the unsold house becomes an expensive white elephant, the builder becomes a more flexible deal maker.

5. *Have a lawyer review the contract.* Most builders present you with a sales document they have created, but you don't have to swallow it whole. Every contract is negotiable, and if it isn't, go to another developer. In particular, make sure your upgrades are included in the contract, along with any other special products or features agreed upon. If necessary, add a statement to the contract allowing you to visit the site at several designated times. (In practice you can probably walk through the construction site on weekends unnoticed. When you do, keep an eye out for screw-ups and unwarranted shortcuts.) And if the contract says the closing will be in April, plan on May. Builders are optimists by nature, and April showers may delay the roof work unavoidably. You can protect yourself by demanding 30–60 days' notice before the formal closing is held.

6. *Schedule a formal final inspection.* Before taking delivery of the finished product, you and an experienced new-home inspector should schedule a top-to-bottom examination of your precious new house. Don't agree to a date if the utilities aren't working yet. During the walk-through, turn on every faucet and every fixture. Each flaw you observe should be entered on a punch list. The builder is supposed to correct these items after

the closing. Stan Harbuck, a home inspector in Salt Lake City, estimates that he usually finds 40–45 noteworthy glitches in a new home (and about 80 in an old one). "Mostly it's subcontractors not finishing their jobs," Harbuck says. "Maybe some vent registers aren't put in or a drain isn't properly connected, but they jury-rig it, then pack up and go to the next site. I've seen customers negotiate $10,000 worth of repairs on closing day." Allow sufficient time to catch all possible errors and omissions. A noon inspection followed by a 2 P.M. closing 15 miles away may not allow enough time for a thorough examination. If you uncover major problems, hold some money in escrow until the faults are made right. A builder (like most of us) acts faster when he has a financial incentive to do so.

7. *Protect your mortgage rate.* If rates are falling, you don't need to worry. If they're rising as your closing date approaches, lock in the interest rate on your loan. You can usually get a rate lock-in for 30–60 days without paying a premium. The lender may grant a few grace days free but will probably charge for a longer lock-in. If construction delays persist, ask the lender to close the loan and hold some of the money in escrow until the appraiser verifies the home is complete. Along the way, don't suffer in silence. Your builder can beef up the work crew to speed completion of your home—but he probably won't unless you raise a fuss.

Commissioning a Custom-Designed Home

Perhaps when you went house shopping nothing satisfied you. Mass-produced new homes struck you as ill made, of poor quality. Older houses didn't suit your taste. So you began considering names of architects. Not a superstar like Frank Gehry, Michael Graves, or Robert A. M. Stern, but maybe one who is well-known in your region—a name that real estate brokers trumpet in ads as a selling point when a house hits the market. Someone who might even land your unhumble abode in the pages of *Architectural Digest* or *Metropolitan Home.* Just as Renaissance banker Cosimo de' Medici commissioned his landmark palazzo (probably from superstar architect Filippo Brunelleschi) around 1440, so you can order up a custom-created dream house today.

Just 2% of homeowners go this route, rather than buying an existing home or selecting from a real estate developer's or home builder's menu. And with good reason: you may need a near Medici–size income to afford it. The National Association of Home Builders estimates that a custom-built house costs about 30% more than a comparable development house, even if you don't use an architect. If you do, his or her fee will add another 10%–15% to the cost. But if the architect is a "name," a local celebrity of sorts, you may well recover that premium at sale time.

And building your own can be a brilliant solution. You may have a onetime shot at the perfect plot of earth. You could end up with a beautifully proportioned design that expands your ideas into a unique living space responsive to you, the site, and to the climate in which the project is built.

Alternatively, of course, you could get stuck in a nightmare of cost overruns and a crossfire between architect and contractor. You could end up with a faddish design that dates quickly and loses salability in a few years—or a dysfunctional design "statement" that leaks in every rainstorm and costs a fortune to heat.

Since this is likely to be a once-in-a-lifetime adventure, don't rush it. Allow ample time to choose the land and the architect and to analyze what you and yours want and need in the new house. Collect pictures; make lists. And stock up on pain relievers. Managing any kind of building project can often be vexatious, time-consuming, and more difficult than most outsiders ever imagine—even when the ending is a happy one. (For an excellent introduction, read Tracy Kidder's *House,* Houghton

Mifflin Company, 1985, a gripping account of ambitious owners, the architect who gives form to their dreams, and the carpenters who pound the nails.) If you determine to proceed, here are practical guidelines to ease the labor pains and lead you to maximum joy with the final result:

CHOOSING THE TURF BENEATH

Typically, land costs alone constitute 25%–35% of the total budget for the construction project. In pricier areas, however, that oh-so-well-located dirt can devour 50% of your funds. If your real estate agent doesn't know what is the common proportion in your community, ask a few local builders. They can be remarkably helpful to you, a possible future customer.

Whatever their answer, don't fall into the trap of buying land in a low-rent location so you can afford a bigger house. This will backfire at sale time, since a luxury residence in a middle-class area won't be priced like a high-end property. Keep your total budget near or just below the market value of existing homes nearby. Be prepared to cough up cash. Many financial institutions won't lend money on raw land, so you may have to buy the lot outright unless you can get private financing.

To avoid nasty surprises, before you buy invite a builder around to estimate various costs, starting with site preparation. If you have to cart away 300 tons of dirt and blast through underground rock to make that hillside site level enough to build on, it could add a withering $25,000 to your total tab. Also discuss the price of tree removal, since you can't nurture a silver birch in your master bedroom. Even plants that don't stand directly where the house will go are routinely cut down by builders to make it easier to bring in supplies and equipment. Talk sewage, too. If you need to put in a septic system, spend $300 or so for an engineer's percolation test before you sign anything. If you're supposed to have access to a town sewer system, find out what it will cost to get hooked up.

The same goes for gaining access to water: Will you have to drill a well, or is it city supplied? What are the costs in either case? Get estimates before you commit to buying the land. To bypass these and related problems, consider buying a plot that already has a house on it and demolishing the existing building. In affluent areas like Houston's River Oaks district, where land prices are high and vacant lots are virtually nonexistent, this has become an increasingly popular solution.

WORKING WITH AN ARCHITECT

Ask about fees in the initial interview, since there's no single method for calculating them. Payments may be structured in one of three ways: as an hourly rate for time and expenses; as a fixed sum; or as a percentage of the construction cost. Many architects use a combination—a fixed fee for the preparation of working drawings and other parts of the project that they have the most control over, and hourly rates for preliminary sketches and conceptual studies that may be scrapped in refining the design. When you've worked out a payment schedule, ask what is *not* included to avoid surprises later.

In deciding what to build, the architect takes into account your budget and compares it to a rough estimate of current per-square-foot building costs. He or she must also incorporate your needs and tastes into the basic design. The legendary Frank Lloyd Wright reportedly intoned to a client, "Madam, you will take what we give you," but his descendants can rarely afford such arrogance. The most responsive practitioners develop communication to a fine art. New York City architect William Richard McGilvray, for instance, resorts to pictures to accommodate architectural illiterates. When designing a weekend retreat in Sharon, Connecticut, for a couple who didn't know a porte cochere from a porterhouse, he sent the clients volumes on English country houses. With the help of Post-it notes and photographs passed back and forth, the couple were better able to articulate their design preferences. And McGilvray used photos to illustrate things they couldn't see or imagine, such as what the bluestone floors and masonry fireplaces might look like in the finished product.

When you have signed off on the house design, the architect prepares working drawings and specifications, including necessary bidding information for contractors. Selecting and hiring this person is your responsibility, but the architect should advise and guide you through the bidding process. (For further guidance on choosing contractors, review the section on fixer-uppers, which begins on page 181.) You may also want a knowledgeable person to supervise the general contractor—you can do it yourself if you have the time and skill, you can enlist the architect for an hourly fee, or you can pay a construction supervisor. Many of those who have been through it swear by the latter choice.

The construction process has been known to escalate into a clash of the Titans, since architects and general contractors both tend toward oversize egos. The architect may bad-mouth your chosen GC as an undereducated, beer-bellied bubba in a pickup truck. The contractor may see only trouble and complain that the carefully wrought plans you and the architect labored over for months are inadequate or impractical. If this kind of conflict arises, try to integrate the two professionals, drawing the best from both. A palazzo that comes together perfectly is usually a combination of excellent intentions and skillful mediation, with a dash of luck besides.

FINDING FINANCING

Your goal is to obtain a construction loan and arrange for a permanent mortgage simultaneously in one attractive package. Expect to pay about three percentage points more than the going mortgage rate for the construction funds. In conjunction with the package, the lender will insist on a preconstruction appraisal to ascertain the amount of the construction loan. As you proceed with the project, the bank will dole out funds and periodically send an inspector to check on the contractor's progress. After you obtain a certificate of occupancy from the local building inspector, the lender issues the mortgage funds, which you use to pay off the construction loan. Then you start making monthly payments like legions of other homeowners.

A final caution: While a custom building job will give you exactly the home you want, or at least what you can afford, these projects almost always seem to cost more and take longer than anyone ever anticipated. Allow for the unexpected: you may have forgotten to factor in the lightning rods, a security system, and other extras in the original budget. You will certainly want to indulge in a few "oh, we might as well's" to enrich the project—putting wiring for a super sound system inside the walls or carving out a special cubbyhole from unused space.

Throughout the process there must be a genuine rapport among architect, builder, and buyer—and the buyer's partner. Marriage counselors, divorce lawyers, and those who have been through the experience seem to agree that the only thing that will test a love relationship more than creating your custom dream home from scratch is creating it from a fixer-upper.

CHECKPOINTS

• When you buy a fixer-upper, get a firm estimate of the time and cost of renovations. If you plan to swing a hammer yourself, be sure of your skills, since a botched job can lower the value of the house. Call in a designer or architect who can advise what kinds of improvements will pay off best at resale time.

• When buying from a home developer, press for upgrades and optional additions like fireplaces or a full garage to replace a carport. Most developers are stubbornly reluctant to cut the official selling price, since it affects future sales and angers earlier buyers.

• If you commission a custom-designed house, be sure you allow for essential costs that may not be included in the original construction budget. Extras like site grading, lightning rods, custom-made draperies for the double-height dining room, or a built-in security system can add thousands to your total outlay.

CHAPTER 16

Buying a Vacation Home

Getting away from it all is a time-tested tradition. Almost as soon as people started living in towns, they felt the need to retreat to the countryside. In the first century A.D., the Roman senator Pliny the Younger praised his hideaway in the Tuscan Hills with sentiments familiar to any stressed-out urban dweller. "I can enjoy a profounder peace there, more comfort, and fewer cares," Pliny wrote. "I need never wear a formal toga and there are no neighbors to disturb me; everywhere there is peace and quiet."

More than seven million Americans bought second homes in the booming 1980s. Roberta Sator, sociology professor at Brooklyn College, notes that the vacation house, once a privilege of the superrich, has become an accepted perk of the $100,000-a-year household.

So it's not surprising that the thought of a second home has crossed your mind. You're just toying with the idea, of course, nothing wrong with that. And you hardly need a Tuscan villa—just a lakeside cottage, perhaps, or a more distant refuge for extended family vacations. Maybe a place where you might resettle in your retirement years.

This will be an indulgence—a big one. You know that a second-home purchase, especially in the short term, isn't likely to be a financial bonanza, right?

Well, not exactly. The long-term investment outlook, say the forecasters, is rosier than you might imagine. If you choose with a cool head and are willing to hang on for a while, your place in the sun—or the ski chalet or the Cape Cod saltbox—might possibly add a sharp, upward punch to your net worth over the next decade or two.

The force behind this upbeat prediction is the voracious baby boomers. When that generation boogied into its thirties, back in the late 1970s, their endless appetite for housing pushed the price of starter homes and trade-ups way, way up. Now they're doing a slow jog into their fifties, which means they are entering their prime second-home-buying years. Get in ahead of the pack, and you could watch them pump up your vacation home equity in the coming decades.

Ingo Winzer, president of Local Market Monitor, a Wellesley, Massachusetts, real estate research firm, predicts that the gains in vacation homes over the next 20 years could exceed the inflation rate by at least 50%. "Demographics are the key, and the boomers are the main catalyst," Winzer says. John Tuccillo, chief economist at the National Association of Realtors, claims that he knows where the 50-plus set is going to get the money. *"Cherchez le* 401(k)," Tuccillo says. "We are going to start seeing retirement savings tapped, and vacation homes that are a tryout for retirement will be on the list of purchases."

So if you are serious about adding a second nest to your assets, your timing is close to impeccable. To be sure, "the steals and deals of the early 1990s have pretty much disappeared," Tuccillo warns, especially where nearby housing markets are healthy. In Hilton Head Island, South Carolina, which draws heavily from people living in Atlanta, the condo market is the strongest it's been in a decade, for example. Nonetheless, pools of well-priced vacation properties in choice locations abound nationwide. A recent survey by Chase Manhattan Personal

Financial Services found that the average price for vacation homes ranged from a modest $92,000 in the Midwest to a still affordable $150,000 in the West.

These sums won't fetch you a showpiece in celeb-studded wonderlands like Aspen or Vail, of course. If you need a trophy ski lodge to hold your head up in the lift line, there recently was a four-bedroom hideout on Vail Mountain being offered for $7 million (furnished). But for every fantasyland like Vail, there's a town like Breckenridge, Colorado, where for about $260,000 you can own a four-bedroom, three-bath, skylit haven in the Rockies. Less than two hours from Denver, Breckenridge has ski runs for snow buffs and, come summer, breathtaking (literally and figuratively) hiking and biking trails among the surrounding 13,000-foot peaks.

You can unearth similar opportunities in other regions of the country if you explore just outside the fashionable hot spots. In old-money Martha's Vineyard, the average home sells for more than $400,000. But 60 miles northeast in Eastham, Massachusetts, on Cape Cod, you could recently find homes selling for less than $250,000 and providing plenty of New England charm, plus access to some of the best beaches on the East Coast. Prefer paddling on the West Coast? Scout out the profusion of $200,000 properties dotted among Washington State's San Juan Islands, within easy striking distance of Seattle.

Are you in the picture now? Then let's turn to how you can get the best vacation quarters for your dollar.

Searching for Your Vacation Home

Your focus changes when you're buying a vacation property. Certainly the commonsense considerations of choosing a permanent residence remain pertinent (so you might want to review some earlier chapters), but a second home demands that you define your needs differently. Are you buying the house for your own enjoyment, or is it an investment that you plan to rent out? Are property values a primary concern—or do family values take pride of place? Perhaps you want a place where your children and grandchildren will flock for celebrations over the years, creating enduring memories. Alternatively you might seek a respite from family pressures.

If you're buying with an eye to strong appreciation, keep the boomers in mind, say the real estate brokers. That generation's definition of a vacation dream house is a roomy, low-maintenance haven with a few extra bedrooms for the kids and grandkids, in a friendly, safe location. Gated communities are popular, especially if they provide easy access to golf, tennis, fishing, swimming, and shopping.

If your vacation house is eventually going to become your retirement residence, then you will need to pay close attention to the lay of the land—literally. In time, a steep hill will become unmanageable for nearly all retirees. You'll want a house on level ground with easy access from the road to the front door, preferably with a bedroom and bath on the first floor. Establishing roots in your new hometown is a key priority, so you'll need a place where you can entertain family and friends comfortably. Consider if you can find congenial companions among the local residents or the weekenders. One New York financial editor, who bought a vacation retreat in a rural part of Pennsylvania's Poconos, eventually sold because he just didn't fit in. "My neighbors were all farmers—nice people, but we had little in common," he recalls. "I had to import friends for company, which meant inviting them for at least 48 hours." Ultimately he replaced his Pocono retreat with a getaway in Connecticut's Litchfield County, where a number of his colleagues, both working and retired, had bought earlier. "I paid more money for less house," he concludes, "but it was worth it to have an easy and fulfilling social life."

In plotting your game plan, take time to explore all the personal and financial aspects of your intended purchase. You want to get it right because you could be living with a mistake for a long time to come. As a start, weigh the following critical points:

LOCATION IS KEY

If your current plan is to use the house as a weekend retreat, then you had best search within a three-hour drive of your primary residence. You want to spend the weekend at the house, not on the highway. (Take a compass and map and circle the area within a 150-mile radius of your hometown. You might be surprised at some of the attractive communities that fall within convenient striking distance.) If you are planning to rent out your space, as about 25% of vacation-home owners do, be sure to keep to within three hours of a metropolitan area, so you'll have a large pool of city dwellers to tap as potential tenants.

GO FOR AMENITIES

The most practical choice is a multiseason home that is insulated for winter and air conditioned, if necessary, for the warm-weather months. If your roost on the shores of Lake Leisure, a mecca for warm-weather water sports, is also less than an hour from the snow-packed slopes of Mount Breakneck, your rental opportunities will double. If that hideaway is meant to be reserved for your personal use, however, realize that your kith and kin may be inviting themselves to visit you in at least two seasons. Is this a blessing you can handle?

DECIDE IF BIGGER IS BETTER

"A vacation home is basically a toy," advises Robert Conlon, a broker at Century 21 Conlon Realtors in Sturgeon Bay, Wisconsin. "Just buy enough house to enjoy yourself." That's practical advice if you are buying a property strictly for personal use and are only moderately gregarious by nature. If you think you might want to rent it out at any time, however, buy a house with lots of bedrooms. Renters are typically a bunch of friends or extended families who travel in packs to defray costs. They need lots of space to fit everyone in. And, in fact, you might end up enjoying your "toy" more if it's big enough to house all your college buddies for your annual July Fourth pig roast. If you're a hard-core business honcho, you may find that playing host is a rewarding investment of your off-duty hours, for both business and personal reasons.

THINK FUN, NOT SUMPTUOUS

Sturdy is important in a vacation home, since multiple friends, relatives, kids, dogs, cats, and possibly renters will be plopping on your chairs, beds, and sofas. Stylish counts, too, if regular rentals are a key part of your financial plan. Remember that strange paradox of vacation houses: People like to feel they're roughing it, but they also want their comforts. So look for reliable plumbing, heating, and cooling systems and modern appliances—especially a good dishwasher (or, better yet two, if you're planning on that pig roast). If your budget permits, you may want to go all out for dramatic fireplaces, double-height living rooms, and other eye-popping features that immediately tell you and your guests that the owner is "off-duty," far from the workaday world. A little make-believe can be a valuable element in getting away from it all.

PRACTICE DUE DILIGENCE

No matter how much you love a specific vacation spot, squelch the urge to buy on the strength of a single visit to an area. The more time you can spend looking and comparing, the better you're likely to do. Renting for a year, or multiple visits in different seasons, will give you a chance to do a thorough market investigation. Talk to all the year-round residents you can find, subscribe to the local newspaper, ask town officials about zoning, future developments, and commercial growth in the area. In winter resort areas ask neighbors or a local police officer how soon your street or road would be plowed. Secluded homes may be left adrift for many days. In a beachfront community, ask city officials about the shoreline's erosion pattern, since you'll want to avoid buying a property that might eventually require an expensive retaining wall.

Use your common sense to locate good value. Don't settle in some deserted spot and imagine that you can start a vacation trend single-handedly. You're best off in an established place where vacationers want to vacation—and where gardeners, repairmen, cleaners, the UPS delivery truck, and the FedEx courier can all get relatively easy access.

At the same time, don't be a victim of the herd mentality in choosing a vacation spot. "If everyone at a cocktail party is talking about the same area, it's going to be overpriced," cautions economist Tuccillo. "The wise move is to buy where it is not yet too popular or expensive." One way to find these places is to consult Table 16-1, which lists the high, medium, and low average prices for homes in more than 200 vacation areas in 43 states.

TABLE 16-1

	Low Price Range	Medium Price Range	High Price Range
ALABAMA			
Gulf Shores	$62,000	$145,000	$390,000
ARIZONA			
Bullhead City	$45,000	$100,000	$195,000
Flagstaff	$85,000	$165,000	$280,000
Prescott	$25,000	$86,000	$240,000
Scottsdale	$100,000	$500,000	$1,000,000
Sedona	$120,000	$260,000	$510,000
Tucson	$100,000	$225,000	$700,000
ARKANSAS			
Beaver Lake	$45,000	$90,000	$150,000
Cherokee Village	$20,000	$45,000	$105,000
Hot Springs	$65,000	$130,000	$225,000
Mountain Home	$42,000	$85,000	$135,000
CALIFORNIA			
Big Bear Lake	$85,000	$150,000	$500,000
Carmel/Monterey Penin.	$192,000	$350,000	$725,000
Del Mar	$160,000	$330,000	$775,000
La Jolla	$175,000	$375,000	$950,000
Lake Arrowhead	$100,000	$225,000	$625,000
Mammoth Lakes	$100,000	$300,000	$500,000
N. Lake Tahoe	$125,000	$275,000	$550,000
Palm Springs	$100,000	$200,000	$500,000
Rancho Bernardo	$150,000	$275,000	$450,000
Rancho Santa Fe	$275,000	$725,000	$1,500,000
S. Lake Tahoe	$80,000	$135,000	$250,000
Squaw Valley	$100,000	$350,000	$750,000
COLORADO			
Aspen	$200,000	$525,000	$1,350,000
Breckenridge	$85,000	$200,000	$400,000
Colorado Springs	$55,000	$125,000	$235,000
Crested Butte	$75,000	$175,000	$480,000
Dillon-Keystone	$85,000	$150,000	$300,000
Durango	$80,000	$185,000	$350,000
Glenwood Springs	$100,000	$175,000	$290,000
Steamboat Springs	$100,000	$225,000	$500,000

	Low Price Range	Medium Price Range	High Price Range
(COLORADO, cont.)			
Telluride	$150,000	$275,000	$725,000
Vail–Avon	$125,000	$225,000	$575,000
DELAWARE			
Bethany-Rehoboth Beach	$85,000	$175,000	$250,000
FLORIDA			
Clearwater	$60,000	$125,000	$250,000
Cocoa Beach	$75,000	$150,000	$275,000
Fernandina Beach/			
Amelia Island	$75,000	$150,000	$300,000
Fort Lauderdale	$80,000	$175,000	$450,000
Fort Myers/Sanibel/			
Captiva	$75,000	$150,000	$325,000
Indian Harbor Beach	$75,000	$150,000	$300,000
Key Biscayne	$200,000	$400,000	$700,000
Key West	$82,500	$155,000	$275,000
Lake Placid	$43,000	$96,000	$175,000
Marco Island	$85,000	$175,000	$350,000
Miami Beach	$85,000	$135,000	$350,000
Palm Coast	$75,000	$130,000	$200,000
Sarasota/Siesta Key	$90,000	$200,000	$500,000
St. Augustine	$35,000	$90,000	$175,000
Vero Beach	$65,000	$125,000	$325,000
West Palm Beach	$75,000	$150,000	$375,000
Winter Park	$80,000	$150,000	$300,000
GEORGIA			
Lake Lanier	$85,000	$165,000	$300,000
Lake Oconee	$50,000	$190,000	$350,000
St. Simons Island	$75,000	$150,000	$275,000
HAWAII			
Kona	$100,000	$250,000	$500,000
Maui, Kihei	$100,000	$250,000	$350,000
Maui, Wailea	$250,000	$400,000	$750,000
Oahu, Honolulu	$150,000	$300,000	$600,000
Oahu, Kaneohe	$135,000	$250,000	$400,000
IDAHO			
Coeur d'Alene	$90,000	$150,000	$300,000
Sandpoint	$75,000	$175,000	$350,000
Sun Valley	$75,000	$175,000	$500,000

	Low Price Range	Medium Price Range	High Price Range
ILLINOIS			
Crystal Lake	$110,000	$200,000	$325,000
Galena	$145,000	$200,000	$300,000
Wonder Lake	$75,000	$130,000	$225,000
INDIANA			
Angola	$50,000	$125,000	$275,000
Warsaw	$50,000	$90,000	$175,000
KENTUCKY			
Cadiz/Lake Barkley	$35,000	$80,000	$135,000
Danville	$57,000	$110,000	$180,000
Eddyville/Kentucky Lake/ Lake Park	$35,000	$76,000	$175,000
Somerset/Lake Cumberland	$40,000	$85,000	$155,000
LOUISIANA			
Lake Charles	$50,000	$110,000	$195,000
MAINE			
Bar Harbor	$65,000	$120,000	$200,000
Waldorf	$125,000	$190,000	$250,000
York Harbor	$95,000	$160,000	$230,000
MARYLAND			
Annapolis	$80,000	$180,000	$480,000
Deep Creek	$80,000	$200,000	$325,000
Ocean City	$75,000	$125,000	$175,000
MASSACHUSETTS			
Cape Cod	$85,000	$150,000	$235,000
Martha's Vineyard Island	$135,000	$230,000	$365,000
Westport	$95,000	$175,000	$375,000
MICHIGAN			
Au Gres	$25,000	$60,000	$125,000
Bellaire	$40,000	$85,000	$200,000
Cadillac	$35,000	$80,000	$175,000
Candian Lakes	$60,000	$125,000	$200,000
Charlevoix	$65,000	$130,000	$280,000
Cheboygan	$55,000	$170,000	$525,000
Coloma	$55,000	$140,000	$325,000

	Low Price Range	Medium Price Range	High Price Range
(MICHIGAN, cont.)			
Escanaba	$35,000	$65,000	$145,000
Glen Arbor	$95,000	$350,000	$550,000
Grand Haven	$75,000	$125,000	$210,000
Grayling	$45,000	$65,000	$125,000
Harbor Springs	$50,000	$175,000	$350,000
Holland	$75,000	$125,000	$250,000
Houghton Lake	$45,000	$65,000	$125,000
Indian River	$100,000	$200,000	$450,000
Ludington	$50,000	$85,000	$175,000
Manistee	$45,000	$90,000	$185,000
Muskegon	$50,000	$95,000	$180,000
New Buffalo	$75,000	$125,000	$300,000
Oscoda	$40,000	$85,000	$175,000
Pentwater	$45,000	$95,000	$185,000
Petoskey	$65,000	$100,000	$275,000
Roscommon	$60,000	$90,000	$250,000
South Haven	$100,000	$150,000	$250,000
St. Joseph	$65,000	$125,000	$225,000
Suttons Bay	$75,000	$200,000	$425,000
Tawas City	$50,000	$75,000	$125,000
Traverse City	$65,000	$125,000	$300,000
MINNESOTA			
Alexandria	$55,000	$110,000	$225,000
Crosby	$70,000	$175,000	$275,000
Grand Rapids	$50,000	$90,000	$175,000
Park Rapids	$50,000	$85,000	$170,000
Pelican Rapids	$50,000	$85,000	$185,000
Pine City	$40,000	$75,000	$150,000
White Bear Lake	$75,000	$125,000	$200,000
MISSISSIPPI			
Gulfport	$40,000	$95,000	$225,000
Ocean Springs	$75,000	$125,000	$200,000
MISSOURI			
Branson	$65,000	$100,000	$250,000
Camdenton	$60,000	$115,000	$180,000
Lake of the Ozarks	$65,000	$110,000	$160,000
Sunrise Beach	$40,000	$87,500	$185,000

BUYING A VACATION HOME

	Low Price Range	Medium Price Range	High Price Range
MONTANA			
Bigfork	$80,000	$185,000	$300,000
Bozeman	$85,000	$185,000	$300,000
Whitefish	$75,000	$140,000	$250,000
NEVADA			
Incline Village	$175,000	$365,000	$900,000
Lake Meade	$80,000	$150,000	$225,000
Las Vegas	$95,000	$175,000	$350,000
NEW HAMPSHIRE			
Hanover	$100,000	$200,000	$375,000
Laconia	$60,000	$125,000	$250,000
Portsmouth	$55,000	$175,000	$300,000
Rye	$30,000	$85,000	$240,000
NEW JERSEY			
Jersey Shore Region	$110,000	$200,000	$350,000
Stone Harbor	$165,000	$325,000	$650,000
NEW MEXICO			
Ruidoso	$75,000	$135,000	$300,000
Santa Fe	$125,000	$215,000	$400,000
Taos	$100,000	$185,000	$285,000
NEW YORK			
Hamptons	$225,000	$425,000	$1,500,000
Lake Ontario	$65,000	$100,000	$200,000
NORTH CAROLINA			
Atlantic Beach	$75,000	$115,000	$190,000
Banner Elk	$40,000	$80,000	$110,000
Boone	$55,000	$110,000	$175,000
Highlands	$85,000	$200,000	$450,000
OHIO			
New Philadelphia	$30,000	$65,000	$115,000
Sandusky	$60,000	$115,000	$210,000
OREGON			
Coos Bay	$60,000	$110,000	$200,000
Grants Pass	$85,000	$165,000	$275,000
Klamath Falls	$50,000	$95,000	$185,000

	Low Price Range	Medium Price Range	High Price Range
(OREGON, cont.)			
Sun River	$90,000	$200,000	$350,000
PENNSYLVANIA			
Mountain Regions,			
Poconos	$75,000	$150,000	$225,000
PUERTO RICO			
Humacao	$65,000	$225,000	$350,000
San Juan	$80,000	$150,000	$300,000
SOUTH CAROLINA			
Hilton Head	$75,000	$175,000	$400,000
Kiawah Island	$60,000	$200,000	$650,000
Myrtle Beach	$50,000	$100,000	$200,000
Seabrook Island	$50,000	$200,000	$750,000
Wild Dunes	$60,000	$225,000	$600,000
SOUTH DAKOTA			
Brookings	$50,000	$100,000	$175,000
TENNESSEE			
Gatlinburg	$55,000	$125,000	$350,000
TEXAS			
Corpus Christi	$45,000	$115,000	$225,000
Galveston	$45,000	$110,000	$225,000
South Padre Island	$50,000	$125,000	$250,000
UTAH			
Deer Valley–Pk City	$125,000	$250,000	$500,000
St. George	$85,000	$220,000	$275,000
VERMONT			
Ludlow	$95,000	$175,000	$225,000
St. Johnsbury	$50,000	$95,000	$165,000
VIRGINIA			
Shenandoah Valley			
Region	$65,000	$95,000	$165,000
Virginia Beach	$75,000	$150,000	$300,000

BUYING A VACATION HOME

	Low Price Range	Medium Price Range	High Price Range
WASHINGTON			
Aberdeen	$50,000	$95,000	$150,000
Gig Harbor	$75,000	$175,000	$275,000
No. Whidbey Island	$100,000	$190,000	$275,000
Orcas Island	$225,000	$425,000	$750,000
Port Angeles	$85,000	$150,000	$250,000
Port Townsend	$85,000	$175,000	$325,000
Sequim	$100,000	$200,000	$325,000
WEST VIRGINIA			
Greenbriar Resort	$75,000	$175,000	$500,000
Harpers Ferry	$75,000	$125,000	$250,000
WISCONSIN			
Eagle River	$65,000	$125,000	$225,000
Hayward	$50,000	$125,000	$275,000
Lake Geneva	$85,000	$165,000	$375,000
Park Falls	$40,000	$75,000	$150,000
Rhinelander	$40,000	$65,000	$95,000
Shawno	$50,000	$85,000	$165,000
Tomahawk	$35,000	$75,000	$150,000
Webster	$45,000	$80,000	$140,000
WYOMING			
Jackson Hole	$150,000	$295,000	$500,000

Source: Coldwell Banker

A close reading of the table will help you separate the established but affordable enclaves from the overpriced palaces in the local Gilded Gulch. Some examples: The medium price range, in Key Biscayne, a short hop south of Miami, averages $400,000 and the high-end homes run more than $700,000. By contrast, in Cocoa Beach, an hour from Orlando, midlevel homes will cost you about $150,000 and the high-end habitations are in the $300,000 range. Similarly, the summer showplaces strung along Lake Michigan in the northern Michigan town of Harbor

Springs fetch half a million, but $150,000 will land you a respectable hideaway on an interior lake in Michigan's northern lake region. "We're talking about large freshwater lakes where you can fish and boat to your heart's content," says Ken Schmidt, a broker with Coldwell Banker in Traverse City, Michigan.

If an area that appeals to you seems too pricey, ask an agent to recommend more affordable spots nearby. Or simply head out yourself with a map and the classified ads to visit places adjacent to the hot spots. Have a salesperson show you a few listings. When you're confident of your intentions, write or call the Chamber of Commerce and tell them you are considering buying a second home in the area. Within days your mailbox will be overflowing.

Before you become wedded to a particular house, however, explore the issue of homeowners insurance. If you're looking in a place where flood and storm damage are frequent threats, it's crucial to talk to an insurance agent familiar with the area in advance of your house hunt. You'll get an idea of what typical premiums are, and the agent may be able to tip you off to certain spots that are prone to flooding or storm damage. If your vacation house gets clobbered by the elements, you can take a beating financially.

Financing Your Vacation Home

Expect to pay a premium to own your own piece of paradise. You'll probably have to pay 20% down, compared with the 10% that's customary on primary homes. Lenders may also hit you up for higher financing costs, especially if you plan to rent out the property. You might face a mortgage rate that's one-eighth to three-quarters of a percentage point higher than the going rate for a comparable primary mortgage, as well as an extra closing point. For example, Interwest Savings Bank in the San Juan Island town of Friday Harbor was recently charging two points on a regular second-home loan and three points if the owner plans to use it as a rental. The bank will also bump up the mortgage rate on the rental property one-half to three-quarters of a percentage point higher than the rate it usually charges for second homes.

The reason is simple. "Lenders typically see the vacation home as a higher-risk proposition," explains Tom Hulbrink, a regional manager of Chase Manhattan Financial Services in Boca Raton, Florida. "We're concerned that if borrowers become overextended, they'll stop making payments on their vacation homes before their primary homes."

Before you even make the appointment with the mortgage banker or other lender, assess your overall financial picture. By the most generous rule, your combined mortgage payments, homeowners insurance, and property taxes for your primary and vacation homes should not exceed 33% of your gross annual income. Moreover, the total payments on all your debts should not eat up more than 40% of gross income. Test those limits and you could find yourself underwater financially.

The Convoluted Tax Treatment

Let's start with the bright spot: if your home away from home is only that—a second residence that's never rented out—your tax benefits come with minimal complications. You can deduct the mortgage interest on your playhouse just as you do on your primary residence. Limit yourself to two homes and combined debt of no more than $1 million. (Once you borrow above that dollar limit, or purchase a third abode, Congress reckons that you don't need the help of a tax deduction.) Interest is also deductible on additional amounts of up to $100,000 in home-equity debt, regardless of how the money is used. Finally, you can deduct property taxes and also casualty losses, should you have them. Take the itemized deductions on Schedule A of your 1040 Form, just as you do with your primary residence. For purposes of the Internal Revenue Code, your vacation home may be a house, apartment, condo, trailer, motor home, boat, or even a garage.

If you decide to mix business and fun by renting out your pleasure palace, then the tax treatment turns tricky. The rules specify three different categories based upon the number of days that the owner rents out the property, compared to the amount of time the owner occupies it. When you figure out the appropriate category for your situation, that will determine the amount of rental expenses you may deduct and the taxes that are due.

• **If you rent out your home for no more than 14 days a year,** you'll owe no taxes on the rental income and are not even required to report it to the IRS.

• **If you rent out your home for more than 14 days but also use it yourself for 15 days** or for more than 10% of the number of days you rent the home, whichever is greater, the IRS will consider it to be your personal vacation home, subject to a set of special mixed-use rules. Mortgage interest and taxes are allocated between personal and rental use of the property. Your rental expenses, however, are deductible only to the extent of your rental income. Thus if you have $5,000 in rental expenses but only $2,500 in rental income, you can deduct only $2,500 worth of expenses.

Moreover, to keep your deductions at a minimum, you are required to claim your expenses in a certain order. You must deduct mortgage interest, property taxes, and casualty losses first; then advertising and commissions, insurance, utilities, repairs, and other operating expenses; and, finally, depreciation (over 27.5 years). Notice that the first items used to offset rental income are deductible anyway if you itemize on Schedule A.

One break: You can carry over excess write-offs to a future year when you have excess rental income or to reduce your gain when you sell it. If your rental income exceeds expenses, of course, your net profit is taxable.

• **If you limit personal use to 14 days or 10% of the number of days the home is rented, whichever is greater,** then your vacation home will be considered a rental property and will be subject to a different set of mixed-use rules. Mortgage interest and taxes are still allocated between personal and rental use of the property. On the plus side, you generally can deduct rental losses up to $25,000 against your income if you actively manage the property—by screening tenants and approving repairs, for example. You qualify for the full $25,000 write-off if your adjusted gross income (AGI) is less than $100,000. The tax benefit is phased out if your AGI is between $100,000 and $150,000. If you earn more than $150,000, you can deduct rental business losses against rental income, but not against your salary, interest, or dividend income. (This limitation does not hold for those in the real estate business professionally. They are permitted to deduct rental business losses against income regardless of how much they earn.)

Rental business expenses, by the way, may include the cost of any trips you take to inspect or repair the property. Personal-use days include any day the dwelling is used by you, a co-owner, or members of your families, whether or not rent is paid. Maintenance days don't count as personal-use days, but be prepared to document that you did significant work on the premises. Receipts from the hardware or paint store, for example, could prove your point. Simply carrying a hammer to the beach for three weeks won't pass muster and might jeopardize your right to claim the house as a rental property.

With a mixed-use home, you allocate expenses between personal and rental days. To calculate the allocation, multiply each expense by a fraction to determine rental deductions. The Internal Revenue Service claims the proper fraction to use is days rented divided by days of use. Some aggressive accountants, however, figure the fraction as days rented divided by 365, the total days in the year, which gives a more favorable financial result for the owner.

For a broader treatment of this complex tax topic, consult IRS Publication 527, "Residential Rental Property." If you're counting on rental income and tax breaks to make your second home financially viable, sit down with a tax professional and get comprehensive advice before you buy. The rules, as you've surely noticed, quickly get convoluted.

Other Forms of Ownership

If you dream of owning a beach cottage or a mountain hide-away, but can't swing the down payment, not to mention the cash drain of two mortgage payments and two sets of utility bills, don't abandon the idea yet. You might be able to own a piece of your dream by buying with friends, purchasing a fractional interest in a property, or buying a time-share in a condo apartment unit. Here's a rundown of how these options work.

BUYING WITH FRIENDS

This is a sociable solution that's become increasingly popular among young buyers. It also has particular appeal in states like Georgia and the Carolinas, where residents have easy access to both the mountains and the ocean. "About half my friends have some sort of combined vacation-house deal," says Ann Mitchell of Augusta, Georgia. She and her husband, John, a physician, own a mountain house in Highlands, North Carolina, with one other couple and a three-bedroom beach condo on Isle of Palms, near Charleston, South Carolina, with seven couples.

If this kind of arrangement appeals to you and your friends, you can take ownership of a vacation home as tenants in common or in a legally constituted partnership. Consult a lawyer to determine which arrangement works best in your circumstances, though a partnership among the co-owners is usually the simpler choice. When the lawyer draws up the papers, make sure the contract addresses the following issues:

• **How ownership will be divided.** If you own a 25% share, then you are generally expected to cover 25% of the down payment and all expenses. The contract should also spell out how any profits from the rent or sale of the property will be distributed and how tax benefits will be apportioned.

• **Who is allowed to use the property when.** Simple fairness dictates that prime holidays like Independence Day or Christmas should be rotated among the owners so every family gets a chance to enjoy them in the house. A stickier point is whether owners can offer the house on "their" weekends to friends, relatives, or children when the owners themselves will not be present. To avoid problems, says Ann Mitchell, only the owners' parents are allowed to occupy their mountain house when they aren't present. "We had some friends who sold their shared house because there were so many problems with the co-owners' college-age children leaving it messy," she notes.

• **How to calculate a fair price if one partner wants out and what to do in the event of death or divorce.** Many owners conclude that they would not want to share with the heirs if a co-owner dies and determine that the surviving owner has an opportunity to buy the share of the deceased at a fair price or that the entire property be put up for sale.

• **Which owner will act as managing partner,** signing checks and paying routine bills. He or she may also coordinate schedules and arrange for maid service and similar chores. In return, the other owners may give that person an extra week or other reward. If no one wants to shoulder the task permanently, owners can rotate the chore on an annual basis. For simplicity's sake, partners should sign 12 predated checks for their share of monthly payments, so there won't be any hassles with collecting expense money.

Even if the legal and managerial tasks are set up smoothly, many vacation-home partnerships founder over simple house-keeping decisions. Weekly or monthly professional maid service can usually prevent such quarrels. Owners are also advised to meet formally twice a year to discuss problems that may arise. At one of these you might want to discuss improvements needed and chip in a few hundred dollars apiece for new purchases and sprucing up—to buy a TV for the master bedroom, for example, or pay for a new paint job.

At the Mitchells' beach condo, shared among eight couples, a few other rules keep the partnership running smoothly. If you break something, *you* replace it—immediately. Only two designated "decorators" are allowed to hang pictures or buy decorative accessories to keep the place from looking junky. Each owner has a big plastic bin to store personal items. "We keep our liquor, wine, spices, and toiletries completely separate, so we always know what will be there on our return," says Mitchell. She adds: "Flexibility is the most important quality. Anyone who is a perfectionist or very uptight should not *even consider* sharing property."

TIME-SHARING

Time-shares are often the cheapest way to buy into a resort. Typically you plunk down from $5,000 to $20,000 for a designated chunk of time—one week is standard—at a resort property, most often a condominium apartment complex. As the time-sharing industry has developed, variations have emerged, and longer intervals, sometimes called **fractionals,** have become increasingly popular. So a skier might buy a "tenth" (a five-week share) of a Colorado resort. A retired couple might choose a quarter share (a thirteen-week interval) of a Florida condo. Owners pay maintenance fees to a management company that handles taxes, pays bills, and tends to repairs and cleaning. If you feel comfortable with the amenities and layout of a resort, and if weekly rentals are expensive, it might be worth your while to plop down some dollars up front and guarantee your place in paradise for the time period you want. You won't have the hassle of making reservations or the disappointment of having to stay at a mediocre hotel because your first choice was booked solid. Over the years, the time-share can be a cheaper way to take a vacation, because you lock in the cost of your accommodations.

There are now more than 1,000 condo and hotel time-share resorts nationwide and about the same number overseas. About 85% of time-share offerings are under a **fee simple plan,** in which the buyer gets title to the real estate. The other kind of time-share, a **right-to-use plan,** is a long lease, usually 20–40 years.

Customers typically put down 10%–25% of the sales price and finance the remainder over five to seven years, often with the help of the developer. Banks rarely (if ever) make conventional mortgage loans on time-share units. If owners use their time-shares as a second home, they are generally entitled to deduct any finance charges. But if they choose a right-to-use plan, finance charges are treated as consumer interest and cannot be written off. Customers who opt for a leasehold arrangement will sometimes finance the deal by taking out a home-equity loan on their primary residence, since interest on these loans remains deductible.

Prospective buyers should allow plenty of time to do their homework. Don't buy into a resort in the back of the boonies, and don't surrender to a hard sell and buy on the spot, say the experts. Take the papers home and have your lawyer review them. Ask for the names of five or 10 people who have owned their share for two or more years, then check out those references.

No matter how enticing the deal sounds, you cannot count on future appreciation with a time-sharing arrangement. Indeed, thousands of time-share owners have struggled to find buyers because the time-share salesman in their resorts have steered potential buyers to the *new,* unsold units. It's not unusual for owners to have to swallow losses of 35%–60% when they finally unload their property. Those who hang on, either from choice or necessity, may find their initial attraction melting away. You may grow tired of visiting the same resort every year or be unable to schedule your vacation during that same week in July. Opportunities to swap may be hard to come by.

If you are still interested in buying a time-share, pay close attention to the following guidelines:

• **Proceed cautiously.** Rent a few times in the development that appeals to you. Try to go during the week that you think you want to own. Let your lawyer and your accountant review the offering terms and advise you on the legal and tax ramifications. Don't rely on verbal assurances from a salesperson. Check the developer's reputation further with the local Better Business Bureau, the attorney general's office, or any state agency that monitors time-sharing.

• **Buy time during the peak season in a popular area.** This will enhance your chances of swapping your unit, renting it out, or selling it.

• **Buy in a place that's easy to reach.** Don't count on potential buyers and swappers driving days to reach your cabin on Lake Oilspill, Louisiana, no matter how good the local jambalaya and zydeco music might be.

• **Don't overpay.** If you are buying a fee simple unit, don't pay more than 10 times the going rate for a comparable week in a local hotel or rental apartment. You can obtain those figures from a real estate agent or from newspaper ads. For a right-to-use time-share, divide the sales price by the number of years offered. If the amount is less than the cost of an equivalent rental, you may be getting a bargain. Before buying from the developer, see whether a time-share resale agent is listing equivalent accommodations at the same project. If so, you can often cut a better deal on the price, since markups on developer sales average 45%.

• **Buy from a proven developer.** Scam operators have muddied the time-share marketplace in the past. Recently, however, the entry of such large operators as Disney, Hilton, and Marriott is forcing out the fly-by-nighters. Stick with an experienced hand and you'll be less likely to find your vacation spoiled by poor maintenance, bad management, or unexpected lawsuits. Big developers are also more likely to maintain rental or resale offices to help you when you need them.

The most satisfied owners seem to be those who bought their time-shares for enjoyment, not as an investment. Jeff Ducker, a certified public accountant in Coral Gables, Florida, spent $7,000 in 1982 for a share of a two-bedroom unit on Sanibel Island, off the Gulf coast of Florida—a price that looks pretty good nowadays. Ducker sold the unit in 1994 for slightly more than he paid for it. "The kids got older, our needs changed," he explains. "But it was great while it lasted."

CHECKPOINTS

• Buy a vacation property primarily for enjoyment, only secondarily as an investment. Pundits say the baby boomers will force second-home prices higher, but don't stake a major chunk of your retirement kitty on those forecasts.

• Test the locale by renting for at least one season before buying property. Talk to other owners in the area and ask if they are happy with their choice.

• Shop in the off season to get better deals. Before purchasing, inspect your prospective vacation home as carefully as you would assess a primary residence.

• If you are buying from a developer, check his or her credentials with the local Better Business Bureau, state and local regulatory agencies, and at least three recent clients.

GLOSSARY

Real estate transactions have a language all their own. Here are definitions of some words and terms that you may encounter in the course of buying your home. Meanings may vary somewhat in different contexts or among regions of the United States.

Abstract of title: A condensed history of the legal title of a piece of real estate.

Acceleration clause: A provision in a mortgage that gives the lender the right to demand payment of the entire outstanding balance if a monthly payment is missed.

Actual cash value: The replacement cost of an item minus depreciation.

Adjustable-rate mortgage: A mortgage loan whose interest rate and payments fluctuate up or down, usually once or twice a year according to changes in a specified index.

Adjustments: Incidental expenses that show up on the settlement sheet that you sign when you buy or sell a house.

Amortization: The payment of a debt, such as a mortgage loan, through regular installment payments that include both principal and interest.

Amortization schedule: A timetable for payment of a mortgage, showing the amount of each payment applied to interest and principal and the remaining balance.

Annual percentage rate (APR): The cost of credit expressed as an annual percentage of the loan amount. It usually includes a combination of the base interest rate, points, and other fees the borrower paid to the lender to acquire a mortgage. The APR, which is usually slightly above the actual interest rate alone, is the most meaningful measure for comparing the cost of mortgage loans offered by different lenders.

Appraisal: A professional opinion of a house's value based on recent, verifiable information of sales (or rentals, if applicable) of comparable properties in its vicinity.

Appreciation: An increase in the value of a house due to changes in market conditions or other causes.

"As is" condition: The seller will make no repairs to the house before settlement.

Assessed value: The valuation placed upon property by a public tax assessor for purposes of taxation.

Assumable loan: An existing mortgage that can be taken over ("assumed") by a buyer, usually on the same terms as those given to the original buyer. An assumable mortgage loan can make a home more attractive to buyers.

Balance: An amount of loan remaining to be paid; sometimes known as the **outstanding balance.**

Balloon mortgage: A loan with monthly payments that are too small to retire the debt within the specified term. The balance must be paid in full when the term expires.

Binder: A preliminary agreement, secured by the payment of earnest money, under which a buyer offers to purchase real estate.

Bridge loan: A 30- to 120-day loan secured by equity in your house. The proceeds are used to make the down payment on a new house when you haven't yet sold the old one.

Broker: A person who has met state real estate licensing standards and can conduct real estate transactions. Many brokers have their own firms.

Buy-down: A payment of interest in advance to temporarily reduce the interest rate on a mortgage loan.

Buyer's broker: A real estate agent who represents the buyer, sometimes for a fee, sometimes for a commission from the listing broker.

Cap: A limit on how much the rate of interest or the monthly mortgage payments can fluctuate during the life of an adjustable-rate mortgage.

Cash reserve: A requirement of some lenders that buyers have sufficient cash remaining after closing to make the first two mortgage payments.

Certificate of occupancy: A certificate issued by the building department of the local or county government to a builder or owner, stating that the building is in proper condition to be occupied and specifying the legally permissible use.

Clear title: A title that is free of liens and legal questions as to ownership of the property.

Closing: The meeting at which title to a property passes from the seller to the buyer. Closing is also known as **settlement.**

Closing costs: Fees and expenses—apart from the actual purchase price of the property—associated with transferring a property from a seller to a buyer, among them lawyers' fees, survey charges, title searches and insurance, and fees to file deeds and mortgages.

Collateral: Something of value that serves as security for a loan.

Commitment letter: A formal offer from a lender stating the terms under which it will lend money to a buyer for the purchase of a home.

Community Home Buyer's Program: An alternative Fannie Mae financing option that allows households of modest means to qualify for mortgages using nontraditional credit histories, 33% housing-to-income and 38% debt-to-income ratios, and the waiver of the standard two-month mortgage payment reserve requirement at closing.

Condominium: A form of property ownership in which the homeowner holds title to an individual dwelling unit, an undivided interest in common areas of a multiunit project, and sometimes the exclusive use of certain limited common areas.

Contingency clause: A condition put on an offer to buy a home. For example, the prospective buyer might make a purchase offer contingent on obtaining financing at a particular rate or an acceptable inspection by a construction engineer.

Contract of sale: A written contract signed by both parties in which the owner agrees to sell and the buyer agrees to buy a specific property under certain specified terms and conditions.

Conventional mortgage: Any mortgage not insured or guaranteed by either the Federal Housing Administration or the Department of Veterans Affairs.

Convertible ARM: An adjustable-rate mortgage that can be converted to a fixed-rate mortgage under specified conditions.

Cooperative (co-op): A property of two or more units whose title is held by a corporation. Residents own shares in the corporation that entitle them to occupy a certain apartment or unit.

Credit report: An account of an individual's credit history prepared by a credit reporting agency and used by a lender in determining a loan applicant's creditworthiness.

Deed: The legal document conveying title to a property.

Default: Failure to make mortgage payments on a timely basis or to comply with other conditions of a mortgage.

Delinquency: A loan in which a payment is overdue but not yet in default.

Depreciation: A decline in the value of a property; the opposite of "appreciation."

Down payment: The part of the purchase price of a house that the buyer pays in cash and does not finance with a mortgage. The down payment commonly ranges from 5% to 20% of the purchase price.

Earnest money: A deposit that the buyer submits with a purchase offer to show the seller that he or she is serious about buying the house. Earnest money is usually placed by the broker in an escrow account until closing, when it becomes part of the down payment or closing costs.

Encumbrance: A claim levied against a property, limiting the owner's ability to transfer the title. Liens and attachments are common forms of encumbrances.

Equity: The difference between the market value of a property and the mortgage plus any other liens against it.

Escrow: A procedure in which documents, cash, or property are put in the care of a neutral third party, one other than the buyer or seller.

FHA mortgage: A loan insured against loss by the Federal Housing Administration (FHA). Such financing usually requires only a 3%–5% down payment.

First mortgage: The mortgage that has first claim in the event of a default.

Fixed-rate mortgage: A mortgage loan with an interest rate and payments that do not vary over the life of the loan.

Fizbos: A FSBO—that is, a house that is for sale by the owner.

Flood insurance: Insurance that compensates for physical property damages resulting from flooding. It is required for properties located in federally designated flood areas.

General contractor: A builder who oversees a renovation or the construction of a house or an addition.

Grading: The slope of the land around the foundation; proper grading causes water to flow away from the house.

Graduated payment mortgage: A mortgage that starts with low monthly payments that increase at a predetermined rate. The initial monthly payments are set at an amount lower than that required for full amortization of the debt.

Gross: Before taxes, as in gross income.

Gutters: Metal or fiberglass channels along the eaves that direct water from the roof into the downspouts.

Half-bath: A small room containing a toilet and sink but no tub or shower.

Handyman's special: A house usually sold in "as is" condition that needs a lot of fixing up.

Home inspector: A trained professional who evaluates the structural soundness of a home, recommends what repairs are needed, and estimates their cost.

Homeowners insurance: Insurance that protects the homeowner from casualty (losses or damage to the home or personal property) and from liability (damages to other people or property). Lenders require the insurance. The premium is usually included as part of the monthly mortgage payment.

Installment debt: Debts with more than a fixed number of months (usually 10 or 11) left to repay.

Interest: The fee charged for borrowing money, often expressed as an annual percentage rate.

Interest rate cap: A provision of an ARM limiting how much interest rates may increase per adjustment period and over the life of the loan.

Joint tenancy: A form of co-ownership giving each tenant equal interest and equal rights in the property, including the right of survivorship.

Lease-option agreement: An arrangement by which you rent a house with an option to buy at the end of a specific period of time at an agreed-upon price.

Lien: A claim against a property that must be paid before the property can be sold.

Lifetime cap: A provision of an ARM that limits the total increase in the interest rate over the life of the loan.

Listing broker: The broker who is retained by the owner to sell a property.

Loan application (or origination) fee: A lender's charge for evaluating, preparing, and submitting a proposed mortgage loan. The prospective borrower pays the fee when he or she applies for a mortgage.

Loan-to-value ratio or percentage (LTV): The relationship between the principal balance of the mortgage and the appraised value or sales price (if it is lower) of the property. If the mortgage is $80,000 and the property is worth $100,000, the loan-to-value ratio is 80%.

Lock-in: A written agreement guaranteeing the buyer a specific interest rate provided the loan is closed within a set period of time. The lock-in also usually specifies the number of points to be paid at closing.

Maintenance: A monthly fee paid by condo and co-op owners for the upkeep of common areas.

Margin: The set percentage the lender adds to the index rate to determine the interest rate of an ARM.

Mortgage: A legal document that pledges a property to the lender as security for payment of a debt.

Mortgage banker: An individual or company that originates mortgages exclusively for resale in the secondary market.

Mortgage broker: An individual or company that for a fee acts as intermediary between borrowers and lenders.

Mortgagee: The lender in a mortgage agreement.

Mortgage insurance: See **private mortgage insurance.**

Mortgagor: The borrower in a mortgage agreement.

Multiple listing service (MLS): A computerized network that gives participating agents information on properties listed for sale with brokers in the area.

Negative amortization: The month-by-month conversion of unpaid mortgage interest into additional loan principal so that the amount of the loan keeps growing with each payment instead of diminishing.

Net: After taxes, as in net income.

No-documentation loan: A program offered by some lenders that requires less extensive verification than a standard loan approval process. Usually available only to borrowers able to make relatively large down payments.

Open listing: A listing agreement under which any broker who sells the property is entitled to a commission.

Owner financing: A purchase in which the seller provides all or part of the financing.

Payment cap: A provision of some ARMs limiting how much a borrower's payments may increase regardless of how much the interest rate increases; this may result in negative amortization.

PITI: A lenders' acronym for principal, interest, taxes, and insurance—the key components of a mortgage payment.

Points: Fees charged by lenders that are expressed as a percentage of the mortgage amount. One point equals 1% of the amount of the mortgage.

Portfolio lender: A lender who originates and retains mortgage loans rather than selling them in the secondary market.

Preapproval: The process of obtaining preliminary approval for a mortgage before the application is complete. May or may not constitute a formal commitment by the lender to make the loan. Don't confuse preapproval with prequalification.

Prepayment penalty: A fee, typically six months' worth of interest, charged by some lenders when a borrower pays off a mortgage ahead of schedule.

Prequalification: An informal estimate of how much money a prospective home buyer could borrow, based on a calculation of available income and existing debt.

Principal: The original amount borrowed, on which interest is calculated.

Private mortgage insurance (PMI): Insurance that protects lenders against loss if a borrower defaults. Fannie Mae generally requires private mortgage insurance for loans with loan-to-value ratios greater than 80%.

Property taxes: Taxes, based on the assessed value of the home, paid by the homeowner for community services and other costs of local government. Included as part of the monthly mortgage payment.

Purchase and sale agreement: A written contract signed by the buyer and seller stating the terms and conditions under which a property will be sold.

Qualifying ratios: Guidelines applied by lenders to determine how large a loan to grant to a home buyer.

Radon: An odorless, colorless gas found in some homes that in sufficient concentration can cause health problems.

Real Estate Settlement Procedures Act (RESPA): A consumer protection law that requires lenders to give borrowers advance notice of closing costs.

Realtor: A member of the National Association of Realtors; usually (but not always) a real estate broker or agent.

Recording fees: The charges for filing the documents effecting the transfer of ownership and clearing the title in a real estate transaction.

Refinancing: The process of obtaining a new mortgage, typically at a lower rate, to repay and replace an existing loan.

Replacement cost: The price of a new item substituted for a damaged one.

Second mortgage: A mortgage whose holder has rights that are subordinate to the rights of the first mortgage holder.

Secondary mortgage market: The buying and selling of existing mortgages.

Security: Something of value pledged to assure loan repayment and subject to seizure if the borrower defaults.

Selling broker: The broker who actually finds the buyer in a real estate transaction.

Stick-built house: One built board by board from the ground up at the site.

Subcontractor: A specialist such as a plumber or roofer who is hired by a general contractor to perform a specific task on a construction job.

Sweat equity: The value added to your property by your own labor.

Teaser: An exceptionally low come-on interest rate for an initial period—often six months or one year—of an adjustable-rate loan.

Tenancy by entirety: A type of joint ownership of property available only to a husband and wife.

Tenancy in common: A type of joint ownership in a property without right of survivorship.

Title: Evidence of ownership.

Title insurance: Insurance that protects lenders and homeowners against loss of their interest in a property if there is a dispute about its title.

Title search: A detailed examination of the ownership documents, undertaken to insure that there are no liens or other encumbrances on the property and no questions about the seller's ownership claim.

Town house: A dwelling that has its own entrance but shares at least one exterior wall with a neighbor.

Transfer tax: State or local tax payable when title passes from one owner to another.

Truth-in-lending: A federal law that requires lenders to fully disclose in writing the terms and conditions of a mortgage, including the APR and other charges.

VA mortgage: A loan guaranteed by the Department of Veterans Affairs against loss to the lender and made through a private lender. It allows an eligible veteran to buy a house without making a down payment.

Yield: The rate of return on an investment over a given time, expressed as an annual percentage rate. Yield is affected by the price paid for the investment as well as by the timing of the principal repayments.

Yield to maturity: The annual percentage rate of return on an investment, assuming it is held to maturity.

INDEX

INDEX

SADLIER-OXFORD

LEVEL D

Vocabulary Workshop

Enhanced Edition

The classic program for:

- *developing* and *enhancing* vocabulary resources

- *promoting* more effective communication in today's world

- *improving* vocabulary skills assessed on standardized and/or college-admission tests

By
Jerome Shostak

NONACCOUNTABLE

FOR CLASSROOM USE ONLY

Sadlier-Oxford

CARLMONT HIGH SCHOOL

3 9050 00223 4854

A Division of William H. Sadlier, Inc.
9 Pine Street
New York, New York 10005-1002
1-800-221-5175

Contents

NOTE: ALL RIGHTS RESERVED. NO PART OF THIS BOOK MAY BE REPRODUCED,
STORED IN A DATABASE OR RETRIEVAL SYSTEM, OR TRANSMITTED IN ANY FORM
BY ANY MEANS, ELECTRONIC, MECHANICAL, PHOTOCOPYING, RECORDING, OR OTH-
ERWISE WITHOUT THE PRIOR WRITTEN PERMISSION OF WILLIAM H. SADLIER, INC.
COPYRIGHT INFRINGERS WILL BE PROSECUTED TO THE FULL EXTENT OF THE LAW
AND MAY BE LIABLE FOR DAMAGES OF UP TO $150,000. REPORT ALL VIOLATIONS,
IN CONFIDENCE, TO THE PUBLISHER AT THE ADDRESS SHOWN BELOW.

Copyright © 1996 by William H. Sadlier, Inc. All rights reserved.

This publication, or any part thereof, may not be reproduced in any form, or by any means,
including electronic, photographic, or mechanical, or by any sound recording system, or by any
device for storage and retrieval of information, without the written permission of the publisher.
Address inquires to Permissions Department, William H. Sadlier, Inc., 9 Pine Street, New York,
New York 10005-1002.

S is a registered trademark of William H. Sadlier, Inc.

Printed in the United States of America.

ISBN: 0-8215-0609-9
10 11 12 13 14/05 04 03 02 01

Foreword

For close to five decades VOCABULARY WORKSHOP has been a highly successful tool for guiding and stimulating systematic vocabulary growth for students. It has also been extremely valuable for preparing students to take the types of standardized vocabulary tests commonly used to assess grade placement, competence for graduation, and/or college readiness. The *Enhanced Edition* has faithfully maintained those features that have made the program so beneficial in these two areas, while introducing new elements to keep abreast of changing times and changing standardized-test procedures, particularly the SAT. The features that make VOCABULARY WORKSHOP so valuable include:

Word List

Each book contains 300 or more basic words, selected on the basis of:
- currency in present-day usage
- frequency on recognized vocabulary lists
- applicability to standardized tests
- current grade-placement research

Units

The words in each book are organized around 15 short, stimulating *Units* featuring:
- pronunciation and parts of speech

New!
- definitions—fuller treatment in the *Enhanced Edition*
- synonyms and antonyms
- usage (one phrase and two sentences)

Reviews

Five *Reviews* highlight and reinforce the work of the units through challenging exercises involving:

New!
- shades of meaning (SAT-type critical-thinking exercise)
- definitions
- synonyms and antonyms
- analogies
- sentence completions
- word families

Cumulative Reviews

Four *Cumulative Reviews* utilize standardized testing techniques to provide ongoing assessment of word mastery, all involving SAT-type critical-thinking skills. Here the exercises revolve around

New!
- shades of meaning
- analogies
- two-word completions

Additional Features

- A *Diagnostic Test* provides ready assessment of student needs at the outset of the term.
- The *Vocabulary of Vocabulary* reviews terms and concepts needed for effective word study.
- The *Final Mastery Test* provides end-of-term assessment of student achievement.
- *Building with Word Roots* introduces the study of etymology.
- *Enhancing Your Vocabulary,* Levels F through H, introduces students to the study of word clusters.

New!
- *Working with Parts of Speech,* Levels F through H, provides further work with word clusters and introduces 50 new words per level.

Ancillary Materials

- An *Answer Key* for each level supplies answers to all materials in the student text.
- A *Series Teacher's Guide* provides a thorough overview of the features in each level, along with tips for using them effectively.
- The *Supplementary Testing Program: Cycle One, Cycle Two* provide two complete programs of separate and different testing materials for each level, so testing can be varied. A *Combined Answer Key* for each level is also available.
- The SAT-type *TEST PREP Blackline Masters* for each level provide further testing materials designed to help students prepare for SAT-type standardized tests.
- An *Interactive Audio Pronunciation Program* is also available for each level.

Pronunciation Key

The pronunciation is indicated for every basic word introduced in this book. The symbols used for this purpose, as listed below, are similar to those appearing in most standard dictionaries of recent vintage. The author has consulted a large number of dictionaries for this purpose but has relied primarily on *Webster's Third New International Dictionary* and *The Random House Dictionary of the English Language (Unabridged)*.

There are, of course, many English words for which two (or more) pronunciations are commonly accepted. In virtually all cases where such words occur in this book, the author has sought to make things easier for the student by giving just one pronunciation. The only significant exception occurs when the pronunciation changes in accordance with a shift in the part of speech. Thus we would indicate that *project* in the verb form is pronounced prə ′jekt, and in the noun form, ′präj ekt.

It is believed that these relatively simple pronunciation guides will be readily usable by the student. It should be emphasized, however, that the *best* way to learn the pronunciation of a word is to listen to and imitate an educated speaker.

Vowels	ā	lake	e	stress	ü	loot, new
	a	mat	ī	kn*i*fe	ủ	foot, pull
	â	care	i	s*i*t	ə	rug, broken
	ä	bark, bottle	ō	flow	ər	b*i*rd, better
	aủ	do*u*bt	ô	all, cord		
	ē	beat, word*y*	oi	o*i*l		

Consonants	ch	*ch*ild, lecture	s	cellar	wh	*wh*at
	g̣	*g*ive	sh	*sh*un	y	*y*earn
	j	*g*entle, bri*dg*e	th	*th*ank	z	i*s*
	ŋ	si*ng*	th̶	*th*ose	zh	mea*s*ure

All other consonants are sounded as in the alphabet.

| **Stress** | The accent mark *precedes* the syllable receiving the major stress: en ′rich |

Parts of Speech	*adj.*	adjective	*int.*	interjection	*prep.*	preposition
	adv.	adverb	*n.*	noun	*v.*	verb
			part.	participle		
			pl.	plural		

The Vocabulary of Vocabulary

Many useful words are commonly employed in connection with the study of vocabulary. Some of these specialized terms that you should know are presented below. The exercises provided in each section will help you to check your knowledge of the "vocabulary of vocabulary."

Synonyms and Antonyms

Synonyms

A *synonym* is a word that is similar in meaning to another word.

Examples:

| go–depart | know–understand |
| listen–hear | hurry–rush |

Exercises

In each of the following groups, encircle the word that is most nearly the **synonym** of the first word in **boldface type.**

1. absurd
a. sensible
b. foolish
c. loud
d. quiet

2. alert
a. seen
b. dull
c. watchful
d. gone

3. blunt
a. stated
b. outspoken
c. sharp
d. unsaid

4. cluster
a. brightness
b. stars
c. clutter
d. group

5. detest
a. hate
b. enjoy
c. embitter
d. examine

6. rebellion
a. uprising
b. failure
c. defeat
d. hatred

7. fragile
a. delicate
b. heavy
c. broken
d. glassy

8. generosity
a. likelihood
b. charity
c. selfishness
d. cleverness

9. grave
a. fault
b. dead
c. visible
d. serious

10. hare
a. horse
b. duck
c. cow
d. rabbit

11. petty
a. unusual
b. slight
c. foreign
d. dry

12. conserve
a. refill
b. use up
c. save
d. throw away

Antonyms

An *antonym* is a word that is opposite in meaning to another word.

Examples:

| go–come | quiet–noisy |
| rush–dawdle | gloomy–cheerful |

Exercises

In each of the following groups, encircle the word that is most nearly the **antonym** of the first word in **boldface type.**

1. abruptly
a. suddenly
b. gradually
c. quickly
d. noticeably

2. amateur
a. veteran
b. beginner
c. professional
d. resident

3. blur
a. dim
b. close
c. open
d. clarify

4. drench
a. wet
b. read
c. dry
d. twist

5. economy
a. waste
b. thrift
c. noise
d. poverty

6. intelligent
a. charming
b. studious
c. stupid
d. lively

7. excessive
a. reasonable
b. unreasonable
c. reasoning
d. unreasoning

8. ferocious
a. juvenile
b. mild
c. angry
d. expensive

Words Pronounced Alike; Words Spelled Alike

Confusion and mistakes in both spoken and written English may result from the fact that different words are *spelled* alike, *pronounced* alike, or *both*.

Homonyms

A *homonym* is a word having the same pronunciation as another word but a different spelling and a different meaning.

Examples:

right–write   beet–beat
meat–meet   strait–straight

Exercises

*In each of the following sentences, encircle the **homonym** that correctly completes the meaning.*

1. A (**loan, lone**) horseman appeared on the distant horizon.
2. It was a (**sight, cite**) for sore eyes.
3. I had hoped to buy the TV set at a lower price during the (**sale, sail**).
4. I'd love to (**wring, ring**) his neck for saying that.
5. She gave me a (**peace, piece**) of her mind at no additional cost.
6. The baseball that was hit foul went through the (**pain, pane**) of glass.
7. May I (**mail, male**) the letter as soon as you have signed it?
8. You must tell the (**hole, whole**) truth and nothing but the truth.
9. Did he announce that the weather would be (**fair, fare**) tomorrow?
10. We walked down the (**aisle, isle**) of the theater.

Homographs

A *homograph* is a word that has the same spelling as another word but a different meaning.

Examples:

Pump may mean a type of shoe.
Pump may mean a machine used to compress or raise liquids and gases.

Pole may mean a long, slender object.
Pole may mean either end of the earth's axis.

Most homographs are not only spelled alike but pronounced alike. There are some, however, that are pronounced differently.

Bow may mean to incline the body; it is pronounced *baủ*, as in *cow*.
Bow, as in "bow and arrow," is pronounced *bō*, as in *row*.

Slough may mean a swamp; it is pronounced *slü*, as in *through*.
Slough may mean to shed or to cast off; it is pronounced *sləf*, as in *rough*.

Homographs that are pronounced differently are sometimes called *heteronyms*.

Exercises   *In Column C, write the **homograph** suggested by the definitions given in Columns A and B. The initial letter of each word is given, and the dashes represent the missing letters.*

	Column A	Column B	Column C
1.	turn or direct	type of cattle	s _ _ _ _
2.	severe, harsh	end of a ship	s _ _ _ _
3.	writing instrument	small enclosure	p _ _
4.	movement of air	to turn, as a clock	w _ _ _
5.	musical instrument	part of a living thing	o _ _ _ _
6.	turn over and over	type of bread	r _ _ _
7.	rips apart	water shed from the eyes	t _ _ _ _
8.	land bordering the sea	ride downhill	c _ _ _ _
9.	dark red color	leave in a helpless position	m _ _ _ _ _
10.	a heavy metal	to conduct or guide	l _ _ _

Parts of a Word

Prefixes   A *prefix* is a syllable or syllables placed at the beginning of a word.

Examples: in- pre- post- contra-

Suffixes   A *suffix* is a syllable or syllables placed at the end of a word.

Examples: -ation -ery -ing -ance

Bases   A *base* (or *root*) is the main part of the word to which prefixes and suffixes may be added.

Examples: -tain- -port- -spire- -fend-

Exercises   *Divide each of the following words into its prefix, root, and suffix. Some of the words may lack a prefix, a suffix, or both. The first word has been done for you.*

	Word	Prefix	Root	Suffix
1.	reporter	re	port	er
2.	overrule	_____	_____	_____
3.	contraction	_____	_____	_____
4.	reversal	_____	_____	_____
5.	contained	_____	_____	_____
6.	interrupt	_____	_____	_____
7.	scribble	_____	_____	_____
8.	inducting	_____	_____	_____
9.	despise	_____	_____	_____
10.	portable	_____	_____	_____

Denotation and Connotation

Denotation   The *denotation* of a word is its specific dictionary definition.

Examples:

Word	Denotation
scholarly	learned
grasping	overly eager for material gain
travel	make a journey

Connotation   The *connotation* of a word is its *tone*—that is, the emotions or associations it normally arouses in people using, hearing, or reading it. Depending on what these feelings are, the connotation of a word may be *favorable (positive)* or *unfavorable (pejorative)*. A word that does not arouse strong feelings of any sort has a *neutral* connotation.

Examples:

Word	Connotation
scholarly	favorable
grasping	unfavorable
travel	neutral

Exercises   *In the space provided, label the connotation of each of the following words **F** for "favorable," **U** for "unfavorable," or **N** for "neutral."*

_____ **1.** conceited   _____ **5.** valiant   _____ **9.** hero

_____ **2.** affectionate   _____ **6.** snob   _____ **10.** willful

_____ **3.** parallel   _____ **7.** excerpt   _____ **11.** spoon

_____ **4.** encroach   _____ **8.** shiftless   _____ **12.** pursue

Literal and Figurative Usage

Literal Usage   When a word is being used in a *literal* sense, it is being employed in its strict (or primary) dictionary meaning in a situation (or *context*) that "makes sense" from a purely logical point of view.

Example: There were logs *floating* in the river after the storm.

Figurative Usage   Sometimes words are used in a symbolic or nonliteral way in situations that do not "make sense" from a purely logical point of view. We call this nonliteral or "extended" application of a word a *figurative* or *metaphorical* usage.

Example: The famous actress *floated* into the room with all the grace and elegance of a prima ballerina.

Exercises   *In the space provided, write **L** for "literal" or **F** for "figurative" next to each of the following sentences to show how the italicized expression is being used.*

_____ **1.** I accidentally put my fingers *in some very hot water* and burned them.

_____ **2.** When the dean suddenly summoned me to his office, I knew I was *in hot water*.

_____ **3.** She kept her hair from falling in her eyes with a *ribbon*.

_____ **4.** A *ribbon* of moonlight suddenly broke through the clouds and illuminated her face.

_____ **5.** I *tiptoed* across the room so as not to awaken my sleeping brother.

_____ **6.** Dawn *tiptoed* across the meadow and drummed her rosy fingertips on my window.

Analogies

An *analogy* is a comparison. For example, we can draw an analogy, or comparison, between the human eye and a camera.

In examinations you may be asked to find the relationship between two words. Then to show that you understand the relationship, you are asked to choose another pair of words that show the same type of relationship.

Example:

back is to **front** as
a. shepherd is to crook
b. star is to sky
c. darkness is to light
d. finger is to hand

Since *back* and *front* are opposites, the correct answer is *c, darkness is to light.* Note that these two words are also opposite in meaning.

Exercises *In each of the following, encircle the item that best completes the analogy.*

1. teenager is to **youth** as
a. judge is to jury
b. baby is to infant
c. cow is to calf
d. boy is to girl

2. catastrophe is to **horror** as
a. achievement is to sorrow
b. tragedy is to laughter
c. question is to pleasure
d. mystery is to puzzlement

3. contempt is to **scorn** as
a. dignity is to ridicule
b. hate is to love
c. reversal is to success
d. understanding is to comprehension

4. cowardly is to **courage** as
a. awkward is to gracefulness
b. fabulous is to intelligence
c. drunk is to intoxication
d. funny is to humor

5. postscript is to **letter** as
a. epilogue is to play
b. overture is to opera
c. cover is to lid
d. sleeve is to coat

6. blunt is to **sharp** as
a. absurd is to ridiculous
b. short is to brief
c. conservative is to radical
d. tall is to fat

7. hammer is to **tool** as
a. typewriter is to machine
b. horse is to cow
c. singer is to soprano
d. trunk is to branch

8. moon is to **Earth** as
a. mountain is to river
b. tide is to sea
c. star is to comet
d. planet is to sun

9. maternal is to **mother** as
a. rural is to fishing
b. colonial is to poverty
c. maritime is to sea
d. terrestrial is to air

10. audacity is to **bold** as
a. vigilance is to watchful
b. hostility is to friendly
c. skill is to clumsy
d. timidity is to shrewd

Context Clues

When you do the various word-omission exercises contained in this book, look for *context clues* built into the passage to guide you to the correct answer.

Restatement Clues

A *restatement clue* consists of a synonym for, or a definition of, a missing word.

Example:

Faithfully reading a weekly news magazine not only <u>broadens</u> my knowledge of current events and world or national affairs but also _____ my vocabulary.

a. decreases   b. fragments   (c.) increases   d. contains

Contrast Clues

A *contrast clue* consists of an antonym for, or a phrase that means the opposite of, a missing word.

Example:

"As you say, my view of the situation may be far too <u>rosy</u>," I admitted. "<u>On the other hand</u>, yours may be a bit (**optimistic, bleak**)."

Inference Clues

An *inference clue* implies but does not directly state the meaning of a missing word.

Example:

"A treat for all ages," the review read, "this wonderful <u>novel</u> combines the _____ of a <u>scholar</u> with the <u>skill</u> and <u>artistry</u> of an expert _____ .

a.   ignorance . . . painter
b.   wisdom . . . beginner
c.   wealth . . . surgeon
(d.) knowledge . . . storyteller

Exercises

Use context clues to choose the word or words that complete each of the following sentences or sets of sentences.

1. I like visiting small towns and rural villages from time to time, but the big city is my _____ home.

a. permanent   b. former   c. original   d. temporary

2. The child's stubborn refusal to do what he was told (**infuriated, delighted**) his normally even-tempered parents.

3. The radio, the television set, and other forms of mass _____ with which we are all familiar today were entirely unknown at the _____ of the 20th century.

a. hysteria . . . end
b. employment . . . middle
c. communication . . . beginning
d. transportation . . . turn

Diagnostic Test

This test contains a sampling of the words that are to be found in the exercises in this Vocabulary Workshop. It will give you an idea of the types and levels of the words to be studied. When you have completed all the units, the Final Mastery Test at the end of the book will assess what you have learned. By comparing your results on the Final Mastery Test with your results on the Diagnostic Test below, you will be able to judge your progress.

Synonyms
*In each of the following groups, encircle the word or expression that is most nearly the **synonym** of the word in **boldface type** in the introductory phrase.*

1. auspicious beginning
a. slow   b. unpleasant   c. favorable   d. strong

2. in a **circumspect** manner
a. careful   b. surrounding   c. loud   d. crude

3. spurious argument
a. logical   b. strong   c. clever   d. false

4. lucrative contract
a. poor   b. profitable   c. long-term   d. expensive

5. fortify a city
a. destroy   b. enter   c. build   d. strengthen

6. causing **obesity**
a. eating   b. fatness   c. diet   d. economy

7. fabricate a product
a. steal   b. consume   c. put together   d. purchase

8. an **eminent** teacher
a. famous   b. youthful   c. elderly   d. experienced

9. incinerate the refuse
a. transport   b. utilize   c. bury   d. burn

10. hoodwink their opponents
a. deceive   b. defeat   c. size up   d. greet

11. biased opinion
a. strong   b. prejudiced   c. hasty   d. fair

12. gave **asylum** to the refugees
a. shelter   b. support   c. freedom   d. sympathy

13. paramount consideration
a. musical   b. chief   c. theatrical   d. final

14. succumb to temptation
a. yield   b. ignore   c. resist   d. enjoy

15. diligent instructor
a. skillful   b. learned   c. experienced   d. untiring

16. supplant an official
a. elect   b. criticize   c. replace   d. keep in office

17. incessant hammering
a. noisy   b. constant   c. unpleasant   d. occasional

18. tenacious fighters
a. persistent   b. dangerous   c. skilled   d. savage

19. apex of fame
a. reward   b. result   c. bottom point   d. top

20. shoddy material
a. inferior   b. colorful   c. drab   d. sturdy

21. meandering stream
a. rushing   b. twisting   c. babbling   d. polluted

22. malign someone
a. praise   b. slay   c. protect   d. slander

23. discarded **dross**
a. idol   b. waste   c. clothing   d. machinery

24. sterling qualities
a. inadequate   b. hidden   c. despised   d. excellent

25. warped mind
a. clever   b. twisted   c. determined   d. educated

26. pensive mood
a. talkative   b. thankful   c. angry   d. thoughtful

27. feign interest
a. pretend   b. increase   c. lose   d. stimulate

28. auxiliary patrol
a. new   b. untrained   c. assisting   d. chief

29. venomous remarks
a. complimentary   b. spiteful   c. intelligent   d. angry

30. plaintiff in the lawsuit
a. judge   b. prosecutor   c. accuser   d. accused

Antonyms   *In each of the following groups, encircle the word or expression that is most nearly* **opposite** *in meaning to the word in* **boldface type** *in the introductory phrase.*

31. relinquish power
a. hand over   b. give up   c. hold on to   d. wish for

32. buoyant outlook
a. cheerful   b. puzzling   c. immature   d. somber

33. a **lucid** explanation
a. muddled   b. long   c. clear   d. trustworthy

34. bogus currency
a. foreign   b. counterfeit   c. genuine   d. worthless

35. a **candid** statement
a. curious   b. misleading   c. frank   d. bitter

36. devitalize a program
a. weaken   b. cancel   c. strengthen   d. revise

37. erratic behavior
a. consistent
b. insulting
c. irregular
d. tactful

38. squander an allowance
a. save
b. waste
c. refuse
d. demand

39. slipshod work
a. sloppy
b. profitable
c. difficult
d. careful

40. a **ghastly** sight
a. remarkable
b. horrible
c. pleasant
d. curious

41. a **momentous** decision
a. serious
b. untimely
c. trivial
d. puzzling

42. chide the children
a. dress
b. compliment
c. scold
d. raise

43. a **humane** act
a. surprising
b. generous
c. praiseworthy
d. cruel

44. an **arduous** task
a. easy
b. endless
c. awful
d. unfinished

45. alien customs
a. unusual
b. pleasant
c. native
d. colorful

46. abridge a novel
a. write
b. expand
c. publish
d. read

47. rancid butter
a. unspoiled
b. expensive
c. imported
d. genuine

48. a **bleak** forecast
a. rosy
b. suspicious
c. believable
d. frightening

49. a **perilous** journey
a. leisurely
b. thrilling
c. costly
d. safe

50. forestall a riot
a. witness
b. prevent
c. incite
d. enjoy

Definitions   Note carefully the spelling, pronunciation, and definition of each of the following words. Then write the word in the blank space in the illustrative phrase following.

1. admonish
(ad 'män ish)

(v.) to caution or advise against something; to scold mildly; to remind of a duty

_____ the noisy students

2. breach
(brēch)

(n.) an opening, gap; a violation or infraction; (v.) to create an opening, break through

_____ the enemy's lines

3. brigand
('brig ənd)

(n.) a bandit

assaulted on the way by _____

4. circumspect
('sər kəm spekt)

(adj.) careful, cautious

try to behave in a _____ fashion

5. commandeer
(käm ən 'dēr)

(v.) to seize for military or official use

the right to _____ private property

6. cumbersome
('kəm bər səm)

(adj.) clumsy, hard to handle; slow-moving

a _____ package

7. deadlock
('ded läk)

(n.) a complete standstill; (v.) to bring to a standstill

a 3-to-3 _____ after 15 innings

8. debris
(də 'brē)

(n.) scattered fragments, wreckage

_____ resulting from the explosion

9. diffuse
(v., dif 'yüz;
adj., dif 'yüs)

(v.) to spread or scatter freely or widely; (adj.) wordy, long-winded, or unfocused; scattered or widely spread

slowly _____ through the room

10. dilemma
(di 'lem ə)

(n.) a difficult or perplexing situation or problem

caught in a painful _____

11. efface
(e 'fās)

(v.) to wipe out; to keep oneself from being noticed

_____ all signs of the struggle

12. muddle
('məd əl)

(v.) to make a mess of; *muddle through:* to get by; (n.) a hopeless mess

a _____ caused by failure to obey my directions

13. opinionated
(ə 'pin yən āt id)

(adj.) stubborn and often unreasonable in holding to one's own ideas, having a closed mind

too _____ to listen to her proposal

14. perennial
(pə 'ren ē əl)

(adj.) lasting for a long time, persistent; (n.) a plant that lives for many years

a _____ favorite of the young

15. predispose
(prē dis 'pōz)

(*v.*) to incline to beforehand

_____ me to colds

16. relinquish
(rē 'liŋ kwish)

(*v.*) to let go, give up

_____ his role in the class show

17. salvage ,
('sal vij)

(*v.*) to save from fire or shipwreck; (*n.*) property thus saved

_____ a few things from the fire

18. spasmodic
(spaz 'mäd ik)

(*adj.*) sudden and violent but brief; fitful, intermittent

_____ rifle fire from the woods

19. spurious
('spyü rē əs)

(*adj.*) not genuine, not true, not valid

reject the _____ will

20. unbridled
(ən 'brīd əld)

(*adj.*) uncontrolled, lacking in restraint

the _____ enthusiasm of the fans

Completing the Sentence

From the words for this unit, choose the one that best completes each of the following sentences. Write the word in the space provided.

1. Though his partner lost everything, he was able to _____ a few dollars from the wreckage of the bankrupt business.

2. He is so _____ that he won't even consider the ideas or suggestions offered by other people.

3. The doctor became more and more fearful that her patient's weakened condition would _____ him to pneumonia.

4. The nurse rushed into the hospital corridor to _____ the visitors who were creating a disturbance.

5. The idea of a(n) _____ like Robin Hood who helps the poor appeals strongly to the popular imagination.

6. I added a few drops of food coloring to the liquid and watched as they slowly _____ through it.

7. The poor animal was subject to sudden seizures, during which its head and legs would jerk about in a wild and _____ manner.

8. Though all modern scholars accept *Macbeth* as Shakespeare's work, one or two of the scenes may be _____ .

9. If I don't get a job, I won't have the money to do what I want; and if I do get a job, I won't have the time. What a(n) _____ !

10. The rug made such a(n) _____ bundle that it took four of us to carry it to the basement.

11. Since we do not want to replace the plants in our garden every year, we favor _____ over annuals.

12. A man of towering pride and _____ ambition, he stopped at nothing to achieve his goals as quickly and directly as possible.

13. We had the heartbreaking task of clearing the _____ after the plane had crashed into the school building.

14. In order to capture the fleeing criminals, the police _____ our car and raced after the vanishing truck.

15. Once Great Britain had given up her vast overseas empire, she found that she had also _____ her position as a world power.

16. Though my memory is getting dimmer and dimmer with the slow passage of time, I doubt that the exciting events of my childhood will ever be totally _____ from my mind.

17. The water pouring through the _____ in the dam threatened to flood the entire valley.

18. The records of our club were in such a(n) _____ that we couldn't even determine which members had paid their dues.

19. The two sides in the labor dispute reached a(n) _____ when neither was willing to meet the other partway.

20. Before Mrs. Kanner makes an investment, she studies all aspects of the situation in a most methodical and _____ manner.

21. The speech rambled on in such a(n) _____ and unfocused manner that, try as I might, I couldn't make out the speaker's point.

Synonyms   *From the words for this unit, choose the one that is most nearly **the same** in meaning as each of the following groups of expressions. Write the word on the line given.*

1. take over, requisition, expropriate, seize   _____

2. rambling, verbose, prolix; to disperse   _____

3. cautious, wary, prudent, careful, guarded   _____

4. to incline, make susceptible to   _____

5. to blot out, erase, expunge, obliterate   _____

6. false, counterfeit, fraudulent, bogus   _____

7. to caution, warn, scold, call on the carpet   _____

8. uncontrolled, unrestrained, unchecked   _____

9. unwieldy, clumsy to handle; ponderous   _____

10. a robber, bandit, highwayman, outlaw _____

11. a standoff, stalemate, impasse _____

12. to rescue, recover, retrieve, reclaim _____

13. to give up, let go, surrender, abandon _____

14. irregular, intermittent, occasional, fitful _____

15. a predicament, quandary, "pickle," "bind" _____

16. enduring, persistent, recurring _____

17. confusion, disorder; to jumble, mess up _____

18. a gap, rupture, rift; to break through _____

19. rubble, detritus, flotsam and jetsam _____

20. obstinate, pigheaded, inflexible _____

Antonyms *From the words for this unit, choose the one that is most nearly **opposite** in meaning to each of the following groups of expressions. Write the word on the line given.*

1. genuine, authentic, bona fide, valid _____

2. incautious, rash, heedless, reckless _____

3. open-minded, reasonable _____

4. an easily solved problem, cinch _____

5. to keep, hold on to, retain, cling to _____

6. to praise, pat on the back _____

7. orderliness, tidiness, neatness _____

8. brief, short-lived, fleeting, ephemeral _____

9. continuous, steady; chronic _____

10. restrained, held in check, muted _____

11. to seal, close _____

12. easy to handle, manageable _____

13. to abandon; to scrap, junk _____

14. brief, concise, succinct; to concentrate _____

15. an agreement, accord; a breakthrough _____

16. to imprint permanently _____

17. to immunize against, shield from _____

Choosing the Right Word   *Encircle the **boldface** word that more satisfactorily completes each of the following sentences.*

1. His attempts to rid his administration of inefficiency were so (**unbridled, spasmodic**) that he came to be called the "reformer by fits and starts."

2. The "robber barons" were a group of 19th-century captains of industry who amassed wealth by means that a (**brigand, salvager**) might use.

3. The evidence intended to show that some races or nationalities are superior to others proved to be completely (**spurious, cumbersome**).

4. How can you expect to succeed at your new job when you are (**diffused, predisposed**) to believe that it is "not right" for you?

5. The dean (**effaced, admonished**) the members of the team for neglecting their homework assignments.

6. The Senator refused to (**efface, relinquish**) the floor to any other speaker before he had finished his statement.

7. Instead of trying to (**commandeer, admonish**) the support of the student body, we must *earn* it by showing our sincerity and ability.

8. Like the rings a pebble makes in a pool of water, the good feelings generated by the speech (**diffused, relinquished**) through the crowd.

9. Since she is so convinced that there is only one right way—her way—I find her too (**circumspect, opinionated**) for my liking.

10. An economy in which the marketplace is considered "open" is one in which competition is more or less (**muddled, unbridled**).

11. Is it too much to expect that I will be able to (**admonish, salvage**) a few shreds of self-respect from my humiliating failure?

12. Developing nations in all parts of the world face the (**perennial, spurious**) problem of gaining a higher level of economic growth.

13. Thus, the nation was faced with a (**dilemma, salvage**) in which either advance or retreat might endanger its vital interests.

14. My mother broke the (**debris, deadlock**) in the quarrel between my brother and me by saying that neither of us could use the car.

15. For the very reason that we are the most powerful nation in the world, we must be extremely (**circumspect, cumbersome**) in our foreign policy.

16. If only I could (**admonish, efface**) the memory of the look of shock and disappointment on my mother's face!

17. Our city government seems to have (**muddled, breached**) into a first-rate financial crisis.

18. The organization of the government is so (**cumbersome, spurious**) that it is all but impossible to know who is responsible for various activities.

19. After the fatal blaze, the fire patrol searched through the (**debris, breach**) for clues that might reveal the cause.

20. Even Sue's refusal to dance with him did not seem to make a (**deadlock, breach**) in his gigantic conceit.

Unit 2

Definitions

Note carefully the spelling, pronunciation, and definition of each of the following words. Then write the word in the blank space in the illustrative phrase following.

1. adjourn
(ə 'jərn)

(v.) to stop proceedings for a time; to move to another place

_____ the session until the next day

2. alien
('ā lē ən)

(n.) a citizen of another country; (adj.) foreign, strange

customs _____ to our way of life

3. comely
('kəm lē)

(adj.) having a pleasing appearance

a _____ child

4. compensate
('käm pən sāt)

(v.) to make up for; to repay for services

_____ him for his losses

5. dissolute
('dis ə lüt)

(adj.) loose in one's morals or behavior

a group of _____ "men-about-town"

6. erratic
(e 'rat ik)

(adj.) not regular or consistent; different from what is ordinarily expected; undependable

upset by his _____ behavior

7. expulsion
(ek 'spəl shən)

(n.) the process of driving or forcing out

order the _____ of aliens

8. feint
(fānt)

(n.) a deliberately deceptive movement; a pretense; (v.) to make a deceptive movement; to make a pretense of

the boxer's extraordinary ability to counter and

_____

9. fodder
('fäd ər)

(n.) food for horses or cattle; raw material for a designated purpose

stored _____ in the silo

10. fortify
('fôr tə fī)

(v.) to strengthen, build up

_____ the city against attack

11. illegible
(i 'lej ə bəl)

(adj.) difficult or impossible to read

an _____ note

12. jeer
(jēr)

(v.) to make fun of rudely or unkindly; (n.) a rude remark of derision

_____ at strangers

13. lucrative
('lü krə tiv)

(adj.) bringing in money, profitable

establish a _____ business

14. mediocre
(mē dē 'ō kər)

(adj.) average, ordinary, undistinguished

a _____ player rather than a star

15. proliferate
(prō 'lif ə rāt)

(v.) to reproduce, increase, or spread rapidly

since some cells _____ more quickly than others

16. subjugate
('səb jü gāt)

(v.) to conquer by force, bring under complete control

a campaign to _____ the rebels

17. sully
('səl ē)

(v.) to soil, stain, tarnish, defile, besmirch

a reputation _____ by scandal

18. tantalize
('tan tə līz)

(v.) to tease, torment by teasing

_____ by goodies in the window

19. terse
(tərs)

(adj.) brief and to the point

a _____ remark

20. unflinching
(ən 'flin chiŋ)

(adj.) firm, showing no signs of fear, not drawing back

faced danger with _____ courage

Completing the Sentence

From the words for this unit, choose the one that best completes each of the following sentences. Write the word in the space provided.

1. The thoroughly disgraceful behavior of a few dissolute officers effectively _____ the honor of the entire unit.

2. In spite of all the adverse criticism her ideas have received, she remains _____ in her determination to improve our community.

3. Despite all my efforts to make this a(n) _____ business, it continues to be a decidedly nonprofit organization.

4. How can you be so cruel as to _____ the poor dog by offering him tidbits that you will never let him have?

5. To enlarge the areas under their control, kings of old sent out their armies to _____ their neighbors.

6. Our doctor's handwriting is so _____ that my brother used one of his prescriptions as a teacher's pass.

7. The speaker advised us not to imitate the _____ kind of person who squanders time and money in the vain pursuit of pleasure.

8. Milton drank quantities of lemon juice and swallowed vitamin C tablets in a valiant attempt to _____ himself against winter colds.

9. A(n) _____ student is one who neither fails any subject nor receives any marks that are above average.

10. Our laws protect not only citizens but also _____ legally residing in this country.

11. When the national economy is expanding, housing developments begin to _____ ; when times are lean, construction slacks off.

12. He was a changed young man after his _____ from West Point for "conduct unbecoming an officer and a gentleman."

13. His only response to my warnings was to _____ at me scornfully and go ahead with his plans.

14. The fact that he says that he is truly sorry does not _____ for the pain I have suffered as a result of his cruelty.

15. Though she is not a beautiful woman by conventional standards, she is certainly _____ and appealing.

16. Since there is a charge for every word used in it, a telegram is usually as _____ as possible.

17. When it is time to end one of our meetings, a member must make a motion to _____ .

18. The farmer must provide storage facilities for the _____ he plans to set aside for his cattle during the long winter.

19. Though he had a great sinker ball, he was so _____ on the mound that fans started to call him "Wild Pitch Hickok."

20. Their so-called "peace initiative" proved to be nothing more than a clever _____ designed to lull the enemy into a false sense of security.

21. The planets move around the heavens in a regular fashion, but the course of a comet is decidedly _____ .

Synonyms   *From the words for this unit, choose the one that is most nearly **the same** in meaning as each of the following groups of expressions. Write the word on the line given.*

1. an ejection, ouster, eviction   _____

2. ordinary, average, run-of-the-mill   _____

3. concise, succinct, crisp, short and sweet   _____

4. irregular, inconsistent, unpredictable   _____

5. foreign; strange, unfamiliar, exotic   _____

6. to multiply, mushroom, burgeon, increase   _____

7. good-looking, attractive, bonny   _____

8. dissipated, debauched; immoral, corrupt   _____

9. a trick, ruse, subterfuge; a bluff, dodge   _____

10. to tempt, lead on, make one's mouth water   _____

11. to pollute, defile, tarnish, taint, smear _____

12. food for animals, feed, provender _____

13. resolute, steadfast, unwavering _____

14. to pay back, reimburse, recompense _____

15. to conquer, subdue, vanquish, master _____

16. to strengthen, reinforce, shore up _____

17. to make fun of, laugh at, mock, taunt _____

18. profitable, gainful, moneymaking _____

19. to postpone, suspend, discontinue _____

20. unreadable, indecipherable, scribbled _____

Antonyms   _From the words for this unit, choose the one that is most nearly **opposite** in meaning to each of the following groups of expressions. Write the word on the line given._

1. unprofitable, losing, in the red _____

2. to be conquered, submit, surrender _____

3. wordy, diffuse, prolix, verbose _____

4. wavering, vacillating, irresolute _____

5. to call to order, open _____

6. virtuous, chaste, moral; seemly, proper _____

7. admittance, admission _____

8. decrease, diminish, slack off, dwindle _____

9. to cleanse, purify, decontaminate _____

10. readable, decipherable, distinct, clear _____

11. to weaken, undermine, sap, impair _____

12. applause, plaudits, accolades _____

13. outstanding, exceptional, distinguished _____

14. native, endemic; familiar _____

15. plain, homely; ugly, repulsive _____

16. steady, consistent, dependable _____

17. to satisfy, fulfill, gratify _____

18. to fail to reward, "stiff" _____

Choosing the Right Word *Encircle the **boldface** word that more satisfactorily completes each of the following sentences.*

1. We all experience fear and panic, but the leader of a great nation must be able to (**tantalize, subjugate**) such emotions.

2. A best-selling book that is then made into a movie may be more (**lucrative, erratic**) than finding the proverbial pot of gold at the end of the rainbow.

3. To keep my self-respect, I must stand (**comely, unflinching**) before the authorities and tell them the truth as I see it.

4. At one point in our fencing match, my opponent unexpectedly (**sullied, feinted**) to the left and threw me completely off guard.

5. Instead of all those long, flowery passages, why don't you try to write more in the (**mediocre, terse**) and direct style of a good newspaper reporter?

6. After the formal dinner was over, we (**tantalized, adjourned**) to the den in order to continue our conversation in a more relaxed atmosphere.

7. When I first noticed how (**illegible, lucrative**) my roommate's handwriting was, I suggested that he sign up immediately for a course in penmanship.

8. I can understand how poor people sometimes feel (**jeered, tantalized**) by the wealth and luxuries they see displayed on TV programs.

9. Over the years I've noticed one thing about rumors: Where the facts are few, fictions (**proliferate, adjourn**).

10. The desire to force everyone to accept the same set of ideas is completely (**illegible, alien**) to the spirit of democracy.

11. All great athletes should know that the same fans who are cheering them today may be (**jeering, unflinching**) them tomorrow.

12. Even though I must work hard for a living, I feel that the company I'm with amply (**compensates, subjugates**) me for my time and effort.

13. "No," said Roger, "I won't (**sully, jeer**) your ears by repeating those mean and nasty rumors."

14. His behavior is so (**mediocre, erratic**) that we never know what to expect from him.

15. In my opinion, his writing is so bad that he will have to improve a great deal just to reach the level of (**mediocrity, compensation**).

16. For centuries people have turned to various kinds of religious literature to (**fortify, proliferate**) themselves against the shocks of daily life.

17. *The Rake's Progress* paints a grim and uncompromising picture of some of the more (**dissolute, comely**) and degrading aspects of human behavior.

18. As soon as I entered that charming little cottage, I noticed that everything in it was neat and (**erratic, comely**).

19. I would be unwilling to vote for the (**expulsion, adjournment**) of club members just because they are behind in their dues.

20. Though a trained veteran is often a well-tuned fighting machine, a raw recruit is sometimes no better than cannon (**feint, fodder**).

Unit 3

Definitions

Note carefully the spelling, pronunciation, and definition of each of the following words. Then write the word in the blank space in the illustrative phrase following.

1. abridge
(ə 'brij)

(v.) to make shorter

to _____ a 1000-page novel

2. adherent
(ad 'hēr ənt)

(n.) a follower, supporter; (adj.) attached, sticking to

has attracted many _____

3. altercation
(ôl tər 'kā shən)

(n.) an angry argument

involved in a noisy _____

4. cherubic
(che 'rü bik)

(adj.) resembling an angel portrayed as a little child with a beautiful, round, or chubby face; sweet and innocent

the _____ smile of a newborn baby

5. condone
(kən 'dōn)

(v.) to pardon or overlook

refuse to _____ bad behavior

6. dissent
(di 'sent)

(v.) to disagree; (n.) disagreement

_____ from the majority view

7. eminent
('em ə nənt)

(adj.) famous, outstanding, distinguished; projecting

an _____ member of the bar

8. exorcise
('ek sôr sīz)

(v.) to drive out by magic; to dispose of something troublesome, menacing, or oppressive

to _____ an evil spirit

9. fabricate
('fab rə kāt)

(v.) to make, manufacture; to make up, invent

learned how to _____ steel

10. irate
(ī 'rāt)

(adj.) angry

try to calm an _____ parent

11. marauder
(mə 'rôd ər)

(n.) a raider, plunderer

a village raided by _____

12. obesity
(ō 'bē sə tē)

(n.) extreme fatness

suffering from _____

13. pauper
('pô pər)

(n.) an extremely poor person

help for the _____ in our community

14. pilfer
('pil fər)

(v.) to steal in small quantities

_____ stamps from the cash box

15. rift
(rift)

(n.) a split, break, breach

an unfortunate _____ in their friendship

3

16. semblance
('sem bləns)

(*n.*) a likeness; an outward appearance; an apparition

tried to create a _____ of order

17. surmount
(sər 'maùnt)

(*v.*) to overcome, rise above

struggle to _____ all obstacles

18. terminate
('tər mə nāt)

(*v.*) to bring to an end

_____ my employment

19. trite
(trīt)

(*adj.*) commonplace; overused, stale

full of clichés and _____ phrases

20. usurp
(yü 'sərp)

(*v.*) to seize and hold a position by force or without right

plot to _____ power

Completing the Sentence

From the words for this unit, choose the one that best completes each of the following sentences. Write the word in the space provided.

1. The only way I could _____ the argument peacefully was to walk away abruptly.

2. It is only through the exercise of their God-given intelligence that people can _____ the difficulties they encounter in daily living.

3. Though he was hurt by the tactless comment, he tried to show pleasure in it by twisting his lips into a feeble _____ of a smile.

4. After driving the lawful ruler out of the country for good, the villainous duke _____ the throne and crowned himself king.

5. No one but a heartless scoundrel would _____ nickels and dimes from the Red Cross collection fund.

6. "That child may have an angel's _____ features, but at heart he is a little devil," I exclaimed in disgust.

7. As the layer of clouds that hung over the city began to break up, the sun came pouring through the _____ .

8. A screenplay or television drama with the same old "boy-meets-girl" plot can certainly be criticized as _____ .

9. During a recent interdenominational service in our community center, the _____ of various faiths met to worship as one.

10. Bands of _____ broke through the frontier defenses of the province and began to plunder the rich farmlands of the interior.

11. Although he has enough money to live on, the loss of most of his great wealth has left him feeling like a(n) _____ .

12. A few of us who disagreed strongly with the committee's conclusions felt compelled to raise our voices in _____ .

13. In this clever spoof of horror movies, the local witch doctor encounters hilarious difficulties when he tries to _____ an evil demon that has taken up residence in the heroine's body.

14. In order to fit the newspaper article into the space available, the editor had to _____ it by omitting secondary details.

15. Although I am not a particularly argumentative person, last week I found myself involved in a serious _____ with a salesclerk.

16. "I am willing to wink at a harmless prank," the dean remarked, "but I will not _____ outright vandalism."

17. The only lasting cure for _____ is to eat a great deal less.

18. I think that the phrase "hot under the collar" aptly describes the typical _____ customer that our complaint department has to deal with.

19. After so many years of distinguished service in the United States Senate, he can properly be called a(n) _____ statesman.

20. It is a real tribute to the ingenuity of the human mind that for thousands of years people have been _____ new and interesting theories of the universe.

Synonyms　　　*From the words for this unit, choose the word that is most nearly **the same** in meaning as each of the following groups of expressions. Write the word on the line given.*

1. to ignore, wink at, turn a blind eye to　　　_____

2. to conquer, overcome, triumph over　　　_____

3. serious overweight, extreme corpulence　　　_____

4. an appearance, air, aura, veneer, façade　　　_____

5. a quarrel, dispute, squabble　　　_____

6. a follower, supporter, disciple　　　_____

7. to steal, rob, filch, swipe, purloin　　　_____

8. illustrious, renowned, distinguished　　　_____

9. to end, conclude, finish, discontinue　　　_____

10. angelic, seraphic, beatific　　　_____

11. angry, incensed, infuriated, enraged, livid _____

12. a poor person, someone destitute _____

13. a crack, fissure, breach, gap, cleft _____

14. to put together, manufacture, devise, contrive, concoct _____

15. commonplace, banal, hackneyed, "corny" _____

16. to shorten, condense, abbreviate _____

17. to seize illegally, commandeer, supplant _____

18. a raider, looter, pirate, freebooter _____

19. to differ, disagree, dispute _____

20. to drive out, expel; to dispel _____

Antonyms *From the words for this unit, choose the one that is most nearly **opposite** in meaning to each of the following groups of expressions. Write the word on the line given.*

1. original, novel, fresh, innovative _____

2. to be vanquished, be defeated, succumb to _____

3. to begin, commence, initiate _____

4. emaciation, gauntness, scrawniness _____

5. to expand, enlarge, augment _____

6. impish, devilish, diabolic, fiendish _____

7. to agree, concur; unanimity, harmony _____

8. an opponent, adversary; critic, detractor _____

9. calm, composed, cool, unruffled _____

10. obscure, nameless, unsung, lowly, humble _____

11. a millionaire, tycoon _____

12. to censure, condemn, disapprove, deprecate _____

13. an agreement, an accord _____

14. to obtain or come to by right _____

15. a dissimilarity, contrast; a total lack _____

16. a reconciliation; a closing of a gap _____

17. to take apart, undo; to destroy, demolish _____

Choosing the Right Word   *Encircle the **boldface** word that more satisfactorily completes each of the following sentences.*

1. The fact that many citizens are (**trite, irate**) over the new taxes does not mean that these taxes are unjustifiable.

2. Unless we repair the (**rifts, fabrications**) in our party and present a united front, we will go down to crushing defeat in the upcoming election.

3. The "robber barons" of an earlier era often acted more like (**adherents, marauders**) than ethical businessmen in their dealings with the public.

4. I feel like a (**usurper, pauper**) now that my part-time job has come to an end and I no longer have any spending money.

5. Like all literary sneak thieves, he has a truly nasty habit of (**pilfering, fabricating**) other people's ideas and then claiming them as his own.

6. The fact that Abraham Lincoln was able to (**surmount, terminate**) the handicap of limited education does not mean that you should quit school.

7. His speech was so (**irate, trite**) that one could almost anticipate the phrases he would use next.

8. I am very much flattered that you have referred to me as "an (**eminent, obese**) educator," but I prefer to think of myself as just a good teacher.

9. One can't become a good writer just by (**surmounting, adhering**) closely to rules laid down in standard grammar books.

10. In a dictatorship, people who (**abridge, dissent**) from the official "party line" usually wind up in prison—or worse.

11. Anyone who wants to dine at that outrageously expensive restaurant had better carry a credit card or a truly (**obese, trite**) wallet.

12. I do not entirely (**usurp, condone**) his misconduct, but I can understand, to a degree, why he behaved as he did.

13. Either party has the right to (**terminate, surmount**) the agreement that has been made whenever the partnership proves unprofitable.

14. It is the sacred duty of all Americans to oppose any attempt to (**abridge, condone**) or deny the rights guaranteed to us in the Constitution.

15. What began as a minor quarrel grew into a serious (**altercation, exorcism**) and then into an ugly brawl.

16. My cousin has so much imagination that he can (**dissent, fabricate**) an excuse that even an experienced Dean of Boys would believe!

17. She had no right to (**exorcise, usurp**) for herself the role of gracious hostess at *my* party!

18. The few words that he grudgingly muttered were the only (**semblance, altercation**) of an apology that he offered for his rude behavior.

19. Their (**irate, cherubic**) faces and ethereal voices almost made me believe that the music they were singing was coming from heaven.

20. The comforting presence of relatives did much to (**exorcise, usurp**) the patient's feelings of alarm at the thought of undergoing major surgery.

Analogies *In each of the following, encircle the item that best completes the comparision.*

1. **rift** is to **breach** as
   a. deadlock is to solution
   b. dilemma is to friction
   c. debris is to wreckage
   d. salvage is to shipwreck

2. **abridge** is to **expand** as
   a. relinquish is to retain
   b. feint is to delay
   c. pilfer is to condone
   d. subjugate is to conquer

3. **angry** is to **irate** as
   a. glum is to predisposed
   b. comely is to ugly
   c. unflinching is to rude
   d. fat is to obese

4. **spurious** is to **genuine** as
   a. lucrative is to wealthy
   b. trite is to original
   c. cumbersome is to costly
   d. terse is to brief

5. **jeer** is to **contempt** as
   a. applaud is to horror
   b. smile is to beauty
   c. yawn is to boredom
   d. wink is to curiosity

6. **exorcise** is to **expulsion** as
   a. breach is to compensation
   b. proliferate is to reduction
   c. subjugate is to liberation
   d. diffuse is to dispersion

7. **illegible** is to **read** as
   a. invisible is to see
   b. immobile is to touch
   c. inaudible is to avoid
   d. inflammable is to count

8. **eminent** is to **favorable** as
   a. spurious is to favorable
   b. unflinching is to unfavorable
   c. erratic is to favorable
   d. mediocre is to unfavorable

9. **fortify** is to **weaken** as
   a. commandeer is to suggest
   b. dissent is to agree
   c. admonish is to caution
   d. tantalize is to command

10. **semblance** is to **likeness** as
    a. dilemma is to solution
    b. expulsion is to acceptance
    c. altercation is to dispute
    d. salvage is to piracy

11. **adjourn** is to **terminate** as
    a. fabricate is to usurp
    b. compensate is to repay
    c. efface is to flourish
    d. proliferate is to abridge

12. **hay** is to **fodder** as
    a. tulip is to perennial
    b. pig is to pauper
    c. feint is to boxing
    d. adherent is to muddle

13. **pauper** is to **millionaire** as
    a. cherub is to imp
    b. brigand is to robber
    c. militant is to adherent
    d. marauder is to doctor

14. **native** is to **alien** as
    a. pleasant is to spurious
    b. mediocre is to remarkable
    c. awkward is to irate
    d. cautious is to circumspect

15. **circumspect** is to **favorable** as
    a. opinionated is to favorable
    b. unbridled is to unfavorable
    c. cumbersome is to favorable
    d. eminent is to unfavorable

16. **pilfer** is to **steal** as
    a. compensate is to cancel
    b. surmount is to remind
    c. commandeer is to reward
    d. sully is to tarnish

17. **spasmodic** is to **continuous** as
    a. dissolute is to dissipated
    b. comely is to early
    c. erratic is to consistent
    d. diffuse is to spurious

18. **adherent** is to **supporter** as
    a. doctor is to patient
    b. champion is to defender
    c. mother is to daughter
    d. admirer is to critic

Definitions   *In each of the following groups, encircle the word that is most nearly* **the same** *in meaning as the introductory expression.*

1. careful to consider all possibilities
   cumbersome   circumspect   spurious   perennial

2. seize for military purposes
   sully   pilfer   commandeer   diffuse

3. rescue property in danger
   proliferate   salvage   abridge   usurp

4. one who lives by plunder or robbery
   commandeer   debris   adherent   brigand

5. loose in one's morals or behavior
   spasmodic   dissolute   comely   erratic

6. rise superior to
   usurp   surmount   fabricate   exorcise

7. owing allegiance to another government
   eminent   debris   deadlock   alien

8. something to be consumed
   breach   expulsion   fodder   pauper

9. make indistinct by wearing away
   fabricate   breach   efface   adjourn

10. choice between two undesirable courses of action
    salvage   brigand   obesity   dilemma

11. distract attention from the intended point of attack
    condone   admonish   feint   tantalize

12. bring to a conclusion
    terminate   relinquish   compensate   jeer

13. holding stubbornly to one's own judgment
    cherubic   opinionated   trite   predisposed

14. without unnecessary words
    unbridled   terse   lucrative   mediocre

15. wink at
    muddle   abridge   condone   subjugate

16. one who invades the territory of another
    marauder   alien   fodder   rift

17. differ in opinion
    tantalize   fortify   compensate   dissent

18. noisy, heated quarrel
    semblance   altercation   muddle   expulsion

19. characterized by anger
    illegible   unflinching   irate   terse

20. bring to a standstill
    proliferate   dissent   deadlock   subjugate

R

Shades of Meaning   *Read each sentence carefully. Then encircle the item that best completes the statement below the sentence.*

In some parts of the world, to decline a dish served at a banquet is considered an unpardonable breach of etiquette. **(2)**

1. In line 2 the word **breach** most nearly means
a. opening   b. assault   c. violation   d. breakthrough

As its name suggests, Frank Lloyd Wright's cantilevered "Fallingwater" house stands eminent above a waterfall. **(2)**

2. The word **eminent** in line 2 is best defined as
a. jutting out   b. distinguished   c. illustrious   d. outstanding

In contrast with the economy of expression that so distinguished the author's early works, the later novels are woefully diffuse. **(2)**

3. The word **diffuse** in line 2 is used to mean
a. uneven   b. spread out   c. dispersed   d. rambling

Some see in TV's power to abridge the distances separating the world's peoples the means of making the earth a "global village." **(2)**

4. The word **abridge** in line 1 most nearly means
a. curb   b. reduce   c. explore   d. erase

The cumbersome wagon trains that plied the Oregon Trail often took weeks just to cross the prairies of Kansas and Nebraska. **(2)**

5. The word **cumbersome** in line 1 is best defined as
a. crude   b. swift   c. unprotected   d. slow-moving

Antonyms   *In each of the following groups, encircle the word or phrase that is most nearly **opposite** in meaning to the word in **boldface type**.*

1. expulsion
a. compulsion
b. farewell
c. admission
d. breathing out

2. obesity
a. thinness
b. starvation
c. overeating
d. disease

3. fortify
a. undermine
b. strengthen
c. narrate
d. listen

4. muddle
a. filth
b. confusion
c. clarity
d. infirmity

5. diffuse
a. scatter
b. accept
c. concentrate
d. originate

6. cherubic
a. friendly
b. impish
c. angelic
d. beautiful

7. trite
a. original
b. foolish
c. meaningless
d. stale

8. erratic
a. angry
b. inconsistent
c. pleasing
d. constant

9. relinquish	11. lucrative	13. condone	15. rift
a. fade	a. unsaid	a. commend	a. opening
b. follow	b. unheard	b. cooperate	b. revenge
c. keep	c. understood	c. create	c. reconciliation
d. try	d. unprofitable	d. condemn	d. escape
10. unflinching	12. unbridled	14. tantalize	16. salvage
a. novel	a. restrained	a. ridicule	a. abandon
b. shaky	b. checkered	b. gratify	b. tame
c. angry	c. interrupted	c. lure	c. save
d. proud	d. prolonged	d. simmer	d. injure

Completing the Sentence   *From the words for this unit, choose the one that best completes each of the following sentences. Write the word in the space provided.*

Group A

deadlock	efface	rift	adjourn
sully	debris	surmount	feint
salvage	relinquish	fortify	compensate

1. With heavy hearts we searched among the _____ of our wrecked apartment building.

2. With faith in the rightness of his cause, he was able to _____ the difficulties that would have discouraged most other men.

3. Harold's agreement to let us try our plan finally broke the _____ that had kept us inactive for several weeks.

4. The disagreement eventually caused the _____ that broke up our friendship.

5. All that I was able to _____ from that humiliating experience was a small measure of self-respect.

Group B

illegible	terse	trite	opinionated
pilfer	mediocre	usurp	proliferate
abridge	muddle	alien	eminent

1. The chaplain emphasized that hatred is _____ to the spirit of all religions.

2. She seems to think that her handwriting is terribly "interesting" and "distinguished," but to me it is merely _____ .

3. In spite of long hours of practice at kicking field goals, his performance during the season was only _____ .

4. The old adage that "Brevity is the soul of wit" seems to have had a profound influence on the humorist's _____ , almost epigrammatic style.

5. I found the television program very boring because of its extremely _____ plot and dialogue.

Word Families

A. *On the line provided, write a **noun form** of each of the following words.*

EXAMPLE: adjourn — **adjournment**

1. admonish _____
2. terminate _____
3. eminent _____
4. subjugate _____
5. circumspect _____
6. comely _____
7. proliferate _____
8. compensate _____
9. illegible _____
10. mediocre _____
11. predispose _____
12. usurp _____
13. exorcise _____
14. diffuse _____

B. *On the line provided, write a **verb form** for each of the following words.*

EXAMPLE: termination — **terminate**

1. expulsion _____
2. adherent _____
3. cumbersome _____
4. alien _____
5. compensation _____
6. dissension _____
7. abridgment _____
8. fortification _____
9. admonition _____

**Filling
the Blanks**
*Encircle the pair of words that best complete the
meaning of each of the following passages.*

1. The earthquake had more or less reduced our house to a pile of worthless
rubble. Nevertheless, we picked carefully through the _____,
trying to _____ items of value. Unfortunately, very little
could be saved.
   a. deadlock . . . relinquish
   b muddle . . . efface
   c. debris . . . salvage
   d. dilemma . . . condone

2. Minor squabbles may cause temporary _____ in our
friendship, but such _____ , however heated and noisy,
have never resulted in a permanent breach.
   a. feints . . . dilemmas
   b. rifts . . . altercations
   c. deadlocks . . . abridgments
   d. dissents . . . semblances

3. Though he began life little better than a(n) _____ , with only
his hands in his pockets, his highly _____ business deals
turned him into a multimillionaire before the age of forty.
   a. adherent . . . cumbersome
   b. usurper . . . spurious
   c. brigand . . . mediocre
   d. pauper . . . lucrative

4. "If you always act cautiously, you should be able to _____
many of life's obstacles," Dad told me. "Still, some difficulties cannot be
overcome, even by the most _____ behavior."
   a. surmount . . . circumspect
   b. abridge . . . alien
   c. commandeer . . . erratic
   d. relinquish . . . mediocre

5. Although the auditorium was packed with the candidate's supporters, who
greeted his remarks with thunderous cheers and applause, there were a
few _____ in the crowd who seemed inclined only to boo
and _____ .
   a. brigands . . . feint
   b. dissenters . . . jeer
   c. paupers . . . condone
   d. adherents . . . admonish

6. Though I am prepared to wink at an occasional petty offense against my
moral code, I absolutely refuse to _____ behavior that is
consistently wicked or _____ .
   a. condone . . . dissolute
   b. efface . . . erratic
   c. abridge . . . unbridled
   d. exorcise . . . circumspect

7. He was thrown out of the club for constantly _____ small
items from the supply room. According to club rules, that type of petty theft
constitutes valid grounds for _____ .
   a. tantalizing . . . termination
   b. sullying . . . subjugation
   c. fabricating . . . admonishment
   d. pilfering . . . expulsion

Unit 4

Definitions

Note carefully the spelling, pronunciation, and definition of each of the following words. Then write the word in the blank space in the illustrative phrase following.

1. abscond
(ab 'skänd)

(*v.*) to run off and hide

_____ with the stolen money

2. access
('ak ses)

(*n.*) approach or admittance to places, persons, things; an increase; (*v.*) to get at, obtain

gain _____ to the secret files

3. anarchy
('an ər kē)

(*n.*) a lack of government and law, confusion

a country suffering from _____

4. arduous
('är jü əs)

(*adj.*) hard to do, requiring much effort

_____ chores

5. auspicious
(ô 'spish əs)

(*adj.*) favorable; fortunate

under _____ circumstances

6. biased
('bī əst)

(*adj.*) favoring one side unduly; prejudiced

a _____ decision

7. daunt
(dônt)

(*v.*) to overcome with fear, intimidate; to dishearten, discourage

not _____ by their threats

8. disentangle
(dis en 'taŋ gəl)

(*v.*) to free from tangles or complications

_____ the fishing net

9. fated
('fā tid)

(*adj.*) determined in advance by destiny or fortune

_____ to rise to the top

10. hoodwink
('húd wiŋk)

(*v.*) to mislead by a trick, deceive

attempt to _____ the child

11. inanimate
(in 'an ə mit)

(*adj.*) not having life; without energy or spirit

stones and other _____ objects

12. incinerate
(in 'sin ər āt)

(*v.*) to burn to ashes

_____ the garbage

13. intrepid
(in 'trep id)

(*adj.*) very brave, fearless, unshakable

_____ explorers of the ocean

14. larceny
('lär sə nē)

(*n.*) theft

found guilty of _____

15. pliant
('plī ənt)

(*adj.*) bending readily, easily influenced

a sapling's _____ branches

16. pompous
('päm pəs)

(*adj.*) overly self-important in speech or manner; excessively stately or ceremonious

a _____ and conceited fool

17. precipice
('pres ə pis)

(*n.*) a very steep cliff; the brink or edge of disaster

peer cautiously over a _____

18. rectify
('rek tə fī)

(*v.*) to make right, correct

_____ a false impression

19. reprieve
(ri 'prēv)

(*n.*) a temporary relief or delay; (*v.*) to grant a postponement

receive a _____ from the Governor

20. revile
(ri 'vīl)

(*v.*) to attack with words, call bad names

_____ their enemies

Completing the Sentence

From the words for this unit, choose the one that best completes each of the following sentences. Write the word in the space provided.

1. No matter how much protective legislation we pass, there will probably always be gullible consumers for swindlers to _____ .

2. The magnetic tape had gotten so badly entwined in the machinery that I had a hard time _____ it.

3. One of the most controversial figures of his time, the former President was revered by some and _____ by others.

4. The guardrail was reinforced to prevent cars from skidding over the edge of the _____ and falling into the abyss below.

5. For someone who believes in astrology, what is _____ to happen to a person is determined by the stars.

6. As soon as I discovered that the project was being mismanaged, I tried my best to _____ the situation.

7. Since I did not feel well prepared, the three-day postponement of final exams was a most welcome _____ .

8. Her extraordinary faith in her own abilities enabled her to overcome many obstacles that would have _____ someone less confident.

9. Though somewhat massively built, the gymnast's body was as supple and _____ as a ballerina's.

10. Without the slightest hesitation, the _____ firefighters entered the flaming building to rescue the children trapped on the second floor.

11. Though many people firmly believe that life forms exist somewhere in outer space, everything that our astronauts have so far encountered has been decidedly _____ .

12. The youths who had "borrowed" the car for joyriding were caught by the police and charged with _____ .

13. The overly ornate style of many 19th-century writers seems rather forced and _____ to us today.

14. The treasurer who had _____ with the company's funds was quickly captured by alert federal agents.

15. It isn't logical to infer that the referee is _____ against State U. just because he makes a few calls against the team.

16. This master key will give you _____ to any of the rooms in the building.

17. With no government around to restore order, the small country remained in a state of _____ for weeks after the revolution.

18. Since everything had gone so smoothly, we felt that the campaign to elect Ellen captain was off to a(n) _____ beginning.

19. Since I'm only an average linguist, mastering the irregular verbs in French was one of the most _____ tasks I have ever undertaken.

20. The steak I'd accidentally left in the broiler too long wasn't just overdone; it was positively _____ .

21. In order to _____ the information I needed for my report, I had the computer call up the "Accounts Payable" file.

Synonyms *From the words for this unit, choose the one that is most nearly **the same** in meaning as each of the following groups of expressions. Write the word on the line given.*

1. promising, encouraging, propitious _____

2. pretentious, highfalutin, bombastic _____

3. to postpone, to delay; a stay, respite _____

4. prejudiced, unfair, partial, bigoted _____

5. to deceive, dupe, put one over on _____

6. supple, flexible, elastic, plastic _____

7. to intimidate, dismay, cow, discourage _____

8. doomed, destined, preordained _____

9. to bolt, make off, skip town _____

10. a cliff, crag, bluff, promontory; a brink, ledge _____

11. to unravel, unwind, unscramble, unsnarl _____

12. to correct, remedy, set right _____

13. lifeless, dead; inert, spiritless _____

14. hard, difficult, laborious, fatiguing _____

15. inveigh against, malign, vilify, denounce _____

16. chaos, disorder, turmoil, pandemonium _____

17. to burn up, cremate, reduce to ashes _____

18. stealing, robbery, theft, burglary _____

19. entry, admittance, entrée _____

20. valiant, courageous, audacious, daring _____

Antonyms   *From the words for this unit, choose the one that is most nearly **opposite** in meaning to each of the following groups of expressions. Write the word on the line given.*

1. timid, cowardly, craven, pusillanimous _____

2. to praise, acclaim; to revere, idolize _____

3. accidental, fortuitous, chance, random _____

4. to tangle up, ensnarl, snag _____

5. to mess up, botch, bungle _____

6. to encourage, embolden, reassure _____

7. total exclusion from something _____

8. to proceed as scheduled _____

9. easy, simple, effortless _____

10. law and order, peace and quiet _____

11. ill-omened, ominous, sinister _____

12. fair, impartial, unprejudiced, just _____

13. rigid, stiff, inflexible, set in stone _____

14. living, alive; energetic, lively, sprightly _____

15. unpretentious, unaffected; plain _____

16. an abyss, chasm, gorge _____

17. to undeceive, disabuse, "clue in" _____

4

Choosing the Right Word   *Encircle the **boldface** word that most satisfactorily completes each of the following sentences.*

1. The team of accountants spent hours trying to locate and then to (**rectify, incinerate**) the error I had so carelessly made.

2. We should begin studying foreign languages at an early age because it is during those years that our minds are most (**fated, pliant**) and receptive.

3. I feared that this latest misfortune would drive him over the (**precipice, access**) and into a depression from which he would not recover.

4. Instead of recognizing that he caused his own failure, he continues to (**revile, hoodwink**) all the people who were "unfair" to him.

5. Anyone who takes the writings of other people and presents them as his or her own is guilty of literary (**anarchy, larceny**).

6. When her eyes suddenly blazed with such fury, I felt that the heat of her glance would all but (**bias, incinerate**) me.

7. Only by admitting your fault and trying to make up for it can you obtain a(n) (**access, reprieve**) from the pangs of conscience.

8. Despite the threats made against his life, the (**arduous, intrepid**) district attorney was able to obtain a conviction of the corrupt officials.

9. Although the hero and the heroine were parted by circumstance, I knew that they were (**intrepid, fated**) to meet again before the last commercial.

10. Like farmers separating the wheat from the chaff, the members of a jury must (**disentangle, daunt**) the truth from the evidence presented to them.

11. A great playwright's characters always seem to come alive; those of a third-rate hack stubbornly remain (**pliant, inanimate**).

12. Far from being "useless," mathematics will give you (**reprieve, access**) to many fields of scientific study.

13. For most retired boxers, the comeback trail is an (**arduous, auspicious**) one that few ever get to the end of.

14. Though the dangers and uncertainties of a westward passage to the Orient cowed many a brave sailor, they did not (**rectify, daunt**) Columbus.

15. How can you accuse me of (**absconding, reprieving**) with all your brilliant ideas when you have never had an original thought in your life!

16. His speech and manners were so (**auspicious, pompous**) and stiff that he cut a somewhat ridiculous figure at our informal little get-together.

17. The voters may seem to be easily deceived, but in the long run they cannot be (**disentangled, hoodwinked**) by self-serving politicians.

18. Spring, with its ever-renewing promise of life, is for me the most (**arduous, auspicious**) of seasons.

19. His narrow education gave him a (**fated, biased**) view of cultures different from his own.

20. There is a vast difference between democracy, under which everyone has duties and privileges, and (**larceny, anarchy**), under which no one has.

Unit 5

Definitions

Note carefully the spelling, pronunciation, and definition of each of the following words. Then write the word in the blank space in the illustrative phrase following.

1. accomplice
(ə ′käm plis)

(*n.*) a person who takes part in a crime

an _____ in the holdup

2. annihilate
(ə ′nī ə lāt)

(*v.*) to destroy completely

_____ the enemy forces

3. arbitrary
(′är bə trer ē)

(*adj.*) unreasonable; based on one's own wishes or whims without regard for reason or fairness

an _____ and high-handed ruler

4. brazen
(′brā zən)

(*adj.*) made of brass; shameless, impudent

a _____ liar

5. catalyst
(′kat əl ist)

(*n.*) a substance that causes or hastens a chemical reaction; any agent that causes change

act as a _____ in the process

6. exodus
(′ek sə dəs)

(*n.*) a large-scale departure or flight

a mass _____ of refugees

7. facilitate
(fə ′sil ə tāt)

(*v.*) to make easier, assist

_____ the efforts of the rescue team

8. incorrigible
(in ′kä rə jə bəl)

(*adj.*) not able to be corrected, beyond control

an _____ optimist

9. latent
(′lāt ənt)

(*adj.*) hidden, present but not realized

a _____ , unexpressed hostility

10. militant
(′mil ə tənt)

(*adj.*) given to fighting; active and aggressive in support of a cause; (*n.*) activist

a _____ campaign against drugs

11. morose
(mə ′rōs)

(*adj.*) having a gloomy or sullen manner; not friendly or sociable

found him in a _____ mood

12. opaque
(ō ′pāk)

(*adj.*) not letting light through; not clear or lucid; dense, stupid

windows that were _____ with grime

13. paramount
(′par ə maůnt)

(*adj.*) chief in importance, above all others

the _____ issue in the election

14. prattle
(′prat əl)

(*v.*) to talk in an aimless, foolish, or simple way; (*n.*) baby talk

the _____ of the child in her crib

15. rebut
(ri 'bət)

(*v.*) to offer arguments or evidence that contradict an assertion, to refute

easy to _____ his shaky case

16. reprimand
('rep rə mand)

(*v.*) to scold, find fault with; (*n.*) a rebuke

_____ the unruly student

17. servitude
('sər və tüd)

(*n.*) slavery, forced labor

penal _____

18. slapdash
('slap dash)

(*adj.*) careless and hasty

did a _____ job on the repairs

19. stagnant
('stag nənt)

(*adj.*) not running or flowing; foul from standing still; inactive, sluggish, dull

bred in _____ pools of water

20. succumb
(sə 'kəm)

(*v.*) to give way to superior force, yield

_____ to pressure

Completing the Sentence

From the words for this unit, choose the one that best completes each of the following sentences. Write the word in the space provided.

1. It is an unfortunate fact that the _____ attitudes of the Kaiser and his saber-rattling cronies helped make World War I inevitable.

2. "If you spent more time and effort on your essays, they would cease to be such _____ affairs," my older sister wisely observed.

3. After the opposing speakers had both presented their cases, they were allowed time to _____ each other's arguments.

4. The second book of the Old Testament is named for the story it recounts of the _____ of the Israelites from the land of Egypt.

5. The doctor warned relatives that if the patient's condition deteriorated any further, she would _____ to pneumonia.

6. Though they had been there all along, Grandma Moses did not discover her _____ artistic talents until well into her seventies.

7. His friends call him "Motormouth" because he has a remarkable capacity to _____ on endlessly about the most trivial matters.

8. Fighting is considered such a(n) _____ violation of the rules of a game that the offending players are usually severely penalized.

9. When he was suddenly deprived of everything he valued in life, the poor man became extremely gloomy and _____ .

10. Dad said nothing when I failed the examination, but the disappointed look on his face hurt more than the most severe _____ .

11. Even though the youngster did not actually steal the vehicle, he acted as one of the thief's _____ .

12. If we are going to use this space as a darkroom for photography, we must have a completely _____ covering over the window.

13. No matter what make of automobile you have, it is of _____ importance that you learn to drive safely before you use it.

14. In certain industrial processes, _____ speed up the desired reaction by lessening the amount of energy needed to produce it.

15. It is a frightening fact of modern life that we now possess the weaponry to _____ not only our enemies, but all mankind, in minutes.

16. The fact that you cannot control those small children does not mean that they are _____ .

17. Many people came to the New World after they had been sentenced to terms of penal _____ for crimes they had committed.

18. The helpful librarian did much to _____ the research for my term paper.

19. In guaranteeing the right to "due process of law," the Constitution protects Americans against _____ arrest and imprisonment.

20. In large areas of the huge swamp, there were _____ pools of water covered with unmoving masses of green slime.

Synonyms *From the words for this unit, choose the one that is most nearly **the same** in meaning as each of the following groups of expressions. Write the word on the line given.*

1. gloomy, sullen, morbid, doleful   _____

2. hazy, cloudy, foggy, murky; dull, obtuse   _____

3. to ease, smoothe the way, simplify   _____

4. a reproof, rebuke; to reprove, reproach   _____

5. still, motionless, inert; foul, fetid   _____

6. captivity, bondage, thralldom, slavery   _____

7. cursory, perfunctory; sloppy, slipshod   _____

8. a partner in crime, confederate   _____

9. to yield, give way, submit; to die, expire   _____

10. aggressive, truculent; an activist _____

11. capricious; high-handed, autocratic _____

12. a stimulus, spur; an instigator _____

13. supreme, foremost, primary, dominant _____

14. to obliterate, decimate, demolish _____

15. dormant, inactive, undeveloped; hidden _____

16. to refute, disprove, confute, shoot holes in _____

17. unruly, intractable; incurable, inveterate _____

18. impudent, saucy, bold; shameless _____

19. an emigration, flight, escape, hegira _____

20. to chatter, babble; to purl; twaddle, gibberish _____

Antonyms   From the words for this unit, choose the one that is most
nearly **opposite** in meaning to each of the following
groups of expressions. Write the word on the line given.

1. transparent, clear; bright, perceptive _____

2. to praise, pat on the back _____

3. to overcome, master, conquer _____

4. secondary, subordinate, ancillary _____

5. flowing, running; fresh, sweet _____

6. freedom, liberty _____

7. reasoned, rational; objective, equitable _____

8. to confirm, corroborate, substantiate _____

9. to foster, promote, encourage, nurture _____

10. deferential, respectful; self-effacing _____

11. an immigration, influx, arrival; an entrance _____

12. unassertive, peaceable; passive _____

13. exposed, manifest, evident _____

14. docile, tractable; curable, reparable _____

15. cheerful, blithe, jaunty, buoyant _____

16. painstaking, meticulous; thorough, in-depth _____

17. to hamper, hinder, obstruct, impede _____

Choosing the Right Word   *Encircle the **boldface** word that more satisfactorily completes each of the following sentences.*

1. On rare occasions, the U.S. Senate will (**reprimand, prattle**) one of its members who has violated its rules.

2. Even people who appear to be free may be in (**exodus, servitude**) to their own passions and prejudices.

3. You may think that his explanation is perfectly clear, but I find it confused and (**brazen, opaque**).

4. The best way to (**facilitate, rebut**) the contention that something is not possible to do is to go out and do it.

5. The brook (**prattling, annihilating**) along its rocky course seemed to be conversing wordlessly with the wind murmuring in the trees.

6. People who never give any assignment more than "a lick and a promise" may be said to belong to the (**militant, slapdash**) school of working.

7. While his (**accomplices, militants**) acted as decoys, one of the youngsters attempted to filch a couple of apples from the unguarded bin.

8. For Africa's starving millions, finding enough food to keep body and soul together has now become the (**paramount, latent**) concern in life.

9. The leaden silence of the afternoon was shattered by the (**opaque, brazen**) voices of trumpets braying fanfares for the returning hero.

10. Most historians agree that military disasters during World War I were the (**exodus, catalyst**) that sparked the Russian Revolution of 1917.

11. Her excellent command of both French and Spanish should (**annihilate, facilitate**) her efforts to get a position in the Foreign Service.

12. It is up to us to get rid of any (**latent, arbitrary**) prejudices that we may still unwittingly hold against members of other races and nationalities.

13. Unemployment will stay at a high level so long as a nation's economy remains (**stagnant, paramount**).

14. I refuse to believe that our society will (**reprimand, succumb**) to the weaknesses that have destroyed other nations.

15. Since they are firmly based on the "logic" of a sentence, the rules of punctuation should not be considered purely (**arbitrary, militant**).

16. (**Accomplices, Militants**) disgusted with the government's policies took to the streets to register a vote of "no confidence."

17. He has deceived me so many times that I am forced to conclude that he is simply a(n) (**incorrigible, latent**) liar.

18. During the summer, urban "sun-worshippers" begin their weekly (**exodus, servitude**) from the city around 3:00 P.M. on Friday.

19. With their bigger, faster, more experienced players, South High simply (**reprimanded, annihilated**) our team, 56 to 7.

20. I don't think it is fair to call him a(n) (**incorrigible, morose**) person just because he was depressed when you met him.

Unit 6

Definitions

Note carefully the spelling, pronunciation, and definition of each of the following words. Then write the word in the blank space in the illustrative phrase following.

1. **atone**
(ə 'tōn)
(*v.*) to make up for

_____ for their mistakes

2. **bondage**
('bän dij)
(*n.*) slavery; any state of being bound or held down

release a slave from _____

3. **credible**
('kred ə bəl)
(*adj.*) believable

a _____ excuse for being late

4. **defray**
(dē 'frā)
(*v.*) to pay for

_____ the shipping charges

5. **diligent**
('dil ə jənt)
(*adj.*) hardworking, industrious, not lazy

a _____ worker

6. **doleful**
('dōl fəl)
(*adj.*) sad, dreary

the losers' _____ faces

7. **ghastly**
('gast lē)
(*adj.*) frightful, horrible; deathly pale

shocked by her _____ appearance

8. **hamper**
('ham pər)
(*v.*) to hold back

_____ our efforts

9. **hew**
(hyü)
(*v.*) to shape or cut down with an ax; to hold to

_____ down the mighty tree

10. **impoverished**
(im 'päv risht)
(*adj.*) poor, in a state of poverty; depleted

_____ by the war

11. **incessant**
(in 'ses ənt)
(*adj.*) never stopping, going on all the time

the _____ crying of the sick baby

12. **intricate**
('in trə kət)
(*adj.*) complicated, difficult to understand

unable to follow his _____ directions

13. **lucid**
('lü sid)
(*adj.*) easy to understand, clear; rational, sane

a _____ explanation

14. **posthumous**
('päs chə məs)
(*adj.*) occurring or published after death

Emily Dickinson's _____ fame

15. **prim**
(prim)
(*adj.*) overly neat, precise, proper, or formal; prudish

in a _____ bonnet and gloves

16. **sardonic**
(sär 'dän ik)
(*adj.*) grimly or scornfully mocking, bitterly sarcastic

the satirist's _____ laughter

17. superfluous
(sü ′pər flü wəs)

(*adj.*) exceeding what is sufficient or required, excess

just so much _____ verbiage

18. supplant
(sə ′plant)

(*v.*) to take the place of, supersede

quickly _____ by a rival

19. taunt
(tônt)

(*v.*) to jeer at, mock; (*n.*) an insulting or mocking remark

_____ by the bully

20. tenacious
(tə ′nā shəs)

(*adj.*) holding fast; holding together firmly; persistent

the bulldog's _____ grasp

Completing the Sentence

From the words for this unit, choose the one that best completes each of the following sentences. Write the word in the space provided.

1. "Someone with such a(n) _____ hold on life doesn't give up the ghost easily," I thought as I watched the old man's struggle to stay alive.

2. During World War II, artificial rubber began to _____ natural rubber in American automobile tires.

3. With a single stroke of his sword, the knight _____ off the monster's head and hung it up on a pole for all to see.

4. A student who is _____ and systematic in study habits will often do better than one who is brilliant but erratic.

5. "Since her heroic deeds clearly speak for themselves," the President remarked, "further comment on my part would be _____ ."

6. He is a rather _____ sort of man whose sensibilities are easily shocked by other people's less exacting standards of conduct.

7. Since my apartment is located on a busy intersection, I have been forced to accustom myself to the _____ hum of traffic outside.

8. The huge piles of snow that cover the roads leading to the site of the accident will greatly _____ the efforts of the rescue team.

9. In a touching scene on the steps of the Capitol, the President awarded _____ Medals of Honor to soldiers who had recently fallen in defense of the country.

10. A man of lofty character and bearing, the prisoner endured the jibes and _____ of his captors with great patience and fortitude.

11. The wily old Senator derived a certain amount of _____ amusement from watching his enemies turn on and destroy one another.

12. When the stock market collapsed in 1929, many a wealthy speculator found himself as _____ as the proverbial church mouse.

6

13. I shall never forget the _____ sight that greeted us when we arrived at the scene of the accident.

14. Although Mrs. McCormick was still in a state of shock after the accident, she was _____ enough to answer the questions posed by the police.

15. Saying "I'm sorry" is a good way to begin to _____ for the suffering or harm that you have done to another person.

16. Lincoln said: "Familiarize yourself with the chains of _____ and you prepare your own limbs to wear them."

17. Our football team would do a great deal better if they mastered a few simple plays, instead of trying to use all those _____ formations.

18. To help _____ the expenses that I would incur on the Senior Class trip to Washington, I became a professional baby-sitter.

19. I suppose bloodhounds may be as happy as other dogs, but they have the _____ look of creatures who have lost their last friend.

20. I know that he will say anything to save his own skin, but I feel that in this case his account of the incident is _____ and should be accepted.

21. For thousands of years the American Indians used stone implements to _____ canoes out of logs and tree trunks.

22. After she lost everything she valued in the world, she began to feel that life had become too _____ to be worth living.

Synonyms　　　*From the words for this unit, choose the one that is most nearly **the same** in meaning as each of the following groups of expressions. Write the word on the line given.*

1. complicated, complex, convoluted　　　_____

2. sorrowful, mournful, melancholy, dolorous　　_____

3. to ridicule, mock, jeer at　　　_____

4. excess, surplus, supererogatory　　　_____

5. to settle, bear the cost, foot the bill　　_____

6. clear, limpid; intelligible; rational　　_____

7. to hinder, obstruct, impede, inhibit　　_____

8. fussy, fastidious; squeamish, prudish　　_____

9. poverty-stricken, destitute, indigent　　_____

10. obstinate, stubborn, dogged, persistent _____

11. dreadful, appalling; gruesome, grisly _____

12. caustic, mordant, acerbic, wry _____

13. occurring after death, post-mortem _____

14. believable, plausible, acceptable, likely _____

15. industrious, assiduous, sedulous _____

16. to chop, hack; to fell; to adhere, conform _____

17. ceaseless, constant, uninterrupted _____

18. captivity, subjection, servitude, dependence _____

19. to make up for, make amends for, expiate _____

20. to replace, displace, supersede, oust _____

Antonyms   From the words for this unit, choose the one that is most nearly **opposite** in meaning to each of the following groups of expressions. Write the word on the line given.

1. occasional, sporadic, intermittent _____

2. simple, uninvolved, uncomplicated _____

3. lazy, indolent; cursory, perfunctory _____

4. murky, muddy; obscure, unintelligible _____

5. necessary, essential, vital, indispensable _____

6. yielding, weak, gentle, lax, slack _____

7. to cheer, applaud, acclaim _____

8. unbelievable, implausible, improbable _____

9. cheerful, blithe, jaunty, buoyant _____

10. dowdy, frumpy; sloppy, untidy; loose, lax _____

11. rich, wealthy, affluent, prosperous _____

12. freedom, liberty; independence _____

13. pleasant, agreeable, attractive, delightful _____

14. prenatal _____

15. to facilitate, ease, smoothe the way _____

16. to make no amends for _____

17. bland, mild; saccharine; good-natured _____

Choosing the Right Word   *Encircle the **boldface** word that more satisfactorily completes each of the following sentences.*

1. What real use is financial independence if a person remains forever in (**bondage, credibility**) to foolish fears and superstitions?

2. He is very slow to form opinions, but once he does he holds on to them (**tenaciously, dolefully**).

3. His feverish and (**lucid, incessant**) activity cannot hide the fact that he doesn't know what he's doing.

4. I know that love is fickle, but I never expected to be (**taunted, supplanted**) in her affections by a crumb like Danny Orr.

5. The novel's grim humor and (**superfluous, sardonic**) portrayal of the futility of all human endeavor make it an intensely disturbing book.

6. In some early societies, people who had committed certain crimes could (**atone, defray**) for them by paying sums of money to their victims.

7. The penniless adventurer is a character so familiar to fiction readers as to render further description of the type (**intricate, superfluous**).

8. "Sticks and stones may break my bones, but names will never hurt me" is an old saying I try to keep in mind whenever someone (**hews, taunts**) me.

9. Even after the most systematic and (**credible, diligent**) search, we could not find the missing documents.

10. Loss of blood very quickly turned the victim's normally rosy face a (**prim, ghastly**) hue of white.

11. The author's writing style is as (**lucid, intricate**) as the sparkling waters of a mountain lake on a spring morning.

12. If we were to lose the basic freedoms guaranteed by the Bill of Rights, we would be truly (**taunted, impoverished**).

13. (**Hampered, Impoverished**) by the weight I had gained over the summer, I was dropped from the football squad after the first practice session.

14. Royalties from a novel that is published (**superfluously, posthumously**) normally go to the author's estate.

15. "The witness has changed his story so often that no jury on earth is likely to find his testimony (**lucid, credible**)," the D.A. observed smugly.

16. I was amazed when I looked through the microscope and observed the (**incessant, intricate**) pattern of blood vessels in the specimen's body.

17. In a totalitarian state, people who do not (**hew, hamper**) firmly to the party line are likely to find themselves in "hot water" with the authorities.

18. That village is famous all over the world for its demure cottages with their well-manicured lawns and (**prim, diligent**) gardens.

19. If we want government to provide services, we must pay taxes to (**defray, hamper**) the costs.

20. Frankly, I am tired of his endless (**credible, doleful**) complaints about all the people who have been unfair to him.

Analogies   *In each of the following, encircle the item that best completes the comparison.*

1. taunt is to **compliment** as
a. supplant is to displace
b. daunt is to defray
c. abscond is to prattle
d. reprimand is to praise

2. bondage is to **servitude** as
a. anarchy is to order
b. larceny is to theft
c. exodus is to arrival
d. precipice is to abyss

3. activist is to **militant** as
a. mourner is to doleful
b. speaker is to pompous
c. accomplice is to prim
d. victor is to morose

4. disentangle is to **intricate** as
a. defray is to tenacious
b. incinerate is to latent
c. rectify is to incorrect
d. hoodwink is to slapdash

5. intrepid is to **favorable** as
a. diligent is to unfavorable
b. arbitrary is to favorable
c. brazen is to unfavorable
d. morose is to favorable

6. opaque is to **lucid** as
a. ghastly is to pleasant
b. stagnant is to murky
c. pliant is to narrow
d. incessant is to constant

7. exodus is to **out of** as
a. anarchy is to above
b. catalyst is to under
c. reprieve is to alongside
d. access is to into

8. exterminate is to **annihilate** as
a. succumb is to overcome
b. hew is to adhere
c. atone is to hasten
d. rebut is to strengthen

9. prattle is to **child** as
a. taunt is to peacemaker
b. gossip is to busybody
c. revile is to hero
d. reprimand is to swindler

10. incorrigible is to **unfavorable** as
a. tenacious is to favorable
b. credible is to unfavorable
c. ghastly is to favorable
d. lucid is to unfavorable

11. diligent is to **industrious** as
a. slapdash is to hasty
b. militant is to intelligent
c. auspicious is to alien
d. pliant is to stubborn

12. racist is to **biased** as
a. cherub is to incorrigible
b. miser is to impoverished
c. actress is to morose
d. daredevil is to intrepid

13. precipice is to **steep** as
a. valley is to high
b. plateau is to flat
c. glacier is to thin
d. volcano is to level

14. bland is to **sardonic** as
a. superfluous is to unnecessary
b. inanimate is to incessant
c. fated is to predetermined
d. dowdy is to prim

15. hamper is to **easy** as
a. facilitate is to arduous
b. rectify is to credible
c. hoodwink is to sardonic
d. hew is to paramount

16. reprieve is to **postponement** as
a. rebuttal is to confirmation
b. bondage is to liberation
c. exodus is to evacuation
d. access is to exclusion

17. tenacious is to **bulldog** as
a. doleful is to monkey
b. pliant is to mule
c. diligent is to bee
d. sardonic is to mouse

18. incinerate is to **ashes** as
a. daunt is to defiance
b. hew is to tree
c. annihilate is to nothing
d. impoverish is to money

Definitions *In each of the following groups, encircle the word that is most nearly **the same** in meaning as the introductory expression.*

1. give relief for a time
disentangle   reprieve   incinerate   revile

2. first and foremost
daunt   inanimate   paramount   servitude

3. unlawful taking away of another's personal property
accomplice   hamper   larceny   latent

4. excessively elevated or ornate
sardonic   pompous   diligent   impoverished

5. hard to achieve
arduous   ghastly   credible   tenacious

6. controlled by destiny
doleful   fated   lucid   incessant

7. off to a good start
biased   pliant   arbitrary   auspicious

8. intensely unpleasant
arduous   incorrigible   ghastly   latent

9. not much fun to be around
paramount   morose   stagnant   opaque

10. correct by removing errors
facilitate   annihilate   hew   rectify

11. slap on the wrist
access   reprimand   exodus   catalyst

12. deceive by a false appearance
revile   hoodwink   prattle   supplant

13. lessen the labor of
facilitate   succumb   taunt   defray

14. quickly and carelessly done
brazen   intrepid   slapdash   intricate

15. expressing sorrow or grief
doleful   lucid   prim   militant

16. absence of a controlling authority
bondage   anarchy   precipice   reprimand

17. yield to force
hamper   rebut   disentangle   succumb

18. make amends
prattle   atone   annihilate   abscond

19. severe or formal rebuke
bondage   reprimand   reprieve   larceny

20. occurring or published after death
incessant   posthumous   superfluous   ghastly

Shades of Meaning   *Read each sentence carefully. Then encircle the item that best completes the statement below the sentence.*

After a period of servitude in a penal colony, he became an evangelical minister and died in the odor of sanctity. **(2)**

1. In line 1 the word **servitude** most nearly means
a. service   b. forced labor   c. illness   d. slavery

Far from being the pliant figurehead that many politicians expected, Lincoln as president firmly proved himself his own man. **(2)**

2. The word **pliant** in line 1 is best defined as
a. elastic   b. flexible   c. weak   d. easily influenced

Is he really so opaque, I wondered, or is he merely pretending ignorance, the better to dupe me? **(2)**

3. The best definition for the word **opaque** in line 1 is
a. obtuse   b. transparent   c. murky   d. unclear

Environmentalists expressed concern that unchecked development would leave the region impoverished of wildlife. **(2)**

4. The word **impoverished** in line 2 most nearly means
a. indigent   b. rich   c. depleted   d. unpopulated

The young playwright was overwhelmed by the sudden access of fame occasioned by the phenomenal success of her second play. **(2)**

5. In line 1 the word **access** is best defined as
a. passage   b. increase   c. approach   d. entry

Antonyms   *In each of the following groups, encircle the word or phrase that is most nearly **opposite** in meaning to the word in **boldface type**.*

1. exodus
a. exit
b. entrance
c. movement
d. home

2. doleful
a. cheerful
b. facile
c. sad
d. angry

3. reprimand
a. compliment
b. answer
c. find fault with
d. punish

4. arbitrary
a. lazy
b. reasonable
c. correct
d. dull

5. disentangle
a. clarify
b. declare
c. enmesh
d. reject

6. morose
a. dark
b. happy
c. frozen
d. kind

7. intrepid
a. fat
b. timid
c. nasty
d. ignorant

8. diligent
a. worried
b. painstaking
c. careless
d. concerned

R

9. superfluous
a. inglorious
b. indispensable
c. insufficient
d. incapable

11. revile
a. hide
b. praise
c. find
d. harden

13. prim
a. sloppy
b. empty
c. tidy
d. lonely

15. servitude
a. bondage
b. liberty
c. poverty
d. cowardice

10. succumb
a. release
b. conquer
c. sicken
d. resign

12. pompous
a. unreal
b. unpretentious
c. unsophisticated
d. unbalanced

14. rectify
a. salute
b. explain
c. correct
d. bungle

16. annihilate
a. destroy
b. repeat
c. foster
d. argue

Completing the Sentence

From the following list of words choose the one that best completes each of the sentences below. Write the word in the space provided.

Group A

abscond	catalyst	doleful	revile
precipice	accomplice	ghastly	access
intricate	latent	hoodwink	atone

1. By pretending to be my friend, she gained _____ to my innermost thoughts.

2. Unless he is willing to tell us who his _____ were, he will have to bear the full weight of the punishment himself.

3. "Without the help of a good road map," Sue confessed, "we never could have followed the _____ route to the picnic area."

4. Some people are deceived fairly easily, but you will find it is pretty difficult to _____ me.

5. That _____ sight will come back to me in nightmares for the rest of my life.

Group B

brazen	arbitrary	bondage	pliant
anarchy	intrepid	reprieve	stagnant
paramount	reprimand	auspicious	incinerate

1. For long ages, mankind has been in a state of _____ to irrational superstitions.

2. I resented her eagerness to _____ me severely, even for minor offenses.

3. The flames of the furnace soon _____ all the old letters that had once been so dear to us.

4. Unless a person finds the world around him interesting and diverse, his life will become _____ and dull.

5. The news that I would not have to take the examination again came as a last-minute _____ .

Word Families

A. *On the line provided, write a **noun form** of each of the following words.*

EXAMPLE: atone — **atonement**

1. intrepid   _____
2. incinerate   _____
3. superfluous   _____
4. diligent   _____
5. tenacious   _____
6. biased   _____
7. pompous   _____
8. credible   _____
9. rectify   _____
10. annihilate   _____
11. incorrigible   _____
12. latent   _____
13. opaque   _____
14. intricate   _____
15. stagnant   _____
16. militant   _____
17. lucid   _____

B. *On the line provided, write a **verb** for of each of the following words.*

EXAMPLE: facility — **facilitate**

1. rebuttal   _____
2. biased   _____
3. bondage   _____
4. impoverished   _____
5. stagnant   _____

Filling the Blanks *Encircle the pair of words that best complete the meaning of each of the following passages.*

1. Though learning a foreign language never comes easily for me, I've found that I can _____ the process if I imitate the ant in the old fable and apply myself to the task as _____ as possible.
   a. defray . . . credibly
   b. rectify . . . brazenly
   c. hamper . . . tenaciously
   d. facilitate . . . diligently

2. "I'm trying to help you, not _____ you," I said. "I want to make your task easier, not more _____ ."
   a. reprieve . . . slapdash
   b. hamper . . . arduous
   c. revile . . . pliant
   d. supplant . . . latent

3. They could no longer sit idly by while a gross injustice went uncorrected. For that reason, they joined a group of _____ reformers actively trying to get the government to _____ the situation.
   a. militant . . . rectify
   b. incorrigible . . . disentangle
   c. biased . . . taunt
   d. morose . . . defray

4. His lies sounded so much like the truth that I was completely taken in by them. If they hadn't seemed so _____ , I don't think I would have been _____ quite so easily.
   a. intrepid . . . impoverished
   b. intricate . . . disentangled
   c. credible . . . hoodwinked
   d. ghastly . . . annihilated

5. A(n) _____ is supposed to _____ the commission of a crime," the burglar growled at his sidekick. (The latter had just set off the alarm system to the bank the pair were robbing.) "But all *you* can seem to do," the burglar continued, "is make this job more difficult!"
   a. catalyst . . . revile
   b. accomplice . . . facilitate
   c. rebuttal . . . incinerate
   d. precipice . . . reprimand

6. Shakespeare's Timon of Athens is a bitter misanthrope who spends much of his time on stage _____ the world and those in it with _____ taunts and caustic jests.
   a. reviling . . . sardonic
   b. reprimanding . . . posthumous
   c. rebutting . . . prim
   d. daunting . . . lucid

7. Tourists always gasp in amazement when _____ Mexican daredevils climb to the top of a lofty _____ in Acapulco and dive fearlessly into the sea hundreds of feet below.
   a. brazen . . . access
   b. intrepid . . . precipice
   c. prim . . . catalyst
   d. pliant . . . exodus

Cumulative Review   Units 1–6

Analogies   *In each of the following, encircle the item that best completes the comparison.*

1. pauper is to **impoverished** as
a. comedian is to sardonic
b. dancer is to obese
c. superstar is to eminent
d. orator is to pompous

2. doleful is to **grief** as
a. intrepid is to fear
b. irate is to anger
c. brazen is to envy
d. morose is to joy

3. prim is to **dissolute** as
a. spurious is to bogus
b. unbridled is to unflinching
c. terse is to curt
d. lucid is to muddled

4. chore is to **arduous** as
a. detail is to superfluous
b. novel is to posthumous
c. note is to legible
d. burden is to cumbersome

5. subjugate is to **bondage** as
a. incarcerate is to prison
b. terminate is to servitude
c. fabricate is to doghouse
d. incinerate is to debt

6. diligent is to **erratic** as
a. alien is to foreign
b. cherubic is to angelic
c. novel is to trite
d. comely is to lively

7. proliferate is to **stagnate** as
a. facilitate is to hamper
b. relinquish is to pilfer
c. supplant is to replace
d. rebut is to mock

8. hew is to **ax** as
a. rectify is to ruler
b. efface is to eraser
c. hoodwink is to pistol
d. defray is to thread

9. spasmodic is to **incessant** as
a. hasty is to slapdash
b. biased is to opinionated
c. lucrative is to profitable
d. latent is to overt

10. circumspect is to **caution** as
a. inanimate is to life
b. credible is to doubt
c. intricate is to simplicity
d. tenacious is to persistence

Shades of Meaning   *Read each sentence carefully. Then encircle the item that best completes the statement below the sentence.*

The author's prim style is poorly matched to the story of overwrought passions it recounts. (2)

1. The best definition for the word **prim** in line 1 is
a. precise   b. exacting   c. crisp   d. fussy

In the first act of *Hamlet* the Prince is visited by the semblance of his murdered father. (2)

2. In line 1 the word **semblance** most nearly means
a. memory   b. relative   c. façade   d. apparition

Rather than trust in an increasingly erratic public transportation system, some commuters have turned to private bus services. (2)

3. The word **erratic** in line 1 is best defined as
a. undependable b. untimely   c. unexpected   d. expensive

Fearing that readers would not grasp what he was up to with his "whale" story, some friends admonished Melville against publishing *Moby Dick*. **(2)**

4. The word **admonished** in line 2 most nearly means
a. scolded   b. reminded   c. cautioned   d. prevented

"Why be content just to muddle through the course," my math teacher asked, "when you might excel if you only put your mind to it?" **(2)**

5. In line 1 the phrase **muddle through** is used to mean
a. mess up   b. get by   c. drop   d. fail dismally

**Filling
the Blanks**
Encircle the pair of words that best complete the meaning of each of the following sentences.

1. In a society that is totally free of prejudice and bigotry, the demons of racial and religious _____ have forever been totally _____ from the minds and the hearts of the people.
a. anarchy . . . reprieved
b. bias . . . exorcised
c. debris . . . salvaged
d. larceny . . . annihilated

2. I regarded the rival who had _____ me in my true love's affections with as much displeasure and dismay as a legitimate heir would look upon the upstart _____ who had stolen his throne.
a. fortified . . . brigand
b. terminated . . . cherub
c. supplanted . . . usurper
d. condoned . . . marauder

3. Though some of our most _____ writers and artists became famous while they were alive, to others such renown was accorded only _____ .
a. eminent . . . posthumously
b. lucrative . . . incorrigibly
c. intrepid . . . superfluously
d. opaque . . . illegibly

4. When the negotiations for a new contract become _____ , the representatives of labor and management in some cases attempt to _____ a settlement by calling on the services of an impartial outside mediator.
a. disentangled . . . hamper
b. defrayed . . . fabricate
c. rectified . . . commandeer
d. deadlocked . . . facilitate

5. Though we had no difficulty _____ small valuables from the old wreck, our efforts to raise the hull itself were _____ by swift currents and heavy seas.
a. accessing . . . compensated
b. breaching . . . tantalized
c. salvaging . . . hampered
d. foddering . . . predisposed

Unit 7

Definitions

Note carefully the spelling, pronunciation, and definition of each of the following words. Then write the word in the blank space in the illustrative phrase following.

1. **adieu**
(ə 'dü; a 'dyü)

(*int., n.*) "Farewell!"; a farewell

offered his _____ before leaving

2. **advent**
('ad vent)

(*n.*) an arrival; a coming into place or view

pleased by the _____ of spring

3. **apex**
('ā peks)

(*n.*) the highest point, tip

the _____ of a triangle

4. **assimilate**
(ə 'sim ə lāt)

(*v.*) to absorb fully or make one's own; to adopt as one's own; to adapt fully

_____ the customs of his new country

5. **bogus**
('bō gəs)

(*adj.*) false, counterfeit

tried to pass _____ money

6. **exorbitant**
(eg 'zôr bə tənt)

(*adj.*) unreasonably high; excessive

charge an _____ fee

7. **interim**
('in tər əm)

(*n.*) the time between; (*adj.*) temporary, coming between two points in time

suspended all activities in the _____

8. **inundate**
('in ən dāt)

(*v.*) to flood, overflow; to overwhelm by numbers or size

_____ the valley to a depth of three feet

9. **malign**
(mə 'līn)

(*v.*) to speak evil of, slander; (*adj.*) evil

_____ her good name

10. **meander**
(mē 'an dər)

(*v.*) to wander about, wind about; (*n.*) a sharp turn or twist

streams that _____

11. **metropolis**
(mə 'träp ə ləs)

(*n.*) a large city; the chief city of an area

highways leading to a major _____

12. **momentous**
(mō 'men təs)

(*adj.*) very important

make a _____ decision

13. **obstreperous**
(əb 'strep ər əs)

(*adj.*) noisy; unruly, disorderly

try to discipline the _____ child

14. **pensive**
('pen siv)

(*adj.*) thoughtful; melancholy

a _____ gaze

15. perilous
('per ə ləs)

(*adj.*) dangerous

find his way out of a _____ situation

16. shoddy
('shäd ē)

(*adj.*) of poor quality; characterized by inferior, dishonest workmanship

reject the _____ goods

17. sprightly
('sprīt lē)

(*adj.*) lively, full of life; spicy, flavorful

play with the _____ kitten

18. surly
('sər lē)

(*adj.*) angry and bad-tempered; rude

lose patience with the _____ waiter

19. tirade
('tī rād)

(*n.*) a long, angry speech, usually very critical

a _____ against his enemies

20. vagrant
('vā grənt)

(*n.*) an idle wanderer, tramp; (*adj.*) wandering aimlessly

asked for a handout by a _____

Completing the Sentence

From the words for this unit, choose the one that best completes each of the following sentences. Write the word in the space provided.

1. Is there anything more unpleasant than to go to a store and find yourself in the hands of a(n) _____ salesperson?

2. The difficult choice between going to college and getting a job is indeed a(n) _____ one for a young person.

3. The record player certainly looked impressive, but its construction was so _____ that within a few months it began to fall apart.

4. Shakespeare's wicked characters often assume the guise of kindness to cloak their _____ natures.

5. In the _____ between Donna's resignation and the election of a new president, I offered to serve in that office.

6. After that _____ charge for a simple motor tune-up, I will never deal with Parson's Garage again.

7. Not until the band struck up a(n) _____ tune did the wedding guests begin to laugh, dance, and have fun.

8. It takes many long hours of study to _____ all the technical information you need to become a computer programmer.

9. King's Highway, an old Indian trail, _____ through Brooklyn, crossing many important streets and almost retracing its path at some points.

10. In the streets of all our great cities, you will find _____ who wander about without homes, jobs, or friends.

11. Baby-sitters often find that children described by their parents as well-behaved become _____ brats as soon as those parents leave.

12. Los Angeles, like every great _____ , has much to offer the visitor, as well as many difficulties and problems.

13. How can you criticize me for the way I behaved during the holdup when you yourself have never been in so _____ a position?

14. Jill interrupted my _____ mood with the quip, "A penny for your thoughts."

15. The appearance of many a main street has been transformed with the _____ of fast-food restaurants.

16. We have evidence that the _____ "English nobleman" is really Elmer Flick, a plumber from Muncie, Indiana.

17. The people living in the valley will have to leave their homes because the area will be _____ when a new dam is constructed across the lake.

18. It is sad to have to bid _____ to friends who have treated us so well.

19. When the head of your golf club has reached the _____ of the swing, pause for a second before you begin the downward motion.

20. The Senator departed from his prepared remarks to deliver an intemperate _____ attacking the administration's foreign policy.

Synonyms *From the words for this unit, choose the one that is most nearly **the same** in meaning as each of the following groups of expressions. Write the word on the line given.*

1. phony, fake, spurious _____

2. a peak, summit, acme; a crowning point _____

3. extreme, inordinate; overpriced _____

4. flimsy, cheap, tacky; imitative _____

5. an arrival, influx _____

6. risky, chancy, hazardous, unsafe _____

7. to submerge, deluge, swamp _____

8. "So long!"; a good-bye _____

9. a drifter, vagabond, hobo, nomad   _____

10. to ramble, wander, roam, zigzag, twist   _____

11. wild, rowdy, uncontrolled; riotous, noisy   _____

12. dreamy, reflective, contemplative, wistful   _____

13. a harangue, diatribe, tongue-lashing   _____

14. to digest, incorporate; to blend in   _____

15. gruff, sullen, cranky, grouchy; hostile   _____

16. an interval, interlude; provisional, stopgap   _____

17. to defame, vilify, badmouth; wicked   _____

18. consequential, weighty, portentous   _____

19. frisky, peppy, spirited, animated, buoyant   _____

20. a large urban center   _____

Antonyms   _From the words for this unit, choose the one that is most nearly **opposite** in meaning to each of the following groups of expressions. Write the word on the line given._

1. polite, gracious, civil; friendly, genial   _____

2. a departure, going away, exodus   _____

3. to proceed in a straight line   _____

4. well-made, solid, durable; superior   _____

5. inexpensive, affordable; reasonable   _____

6. trivial, slight, inconsequential, unimportant   _____

7. sullen, spiritless, dull, morose, sluggish   _____

8. safe, secure, harmless   _____

9. quiet, well-behaved, docile   _____

10. to praise, commend; kind, benevolent   _____

11. the bottom, nadir   _____

12. genuine, authentic   _____

13. "Hello!"; a greeting   _____

14. a hamlet, village   _____

15. a stay-at-home, homebody; a resident   _____

Choosing the Right Word   *Encircle the **boldface** word that more satisfactorily completes each of the following sentences.*

1. I lay there quietly, looking at the clouds and allowing (**vagrant, shoddy**) thoughts to pass through my mind.

2. One of the glories of America has been its ability to (**assimilate, inundate**) immigrants from every part of the globe.

3. It was amazing to see how that quiet, (**pensive, exorbitant**) girl changed into a tough, hard-driving leader.

4. I don't know which was worse—your failure to keep your promise to me or your (**shoddy, momentous**) excuse for lying about it.

5. His talk (**maligned, meandered**) aimlessly through memories of his youth, descriptions of his children, and criticisms of the administration.

6. Though Grandmother is well into her eighties, she is still as (**exorbitant, sprightly**) as a teenager.

7. I have no respect for a person who is unfailingly courteous to his superiors but (**sprightly, surly**) to the employees under him.

8. With the (**tirade, advent**) of competitive team sports for girls, our school's athletic budget may have to be readjusted.

9. When the new recruits refused to budge from their foxholes, the enraged sergeant let loose with a(n) (**apex, tirade**) of insults and abuse.

10. The by-laws state that any member who speaks in a(n) (**obstreperous, perilous**) manner is to be quieted by the sergeant-at-arms.

11. When we asked for suggestions on how to improve the sports program, we were (**assimilated, inundated**) by "bright ideas" from all sides.

12. We can all agree that Elizabethan drama reached its (**apex, metropolis**) in the matchless plays of Shakespeare.

13. I feel that a symphony orchestra is just as important to a (**vagrant, metropolis**) as a big department store or a major-league sports team.

14. Was any event in history more (**momentous, exorbitant**) than the decision of the Continental Congress in 1776 to break away from Great Britain?

15. You have reached the stage of life where you must expect to say (**interim, adieu**) to childhood, and to take on the responsibilities of a young adult.

16. I suffered a substantial financial loss, and an even greater loss of faith in human nature, when I tried to cash his (**obstreperous, bogus**) check.

17. Churchill once said that if a nation tries to avoid everything that is hard and (**shoddy, perilous**), it will weaken its own security.

18. The Governor has appointed Mrs. Henry Wormser to serve as a(n) (**bogus, interim**) Senator until a new election can be held.

19. Yes, it's a pretty dress, and I know that you're eager to have it for the Junior Prom, but don't you think the price is a little (**perilous, exorbitant**)?

20. Only after Lincoln's death did most people appreciate the great qualities of the man who had been so (**maligned, inundated**) in his own lifetime.

Unit 8

Definitions | *Note carefully the spelling, pronunciation, and definition of each of the following words. Then write the word in the blank space in the illustrative phrase following.*

1. assurance
(ə 'shùr əns)

(n.) a pledge; freedom from doubt, self-confidence

speak with _____ on various topics

2. asylum
(ə 'sī ləm)

(n.) an institution for care of children, elderly people, etc.; a place of safety

offer _____ to the oppressed

3. console
(v., kən 'sōl; n., 'kän sōl)

(v.) to comfort; (n.) the keyboard of an organ; a control panel for an electrical or mechanical device

tried to _____ the grieving child

4. dilate
(dī 'lāt)

(v.) to make or become larger or wider; to expand upon

_____ the pupil of the injured eye

5. dross
(drôs)

(n.) refuse, waste products

throw away the _____

6. dwindle
('dwin dəl)

(v.) to lessen, diminish

_____ in size

7. flippant
('flip ənt)

(adj.) lacking in seriousness; disrespectful, saucy

resent their _____ attitude

8. immunity
(i 'myü nə tē)

(n.) resistance to disease; freedom from some charge or obligation

build up an _____ to the flu

9. institute
('in stə tüt)

(v.) to establish, set up; (n.) an organization for the promotion of learning

_____ a new policy

10. liability
(lī ə 'bil ə tē)

(n.) a debt; something disadvantageous

became a _____ to the company

11. preposterous
(prē 'päs tər əs)

(adj.) ridiculous, senseless

a _____ notion

12. pugnacious
(pəg 'nā shəs)

(adj.) quarrelsome, fond of fighting

put off by his _____ attitude

13. rabid
('rab id)

(adj.) furious, violently intense, unreasonably extreme; mad; infected with rabies

a _____ baseball fan

14. realm
(relm)

(n.) a kingdom; a region or field of study

in the _____ of science

15. rejuvenate
(ri ′jü və nāt)

(*v.*) to make young again; to renew

_____ one's flagging spirits

16. remunerate
(ri ′myü nə rāt)

(*v.*) to reward, pay, reimburse

_____ him handsomely for his work

17. sparse
(spärs)

(*adj.*) meager, scant; scattered

an area with a _____ population

18. sterling
(′stər liŋ)

(*adj.*) genuine, excellent; of standard quality

man of _____ character

19. venture
(′ven chər)

(*n.*) a risky or daring undertaking; (*v.*) to expose to danger; to dare

_____ forth at night

20. warp
(wôrp)

(*v.*) to twist out of shape; (*n.*) an abnormality

a _____ mind

Completing the Sentence

From the words for this unit, choose the one that best completes each of the following sentences. Write the word in the space provided.

1. He is such a(n) _____ chess player that he spends almost all of his spare time either playing or studying to improve his game.

2. When I arrived in California, I found employment opportunities there so _____ that I soon decided to return home.

3. The wooden staircase we had worked so hard to build was now irregularly curved because the boards had _____ .

4. Many members have lost interest in our club, but I am confident that we can _____ their enthusiasm with a worthwhile program.

5. Because his army was stronger than his rival's, the pretender to the throne was able to seize power throughout the entire _____ .

6. For many years, Mrs. Raimondi has devoted her time, her energies, and her funds to establishing a(n) _____ for promoting world peace.

7. The idea that an incoming President can miraculously solve all of the nation's problems is simply _____ .

8. Although I cannot support her in the election, I fully appreciate her many _____ qualities.

9. I consider myself a very peaceful person, but if anyone approaches me in a(n) _____ manner, I am prepared to defend myself.

10. Calling upon his many years of experience, the retired warden discussed with great _____ the topic of the evening—"Can Criminals Be Rehabilitated?"

11. Can any amount of money _____ me for the years of my life I have given to that hopeless cause?

12. When we are discussing a serious problem like drug abuse, I feel that _____ remarks are in bad taste.

13. He is an excellent ball handler and a very good shot; his only serious _____ as a basketball player is lack of speed.

14. The English word *bedlam* was taken from the name of an infamous _____ for the insane in medieval London.

15. When Horace, my favorite hamster, died suddenly, my friends were unable to _____ me during my hours of grief.

16. As days passed with no signs of life from the men trapped in the mine, hopes for their rescue _____ and eventually vanished.

17. We hope to lessen the number, length, and severity of common colds, even if we cannot provide complete _____ from them.

18. All the riches of this world, said the minister, are so much worthless _____ without spiritual values and faith.

19. As the snake came into view and slithered across our path, Ralph's eyes _____ with fear.

20. You will need experience, ability, financing, and good luck to have any chance of succeeding in so risky a business _____ .

Synonyms   *From the words for this unit, choose the one that is most nearly **the same** in meaning as each of the following groups of expressions. Write the word on the line given.*

1. to found, bring about; an academy   _____

2. to soothe, solace, alleviate   _____

3. first-rate, outstanding, worthy; pure   _____

4. to decrease, shrink, fade, peter out   _____

5. to try, chance, undertake; a gamble   _____

6. to enlarge, expand, swell, prolong   _____

7. to compensate, satisfy, profit, benefit   _____

8. a handicap, difficulty, impediment, drawback   _____

9. to renew, revitalize, breathe new life into _____

10. to bend, distort, misshape; an irregularity _____

11. exemption, impunity, excusal _____

12. rubbish, trash, detritus; dregs, scum _____

13. a domain, duchy, bailiwick, jurisdiction _____

14. a sanctuary, refuge; a sanatorium _____

15. fanatical, zealous; raving, infuriated, berserk _____

16. thin, scanty, few and far between _____

17. impudent, impertinent, insolent; frivolous _____

18. sureness, poise, self-possession; a promise _____

19. argumentative, combative, belligerent _____

20. nonsensical, absurd, incredible _____

Antonyms *From the words for this unit, choose the one that is most nearly **opposite** in meaning to each of the following groups of expressions. Write the word on the line given.*

1. to withdraw, retire, shrink from, shy away _____

2. plentiful, abundant, profuse, teeming _____

3. to straighten, unbend; to rectify _____

4. peace-loving, friendly, amicable, congenial _____

5. to wear out, exhaust, enervate, debilitate _____

6. mediocre, shoddy, second-rate, sham _____

7. sensible, reasonable, realistic, plausible _____

8. to terminate, discontinue; to demolish, raze _____

9. moderate, restrained, blasé, indifferent _____

10. vulnerability, susceptibility, exposure _____

11. an advantage, asset _____

12. to increase, enlarge, swell, proliferate _____

13. uncertainty, doubt, insecurity _____

14. to distress, aggravate, bother, vex, torment _____

15. to contract, compress, constrict _____

16. serious, respectful, deferential, obsequious _____

Choosing the Right Word — *Encircle the **boldface** word that more satisfactorily completes each of the following sentences.*

1. When you write so imaginatively about "life on other planets," you are entering the (**realm, immunity**) of science fiction.

2. My father should have known better than to (**venture, warp**) into a canoe that I was going to paddle upstream against a crosswind.

3. Today scientists smile wryly at the (**preposterous, sterling**) notion that the earth is flat, but in earlier times it was an accepted fact.

4. As usual, there are plenty of *talkers*, but the supply of *doers* is (**flippant, sparse**).

5. Patriotism is a fine quality, but not when it is (**instituted, warped**) into a hatred of other nations.

6. Walt's (**pugnacious, sterling**) behavior on the football field was more effective in drawing penalties than in gaining ground.

7. I agree with some of his ideas, but I often find that his (**sparse, rabid**) enthusiasm for crackpot causes is hard to take.

8. A sound understanding of the principles of freedom and self-government is the best way to gain (**immunity, asylum**) from totalitarian propaganda.

9. I like humor as well as anyone, but I don't believe in being (**flippant, rabid**) on so solemn an occasion.

10. I support Rick for team captain because of the (**remunerative, sterling**) leadership he has given us during the long, hard season.

11. In spite of all his talk about his great wealth, I noticed that he did not offer to (**remunerate, institute**) us for the cost of the gas.

12. Do you expect me to be (**dilated, consoled**) by the fact that I was not the only one to fail the exam?

13. His worst (**liability, realm**) as a leader is his unwillingness to listen to suggestions from others.

14. Many Americans think that the United States should continue to provide (**assurance, asylum**) for people fleeing from tyranny in other lands.

15. She did not agree to run for Mayor until she had received (**assurance, institute**) of support from important groups in the community.

16. No doubt he knows a great deal about ecology, but is there any need for him to (**console, dilate**) at such length on threats to the environment?

17. In order to meet stricter industry standards, the auto manufacturer had to (**institute, remunerate**) a tough new system of quality controls.

18. We must clear away the (**sterling, dross**) of false ideas from our minds and take a long, hard look at the problem as it actually exists.

19. How quickly their interest in the program (**dwindled, remunerated**) when they realized that it called for so much work, with little chance for glory!

20. The outworn ideas of the past cannot be (**rejuvenated, dilated**) simply by expressing them in snappy, modern slang.

Unit 9

Definitions *Note carefully the spelling, pronunciation, and definition of each of the following words. Then write the word in the blank space in the illustrative phrase following.*

1. **auxiliary**
(ôg ′zil yə rē)
(*adj.*) giving assistance or support; (*n.*) a helper, aid
turn on the _____ motor

2. **candid**
(′kan did)
(*adj.*) frank, sincere; impartial; unposed
be _____ with one's friends

3. **cubicle**
(′kyü bə kəl)
(*n.*) a small room or compartment
worked in a tiny _____

4. **drudgery**
(′drəj ə rē)
(*n.*) work that is hard and tiresome
wearied by the endless _____

5. **envoy**
(′en voi; ′än voi)
(*n.*) a representative or messenger (as of a government)
a special _____ to the UN

6. **escalate**
(′es kə lāt)
(*v.*) to elevate; to increase in intensity
_____ into a major conflict

7. **expedient**
(ek ′spē dē ənt)
(*n.*) a means to an end; (*adj.*) advantageous, useful
do whatever is _____

8. **feign**
(fān)
(*v.*) to pretend
_____ an illness

9. **flair**
(flâr)
(*n.*) a natural quality, talent, or skill; a distinctive style
a _____ for the dramatic

10. **grievous**
(′grē vəs)
(*adj.*) causing sorrow or pain; serious
avoid making a _____ error

11. **heterogeneous**
(het ə rə ′jē nē əs)
(*adj.*) composed of different kinds, diverse
_____ group of students

12. **horde**
(hôrd)
(*n.*) a vast number (as of people); a throng
attacked by a _____ of warriors

13. **impel**
(im ′pel)
(*v.*) to force, drive forward
_____ by hunger

14. **incredulous**
(in ′krej ə ləs)
(*adj.*) disbelieving, skeptical
an _____ stare

15. **inscribe**
(in ′skrīb)
(*v.*) to write or engrave; to enter a name on a list
_____ his name on the watch

16. **monologue**
(′män ə läg)
(*n.*) a speech by one actor; a long talk by one person
one of Hamlet's famous _____

9

17. prognosis
(präg ′nō səs)

(*n.*) a forecast of the probable course and outcome of a disease or situation

a _____ of a speedy recovery

18. rasping
(′ras piŋ)

(*adj.*) with a harsh, grating sound; (*n.*) a harsh sound

unable to stand his _____ tone

19. repugnant
(rē ′peg nənt)

(*adj.*) offensive, disagreeable, distasteful

their _____ lack of cleanliness

20. scuttle
(′skət əl)

(*v.*) to sink a ship by cutting holes in it; to get rid of something in a decisive way; (*v.*) to run hastily, scurry; (*n.*) a pail

_____ the captured galleon

Completing the Sentence

From the words for this unit, choose the one that best completes each of the following sentences. Write the word in the space provided.

1. Hopelessly cut off from the main fleet, the captain of the vessel decided to _____ his ship rather than allow it to fall into enemy hands.

2. The names of all four members of the record-breaking relay team will be _____ on the trophy awarded to our school.

3. A strong sense of fairness has _____ our representative at the UN to admit that a mistake was made.

4. Though many people relish Limburger cheese, I find its strong odor truly _____ .

5. It is the _____ population of New York City that accounts for the wide variety of cultures found in its neighborhoods.

6. We must have the courage and the clear-sightedness to realize that what is _____ is not always right.

7. In times of rapid inflation, the prices of goods _____ at a dizzying rate.

8. In his opening _____ , the talk-show host poked mild fun at all the candidates for President.

9. The New York City Marathon begins with a(n) _____ of runners swarming across the Verrazano Narrows Bridge.

10. In many cities, groups of private citizens have volunteered to serve as _____ police to help combat crime.

11. He says that his _____ in the dormitory is so small that he has to walk into the hallway to change his mind or stretch his imagination.

12. It is all very well to be _____ , but there are times when you should keep certain thoughts and opinions to yourself.

13. An unwilling pupil is apt to look upon hours of practice at the piano as so much boredom and _____ .

14. Her voice was so _____ that I found it painful to listen to her.

15. An indispensable asset to an aspiring dress designer is a remarkable _____ for color and texture.

16. My rather lame excuse for failing to complete my homework was greeted with a(n) _____ snort by the teacher.

17. A special _____ was named by the President to negotiate a settlement in the war-torn Middle East.

18. Peter listened attentively to my dire _____ of the probable effect a third bowl of chili would have on his digestion.

19. I couldn't help admiring her ability to _____ interest as he continued with his endless explanation of German irregular verbs.

20. When Lincoln had been in the White House about a year, he suffered a(n) _____ loss in the death of his youngest son.

21. We will use any _____ we can think of to help us get through this extremely difficult time.

Synonyms — *From the words for this unit, choose the one that is most nearly **the same** in meaning as each of the following groups of expressions. Write the word on the line given.*

1. to urge, push, spur, propel, incite   _____

2. dubious, mistrustful, doubting   _____

3. toil, labor; a grind   _____

4. a prediction, forecast, projection   _____

5. hateful, odious, revolting, repulsive   _____

6. to engrave, imprint; to enroll, enlist   _____

7. an agent, ambassador, emissary, minister   _____

8. to fake, sham, affect, simulate   _____

9. an enclosure, hole-in-the-wall   _____

10. a soliloquy, recitation   _____

11. a crowd, mass, multitude, host, swarm   _____

12. an aptitude, bent, knack, gift; style, panache _____

13. forthright, plainspoken; unbiased _____

14. additional, back-up; a reserve, accessory _____

15. a contrivance, device; serviceable _____

16. miscellaneous, mixed, variegated _____

17. scratchy, scraping, abrasive, gravelly _____

18. to abandon, discard, scrap, ditch, dump _____

19. painful, heartrending, onerous; flagrant _____

20. to climb, raise, ascend, mount _____

Antonyms *From the words for this unit, choose the one that is most nearly **opposite** in meaning to each of the following groups of expressions. Write the word on the line given.*

1. inconvenient, untimely, disadvantageous _____

2. uniform, homogeneous, of a piece _____

3. believing, trustful, gullible _____

4. play, frolic, amusement, recreation, fun _____

5. to decrease, lessen, descend, defuse _____

6. a dialogue, conversation, colloquy _____

7. pleasing, attractive, tempting; wholesome _____

8. insincere, evasive, misleading; artful _____

9. to discourage, check, restrain, curb _____

10. sonorous, smooth, satiny, silky, mellow _____

11. to erase, rub out, delete, efface, obliterate _____

12. to keep afloat, salvage, rescue, preserve _____

13. joyful, uplifting, cheery, upbeat, comforting _____

14. a few, handful _____

15. a vast hall or auditorium _____

16. main, primary, principal _____

17. an inability or incapacity _____

Choosing the Right Word   *Encircle the **boldface** word that more satisfactorily completes each of the following sentences.*

1. I searched in vain through the (**grievous, heterogeneous**) pile of odds and ends for the spare part I had inadvertently thrown away.

2. The poet Browning tells us that if we were to open his heart, we would find the word "Italy" (**inscribed, escalated**) inside it.

3. Cut off from all supplies, the soldiers had to use various (**expedients, cubicles**) to keep their equipment in working order.

4. It's one thing to be interested in writing; it's quite another to have a (**flair, monologue**) for it.

5. As soon as I heard (**candid, rasping**) noises coming from the workshop, I knew that Peter was filing off the rough edges on the lamp he was making.

6. Was it patriotism, a desire to show off, or just self-interest that (**inscribed, impelled**) him to take those terrible risks?

7. I work in an office compartment, travel in a midget car, and sleep in a tiny bedroom. My life seems to take place in a series of (**envoys, cubicles**)!

8. Fortunately, the coolness and good sense of those involved prevented a minor border incident from (**escalating, scuttling**) into a full-scale war.

9. I stared at the clerk (**increduously, expediently**) as he smugly assured me that the coat was worth the preposterous sum the store was asking for it.

10. An army without strong leadership and firm discipline is no more than an armed (**horde, auxiliary**).

11. People who boast of their high moral principles are often the ones who will (**scuttle, escalate**) them most quickly to serve their own interests.

12. Since the person I was trying to interview wouldn't let me get a word in edgewise, our conversation quickly turned into a (**prognosis, monologue**).

13. "The noble Brutus has told you Caesar was ambitious; if it were so, it was a (**grievous, rasping**) fault."

14. Despite the doctor's gloomy (**prognosis, flair**) when I entered the hospital, I was up and about in a matter of days.

15. The building is equipped with a(n) (**repugnant, auxiliary**) generator, ready to go into service whenever the main power source is cut off.

16. How can you say that the TV interview was spontaneous and (**feigned, candid**) when it was all carefully rehearsed?

17. The expression of satisfaction that comes over his face when he talks of the failures of other people is highly (**expedient, repugnant**) to me.

18. Instead of sending your little sister as a(n) (**envoy, drudge**) to explain what went wrong, why don't you stand up and speak for yourself?

19. I don't consider it (**drudgery, scuttle**) to prepare meals every day because I love good food and good cooking.

20. I must admit now that I was hurt when the coach took me out in the last minutes of the game, but I tried to (**inscribe, feign**) indifference.

Analogies *In each of the following, encircle the item that best completes the comparison.*

1. **bogus** is to **authentic** as
a. candid is to frank
b. pensive is to thoughtful
c. momentous is to trivial
d. rasping is to grating

2. **escalate** is to **up** as
a. dilate is to down
b. institute is to down
c. remunerate is to down
d. dwindle is to down

3. **malign** is to **hateful** as
a. console is to kind
b. assimilate is to expedient
c. warp is to merciful
d. rejuvenate is to grievous

4. **asylum** is to **safety** as
a. drudgery is to pleasure
b. assurance is to doubt
c. venture is to risk
d. interim is to success

5. **sprightly** is to **favorable** as
a. sterling is to unfavorable
b. sparse is to favorable
c. surly is to unfavorable
d. shoddy is to favorable

6. **immunity** is to **liability** as
a. prognosis is to disease
b. metropolis is to hamlet
c. flair is to dross
d. monologue is to tirade

7. **cubicle** is to **small** as
a. realm is to large
b. metropolis is to small
c. expedient is to large
d. horde is to small

8. **"Welcome!"** is to **advent** as
a. "Adieu!" is to disaster
b. "Adieu!" is to defeat
c. "Adieu!" is to delay
d. "Adieu!" is to departure

9. **feign** is to **pretend** as
a. institute is to instruct
b. inscribe is to worship
c. inundate is to flood
d. impel is to restrain

10. **meander** is to **winding** as
a. venture is to straight
b. warp is to twisted
c. scuttle is to straight
d. dilate is to twisted

11. **exorbitant** is to **reasonable** as
a. pugnacious is to excited
b. perilous is to safe
c. incredulous is to distasteful
d. preposterous is to bright

12. **flippant** is to **unfavorable** as
a. candid is to favorable
b. heterogeneous is to unfavorable
c. obstreperous is to favorable
d. auxiliary is to unfavorable

13. **vagrant** is to **wander** as
a. spoilsport is to travel
b. spendthrift is to economize
c. daredevil is to cower
d. busybody is to meddle

14. **dilate** is to **widen** as
a. malign is to praise
b. venture is to claim
c. remunerate is to reward
d. dwindle is to spin

15. **bully** is to **pugnacious** as
a. officer is to bogus
b. auxiliary is to momentous
c. thinker is to pensive
d. envoy is to rabid

16. **apex** is to **triangle** as
a. floor is to ceiling
b. diameter is to circle
c. ditch is to road
d. crest is to wave

17. **surly** is to **politeness** as
a. candid is to honesty
b. flippant is to seriousness
c. repugnant is to cruelty
d. sprightly is to liveliness

18. **incredulous** is to **belief** as
a. informal is to attire
b. insensitive is to feeling
c. invincible is to victory
d. insincere is to skill

Definitions   In each of the following groups, encircle the word that is most nearly **the same** in meaning as the introductory expression.

1. bend out of shape
   inundate   warp   assimilate   meander

2. freedom from doubt
   asylum   metropolis   vagrant   assurance

3. farewell
   interim   immunity   prognosis   adieu

4. person who represents one government in dealings with another
   dross   envoy   liability   console

5. contrary to common sense
   pensive   sparse   sterling   preposterous

6. the very summit
   auxiliary   console   cubicle   apex

7. area of control
   monologue   cubicle   flair   realm

8. causing severe pain or suffering
   candid   heterogeneous   momentous   grievous

9. provide payment
   dwindle   remunerate   assimilate   institute

10. involving danger
    flippant   sterling   perilous   incredulous

11. urge forward
    impel   rejuvenate   warp   venture

12. enter on a list
    escalate   scuttle   impel   inscribe

13. long, violently critical speech
    advent   tirade   dross   horde

14. having no fixed course
    rasping   vagrant   bogus   pugnacious

15. undertaking involving risk or danger
    institute   auxiliary   venture   envoy

16. place of protection
    scuttle   institute   asylum   drudgery

17. suitable for achieving a desired end
    flippant   expedient   exorbitant   pensive

18. hastily or poorly done
    rabid   obstreperous   surly   shoddy

19. utter false reports about
    feign   dilate   malign   meander

20. extremely unpleasant
    candid   sprightly   repugnant   expedient

**Shades of
Meaning**

*Read each sentence carefully. Then encircle the item
that best completes the statement below the sentence.*

Scouts came upon a Pawnee hunting party encamped near a meander of
the Platte River. **(2)**

1. In line 1 the word **meander** most nearly means
a. ramble   b. turn   c. rapids   d. wandering

As a longtime friend of one of the participants, I don't think I can be an
entirely candid judge of the debate. **(2)**

2. The word **candid** in line 2 is used to mean
a. forthright   b. sincere   c. unposed   d. impartial

Though the few defenders remaining fought bravely and well, they were
inundated by wave upon wave of shock troops. **(2)**

3. In line 2 the word **inundated** is best defined as
a. overwhelmed   b. saturated   c. relieved   d. harried

"I should have been a pair of ragged claws
scuttling across the floors of silent seas." (T.S. Eliot) **(2)**

4. The word **scuttling** in line 2 most nearly means
a. slinking   b. scraping   c. scurrying   d. salvaging

The rich flavor of the fish was heightened by the sprightly sauce with
which it was served. **(2)**

5. In line 1 the word **sprightly** is best defined as
a. spicy   b. secret   c. animated   d. frisky

Antonyms

*In each of the following groups, encircle the word or
phrase that is most nearly **opposite** in meaning to the
word in **boldface type**.*

1. flippant
a. respectful
b. long
c. puzzling
d. clever

2. bogus
a. mandatory
b. homemade
c. machine-made
d. genuine

3. drudgery
a. dull work
b. hard work
c. fun
d. artistry

4. repugnant
a. peaceful
b. brief
c. attractive
d. expensive

5. pensive
a. thoughtful
b. sad
c. carefree
d. pleased

6. sparse
a. lasting
b. first
c. plentiful
d. important

7. rabid
a. slow
b. tepid
c. extreme
d. foolish

8. rasping
a. loud
b. hysterical
c. mellow
d. hushed

9. momentous
a. long-lasting
b. brief
c. inconsequential
d. tremendous

11. malign
a. hide
b. pretend
c. praise
d. repulse

13. incredulous
a. skeptical
b. gullible
c. faithful
d. disloyal

15. scuttle
a. sink
b. rescue
c. torpedo
d. drift

10. surly
a. clean
b. clear
c. clever
d. polite

12. dwindle
a. ape
b. mushroom
c. pine
d. hog

14. liability
a. truth
b. advantage
c. impossibility
d. drawback

16. advent
a. preparation
b. arrival
c. interim
d. departure

Completing the Sentence

From the following list of words choose the one that best completes each of the sentences below. Write the word in the space provided.

Group A

advent	**candid**	**momentous**	**immunity**
metropolis	**vagrant**	**adieu**	**warp**
apex	**interim**	**dilate**	**realm**

1. His eyes _____ with surprise when we walked into the room so unexpectedly.

2. The _____ of the flu season is often marked by a sharp increase in the number of students absent from school.

3. Education and experience should provide _____ against the poison of racial prejudice.

4. When the President spoke of Mrs. Thomas's achievements in a nationwide television address, she felt she had reached the _____ of her career.

5. In the _____ between the end of the fall term and the beginning of the spring term, we plan to take a trip to Washington.

Group B

institute	**dwindle**	**assimilate**	**rejuvenate**
sparse	**heterogeneous**	**flippant**	**escalate**
repugnant	**pensive**	**meander**	**inundate**

1. As the hair on his head became more and more _____ , he began to use all kinds of tonics and lotions.

2. The local planning commission has _____ strict regulations governing development in the city's historic district.

R

3. The union contract has a clause that pay rates are to _____ automatically whenever the cost of living rises.

4. Although she seems to learn very rapidly, the fact is that she does not really _____ the material.

5. I think the phrase "people coming from all walks of life" aptly describes the _____ group of individuals attending the conference.

Word Families

A. *On the line provided, write a **noun form** of each of the following words.*

EXAMPLE: dilate — **dilation**

1. sprightly _____
2. surly _____
3. escalate _____
4. expedient _____
5. assimilate _____
6. candid _____
7. remunerate _____
8. exorbitant _____
9. inundate _____
10. console _____
11. flippant _____
12. institute _____
13. rejuvenate _____
14. repugnant _____
15. inscribe _____

B. *On the line provided, write a **verb form** of each of the following words.*

EXAMPLE: expedient — **expedite**

1. immunity _____
2. prognosis _____
3. assurance _____
4. grievous _____
5. perilous _____
6. rasping _____

**Filling
the Blanks**   *Encircle the pair of words that best complete the
meaning of each of the following passages.*

1. Some people really enjoy doing all the tiresome and time-consuming
   chores associated with housework, but to me such _____
   is truly _____ .
   a. drudgery . . . repugnant   c. liability . . . boorish
   b. immunity . . . obstreperous   d. assurance . . . pensive

2. "They're asking far too much for this _____ merchandise,"
   I remarked. "I'd be a fool to pay such an _____ price for
   goods that are so badly made."
   a. bogus . . . rasping   c. shoddy . . . exorbitant
   b. sterling . . . expedient   d. grievous . . . auxiliary

3. "Over the years, consumer prices have soared, while the real purchasing
   power of the dollar has _____ ," the speaker said. "If the
   cost of living continues to _____ , the value of our money
   must surely shrink even more."
   a. dwindled . . . dwindle   c. escalated . . . escalate
   b. escalated . . . dwindle   d. dwindled . . . escalate

4. As soon as the robins and the crocuses herald the _____ of
   spring, our personnel department is _____ with a veritable
   deluge of letters from college students asking about summer employment.
   a. interim . . . impelled   c. prognosis . . . rejuvenated
   b. advent . . . inundated   d. flair . . . consoled

5. Does the old saying, "Nothing _____ , nothing gained,"
   mean that someone who expects to be _____ well for his
   or her efforts must be prepared to take some risks?
   a. scuttled . . . maligned   c. ventured . . . remunerated
   b. feigned . . . impelled   d. assimilated . . . inundated

6. After fighting my way all year along the noisy, crowded streets of a bustling
   modern _____ like Tokyo or New York, I find it quite a
   pleasure to _____ aimlessly along a winding country road.
   a. realm . . . dilate   c. asylum . . . impel
   b. metropolis . . . meander   d. cubicle . . . venture

7. Roman governors had at their command both regular legionary troops and
   _____ units drawn from the native population to repel the
   _____ of savage barbarians that from time to time swarmed
   into the provinces of the Empire like an invasion of locusts.
   a. pugnacious . . . tirades   c. vagrant . . . realms
   b. heterogeneous . . . envoys   d. auxiliary . . . hordes

Cumulative Review   Units 1–9

Analogies   *In each of the following, encircle the item that best completes the comparison.*

1. salvage is to **scuttle** as
a. dilate is to feign
b. proliferate is to dwindle
c. dissent is to escalate
d. abridge is to reprieve

2. brazen is to **modesty** as
a. candid is to honesty
b. rabid is to enthusiasm
c. biased is to prejudice
d. flippant is to earnestness

3. exodus is to **adieu** as
a. anarchy is to good-bye
b. metropolis is to bon voyage
c. advent is to hello
d. servitude is to welcome

4. arduous is to **difficulty** as
a. inanimate is to strength
b. sterling is to intensity
c. perilous is to danger
d. pompous is to simplicity

5. intrepid is to **daunt** as
a. diligent is to tantalize
b. incredulous is to hoodwink
c. incorrigible is to surmount
d. obstreperous is to rejuvenate

6. compensate is to **remunerate** as
a. taunt is to jeer
b. malign is to supplant
c. hew is to relinquish
d. warp is to rectify

7. inundate is to **water** as
a. defray is to wind
b. assimilate is to lightning
c. incinerate is to fire
d. annihilate is to snow

8. spurious is to **bogus** as
a. mournful is to doleful
b. superfluous is to essential
c. exorbitant is to minimal
d. lucid is to opaque

9. institute is to **terminate** as
a. atone is to succumb
b. facilitate is to hamper
c. impel is to inscribe
d. revile is to fortify

10. shoddy is to **quality** as
a. trite is to novelty
b. spasmodic is to interest
c. eminent is to renown
d. credible is to belief

Shades of Meaning   *Read each sentence carefully. Then encircle the item that best completes the statement below the sentence.*

Consumer advocates demanded that the manufacturer either retract or substantiate the exorbitant claims advanced for the product.   (2)

1. In line 2 the word **exorbitant** most nearly means
a. overpriced   b. unproven   c. excessive   d. modest

Scholars and students alike now use computers to access vast stores of information housed in libraries all over the world.   (2)

2. The best definition for the word **access** in line 1 is
a. approach   b. gain entry to   c. admit   d. communicate

After a decade of neglect the once splendid hotel had taken on a decidedly shoddy appearance.   (2)

3. The word **shoddy** in line 2 is best defined as
a. flimsy   b. tacky   c. mediocre   d. run-down

In her talk the psychiatrist described the brain as the "console of human perception." (2)

4. In line 1 the word **console** most nearly means
   a. monitor b. comfort c. origin d. solace

It was not his behavior so much as the rabid nature of his talk that gave him away as a madman. (2)

5. In line 1 the word **rabid** is used to mean
   a. furious b. diseased c. insane d. odd

Filling the Blanks *Encircle the pair of words that best complete the meaning of each of the following sentences.*

1. In a famous _____ towards the end of the play, the deposed and incarcerated king laments the fact that the vast _____ over which he once ruled has shrunk to the dimensions of a narrow prison cell.
   a. tirade . . . precipice c. monologue . . . realm
   b. interim . . . rift d. catalyst . . . debris

2. After the beauty pageant was over, _____ of reporters swarmed into the backstage area hoping to get a few words with the _____ winner of the contest.
   a. dilemmas . . . surly c. muddles . . . prim
   b. hordes . . . comely d. deadlocks . . . sprightly

3. As order gave way to _____ in that strife-torn country, the stream of refugees seeking _____ from the turbulence of the times swelled to a mighty torrent.
   a. liability . . . immunity c. deadlock . . . assurance
   b. bondage . . . access d. anarchy . . . asylum

4. Though he has no real _____ for teaching, he's a very hard worker whose _____ and persistence make up handsomely for what he lacks in talent.
   a. repugnance . . . tenacity c. bias . . . obesity
   b. flair . . . diligence d. predisposition . . . mediocrity

5. Instead of giving me the gist of his complaint in a few _____ and pithy sentences, he launched into a long and bitterly abusive _____ against all the people he claimed were "out to get him."
   a. lucid . . . venture c. terse . . . tirade
   b. erratic . . . feint d. opaque . . . altercation

Unit 10

Definitions

Note carefully the spelling, pronunciation, and definition of each of the following words. Then write the word in the blank space in the illustrative phrase following.

1. **adept**
   (*adj.*, ə ʹdept;
   n., ʹa dept)

   (*adj.*) thoroughly skilled; (*n.*) an expert

   an _____ musician

2. **aspire**
   (ə ʹspīr)

   (*v.*) to have ambitious hopes or plans, strive toward a higher goal, desire earnestly; to ascend

   _____ to be an honors student

3. **bleak**
   (blēk)

   (*adj.*) bare, dreary, dismal

   depressed by the _____ landscape

4. **chide**
   (chīd)

   (*v.*) to blame, scold

   _____ the student for his rudeness

5. **despicable**
   (di ʹspik ə bəl)

   (*adj.*) worthy of scorn, contemptible

   shocked by his _____ selfishness

6. **diminutive**
   (də ʹmin yə tiv)

   (*adj.*) small, smaller than most others of the same type

   the _____ lapdog

7. **emancipate**
   (ē ʹman sə pāt)

   (*v.*) to free from slavery; to release or liberate

   _____ from superstitions

8. **erroneous**
   (e ʹrō nē əs)

   (*adj.*) incorrect, containing mistakes

   prove his statement to be _____

9. **exploit**
   (*v.*, ek ʹsploit;
   n., ʹek sploit)

   (*v.*) to make use of, develop; to make improper use of for personal profit; (*n.*) a feat, deed

   _____ the mineral deposits

10. **extemporaneous**
    (ek stem pə ʹrā
    nē əs)

    (*adj.*) made or delivered on the spur of the moment

    an _____ speech

11. **impair**
    (im ʹpâr)

    (*v.*) to make imperfect, damage, harm

    _____ his confidence

12. **invincible**
    (in ʹvin sə bəl)

    (*adj.*) not able to be defeated, unbeatable

    cheered the _____ champion

13. **languid**
    (ʹlaŋ gwid)

    (*adj.*) drooping; without energy, sluggish

    felt _____ late in the afternoon

14. **mire**
    (mīr)

    (*n.*) mud; wet, swampy ground; a tough situation; (*v.*) to get stuck

    sink into the _____

15. **obtrusive**
    (əb ʹtrü siv)

    (*adj.*) forward; undesirably prominent; thrust out

    put off by his _____ behavior

16. preamble
('prē am bəl)

(*n.*) an introduction to a speech or piece of writing

the _____ to the Constitution

17. render
('ren dər)

(*v.*) to cause to become; to perform; to deliver officially; to process, extract

wait for the jury to _____ the verdict

18. rugged
('rəg əd)

(*adj.*) rough, irregular; severe, stern; strong; stormy

climbed some _____ mountains

19. skeptical
('skep tə kəl)

(*adj.*) inclined to doubt, slow to accept something as true

_____ of the rumors

20. slipshod
('slip shäd)

(*adj.*) untidy in dress, personal habits, etc.; careless, sloppy

_____ construction methods

Completing the Sentence

From the words for this unit, choose the one that best completes each of the following sentences. Write the word in the space provided.

1. The many inconsistencies in the suspect's story made the police highly _____ of his alibi.

2. We learned that the matchless discipline and superior leadership of the Roman legions made them all but _____ .

3. The warmth of the June sun made him feel so _____ that he scarcely had the energy to brush away the flies.

4. Poor diet, lack of exercise, and insufficient rest have done a great deal to _____ his health.

5. She understands math very well, but she did poorly on the examination because of _____ work in computation.

6. To improve their standard of living, the people of that underdeveloped country must learn to _____ the resources of their land.

7. Against the solemn hush of the memorial service, Marcia's boisterous laughter was singularly _____ .

8. Marching over the _____ terrain under a broiling sun, we were soon on the verge of exhaustion.

9. The _____ but powerful halfback from Syracuse was one of the lightest men ever to play professional football.

10. Why do you take it on yourself to _____ me whenever I sav or do anything even slightly out of line?

11. Before we get into the specific details of our proposal, we should write a(n) _____ that will explain in general terms what we want to do.

12. How can you _____ to work in the space program when you haven't even been able to pass your science and math courses?

13. The social worker said with great emphasis that anyone who would take advantage of a blind person is utterly _____ .

14. His after-dinner speech was so polished and sure that we never guessed it was _____ .

15. The Welsh mining village, with its rows of drab cottages, seemed terribly _____ and uninviting in the cold autumn rain.

16. The master silversmith was fantastically _____ in the use of his simple hand tools.

17. There are many millions of people throughout the world still waiting to be _____ from the bonds of grinding poverty.

18. Since it had rained heavily all night, the newly plowed fields were by now an almost impassable _____ .

19. After hearing the charges against the accused student, the Principal said she would _____ her decision shortly.

20. Instead of admitting openly that he didn't know how to get to Lake Placid, he gave us completely _____ directions.

Synonyms   From the words for this unit, choose the one that is most nearly **the same** in meaning as each of the following groups of expressions. Write the word on the line given.

1. mistaken, fallacious, all wrong _____

2. low, vile, cheap, sordid, detestable _____

3. rocky, craggy; blunt, harsh; hardy, tough _____

4. dubious, suspicious, incredulous _____

5. to injure, mar, disable, cripple, enervate _____

6. messy, untidy, slovenly, slapdash, cursory _____

7. masterful, accomplished, proficient _____

8. brash, impudent; conspicuous; protruding _____

9. spontaneous, impromptu, off-the-cuff _____

10. grim, cheerless, gloomy; desolate, barren _____

11. to set loose, unchain, unshackle, unfetter _____

12. an opening, preface, prologue, preliminary _____

13. to upbraid, reprimand, rebuke, chastise _____

14. to seek, yearn, aim for; soar _____

15. lazy, sluggish, listless; slack, lethargic _____

16. undersized, miniature, tiny, compact _____

17. to utilize, turn to advantage; to misuse _____

18. a marsh, swamp, bog, slough _____

19. to present, furnish, submit; to make, effect _____

20. unconquerable, indomitable, insuperable _____

Antonyms *From the words for this unit, choose the one that is most nearly **opposite** in meaning to each of the following groups of expressions. Write the word on the line given.*

1. planned, rehearsed, prepared _____

2. lively, energetic, vigorous, enlivening _____

3. tidy, neat, orderly; careful, painstaking _____

4. smooth, flat; soft, mild; tender, delicate _____

5. to improve, strengthen, promote, advance _____

6. believing, credulous, gullible, ingenuous _____

7. clumsy, unskilled, inept, maladroit; a novice _____

8. praiseworthy, commendable, meritorious _____

9. accurate, correct, exact, unerring _____

10. rosy, cheerful, sunny; promising, encouraging _____

11. to approve, praise, compliment, pat on the back _____

12. oversized, gigantic, huge, enormous _____

13. to enslave, snare, chain, shackle _____

14. vulnerable, conquerable, surmountable _____

15. meek, reserved, deferential; recessed _____

16. a conclusion, ending, closing, epilogue _____

Choosing the Right Word *Encircle the **boldface** word that more satisfactorily completes each of the following sentences.*

1. I could see that his long, sad story about his bad luck was only the (**impairment, preamble**) to a request for a loan.

2. There is a theory that because Napoleon was so (**obtrusive, diminutive**), he was determined to outdo all the taller men around him.

3. I do not accuse him of deliberately lying, but I can prove beyond doubt that his charges are (**skeptical, erroneous**).

4. I would never entrust my funds to anyone who is so (**adept, slipshod**) in managing his own affairs.

5. In the (**slipshod, extemporaneous**) give-and-take of a televised debate, it is easy for a nervous nominee to make a slip of the tongue.

6. A good scientist will always be (**skeptical, erroneous**) about any theory that is not backed up by convincing evidence.

7. His huge bulk, combined with his (**extemporaneous, languid**) manner, made me think of a tired whale.

8. When Emerson said "Hitch your wagon to a star!" he meant that we should (**aspire, mire**) to reach the very highest levels of which we are capable.

9. The goalie's reflexes were as sharp as ever, but the knee injury had plainly (**impaired, aspired**) his ability to maneuver.

10. Sergeant Alvin York was awarded this nation's highest honors for his many daring (**preambles, exploits**) during World War I.

11. Passengers trying to leave the bus kept tripping over some very large packages that jutted out (**obtrusively, languidly**) into the aisle.

12. It is worse than useless to (**render, chide**) children for misbehaving without giving them an opportunity to behave better.

13. That monologue about the young teacher on her very first day in school (**rendered, emancipated**) me helpless with laughter.

14. When we tried to straighten out that mess, we found ourselves (**mired, exploited**) in a mass of inaccurate, incomplete, and mixed-up records.

15. The sculptor has done a superb job of representing the strong, rough planes of Lincoln's (**languid, rugged**) features.

16. It is up to all of us to (**impair, emancipate**) ourselves from prejudices and false ideas acquired early in life.

17. Our basketball team, with its well-planned attack, tight defense, and 7-foot center, proved all but (**invincible, adept**).

18. When I asked him why he wasn't going to the Senior Prom, he answered only with a (**bleak, slipshod**) little smile.

19. Far from admiring the way he got those letters of recommendation, I must say that I consider his deception utterly (**skeptical, despicable**).

20. After four years as the President's press secretary, I have become an accomplished (**adept, skeptic**) in the art of fielding questions.

Unit 11

Definitions

Note carefully the spelling, pronunciation, and definition of each of the following words. Then write the word in the blank space in the illustrative phrase following.

1. brevity
('brev ə tē)

(*n.*) shortness

    admire the _____ of the speech

2. comport
(kəm 'pôrt)

(*v.*) to conduct or bear oneself, behave; to be in agreement

    _____ themselves with dignity

3. concise
(kən 'sīs)

(*adj.*) expressing much in a few words

    put your ideas into a _____ statement

4. demure
(di 'myür)

(*adj.*) sober or serious in manner, modest

    attracted by her _____ smile

5. depreciation
(di prē shē 'ā
shən)

(*n.*) a lessening in value; a belittling

    computed the annual _____ in value of the property

6. deteriorate
(di 'tir ē ə rāt)

(*v.*) to lower in quality or value; to wear away

    watched his health _____

7. divulge
(di 'vəlj)

(*v.*) to tell, reveal; to make public

    _____ our secret formula to no one

8. enlightened
(en 'līt ənd)

(*adj.*) free from ignorance and false ideas; possessing sound understanding

    an _____ attitude

9. forestall
(fōr 'stôl)

(*v.*) to prevent by acting first

    _____ an argument

10. garble
('gär bəl)

(*v.*) to distort in such a way as to make unintelligible

    confuse us with a _____ report

11. proponent
(prō 'pō nənt)

(*n.*) one who puts forward a proposal; one who supports a cause or belief

    a _____ of tax reform

12. quaver
('kwā vər)

(*v.*) to shake, tremble; to trill

    a voice that _____ with anger

13. recoil
(*v.*, ri 'koil;
n., 'rē koil)

(*v.*) to spring back, shrink; (*n.*) the act of springing back

    _____ at the sound of the shot

14. recoup
(ri 'küp)

(*v.*) to make up for, regain

    a scheme to _____ his lost fortune

15. reek
(rēk)

(n.) an unpleasant smell; (v.) to give off unpleasant smells; to give a strong impression

clothes that _____ of tobacco

16. relentless
(ri 'lent ləs)

(adj.) unyielding, harsh, without pity

a _____ pursuit of excellence

17. rivulet
('riv yü lət)

(n.) a small stream

dipped my toe in the _____

18. squander
('skwän dər)

(v.) to spend foolishly, waste

_____ a fortune on gambling

19. staccato
(stə 'kät ō)

(adj.) detached or disconnected in sound or style

_____ bursts from a machine gun

20. statute
('stach üt)

(n.) a law

a _____ passed by the legislature

Completing the Sentence

From the words for this unit, choose the one that best completes each of the following sentences. Write the word in the space provided.

1. The program featured a debate between _____ of gun control and critics of legislation restricting ownership of firearms.

2. Now that the storm has damaged the crops, it's up to us to work twice as hard to _____ our losses.

3. How often have we heard candidates for public office promise that they will be tough and _____ in fighting organized crime!

4. In a passage that a composer has marked _____ every note should sound like the quick thrust of a knife.

5. "I'm not afraid of anyone!" the boy piped up bravely, but we noticed that his voice _____ as he said it.

6. As it wound its way through the desert, the mighty river became a mere _____ that travelers could easily wade across.

7. What we need is not a lot of new legislation but tough enforcement of the _____ already on the books.

8. The statements that appeared in the local newspapers were so badly _____ we could not be sure what the witnesses had said.

9. A(n) _____ public opinion, said Jefferson, is essential to a democratic society.

10. Leaders are judged by how well they _____ themselves in times of crisis.

11. Since you are charged for every word you use in a telegram, it pays to be as _____ as possible.

12. The child _____ in fear and disgust as the harmless water snake slithered over the floor.

13. Economists will tell you that inflation results in an increase in the supply of money but a(n) _____ in its value.

14. The assertive heroines portrayed in many TV programs are a far cry from the _____ young ladies depicted in 19th-century novels.

15. The telltale _____ of gas reminded us that someone had left a burner open on the stove.

16. Since you worked so long and hard for the money you earned, it's doubly foolish to _____ it on things you don't really want or need.

17. A President will often try to _____ the defeat of a legislative program by appealing for the public's support on TV.

18. In saying that "_____ is the soul of wit," Shakespeare was reminding comedians to keep their jokes short and snappy.

19. Despite the creature comforts we now enjoy, I feel that the quality of life has somehow _____ in recent years.

20. The witnesses have testified at great length, but how much really valuable information have they _____ to the investigating committee?

Synonyms   *From the words for this unit, choose the one that is most nearly **the same** in meaning as each of the following groups of expressions. Write the word on the line given.*

1. to quiver, vibrate, shiver, quake, palpitate   _____

2. to worsen, decline, degenerate; to debase   _____

3. a rule, ordinance, enactment   _____

4. shy, diffident, sedate; seemly, decorous   _____

5. stern, merciless; persistent, unremitting   _____

6. to hinder, thwart, preclude, ward off   _____

7. abrupt, disconnected, disjointed   _____

8. to deport oneself; to agree, concur   _____

9. to jumble, scramble, confuse, misrepresent   _____

10. a cheapening, lowering, devaluation   _____

11. brief, succinct, terse, pithy, to the point   _____

12. knowing, informed, aware, cultivated   _____

13. a brook, creek, rill   _____

14. to recover, retrieve   _____

15. conciseness, terseness, pithiness   _____

16. to misspend, dissipate   _____

17. to shrink, flinch, retreat; a kickback   _____

18. to disclose, impart, spill the beans, "leak"   _____

19. a stench; to stink, smell   _____

20. a supporter, advocate, exponent   _____

Antonyms   _From the words for this unit, choose the one that is most nearly **opposite** in meaning to each of the following groups of expressions. Write the word on the line given._

1. merciful; accommodating, indulgent   _____

2. continuous, flowing, unbroken   _____

3. to welcome, accept, allow, submit, abide by   _____

4. ignorant, unaware, untaught, benighted   _____

5. a perfume, fragrance, bouquet   _____

6. to save, economize, hoard, squirrel away   _____

7. an increase, appreciation, enhancement   _____

8. to advance, proceed, gain ground   _____

9. to improve, fix up, enhance   _____

10. verbosity, long-windedness, prolixity   _____

11. to lose, default, forfeit, kiss goodbye   _____

12. wordy, verbose, long-winded, prolix   _____

13. an opponent, critic, foe, adversary   _____

14. to clarify, elucidate, articulate   _____

15. bold, forward, assertive, immodest   _____

16. to hide, conceal, cover up, secrete, keep under wraps   _____

Choosing the Right Word *Encircle the **boldface** word that more satisfactorily completes each of the following sentences.*

1. Seeing my childhood friend so gray and infirm, I became keenly aware of the (**relentless, demure**) passage of the years.

2. In an attempt to mislead the enemy, the crafty prisoner of war deliberately (**garbled, divulged**) his account of how the attack had been planned.

3. I had no idea how much he envied my success in college until I overheard him bitterly (**depreciating, forestalling**) my accomplishments.

4. The charitable programs sponsored by this organization (**comport, recoil**) well with our conception of a just and compassionate society.

5. In order to (**recoil, forestall**) criticisms of my proposal, I prepared myself with relevant facts and figures before the meeting.

6. William Shakespeare expressed the tragic (**brevity, statute**) of life by comparing it to a candle that must soon go out.

7. When I learned how the air and water were being polluted, I became a strong (**divulger, proponent**) of ecological reforms.

8. The debate between the candidates was interesting, but I am not sure that it did much to (**reek, enlighten**) the voters on the issues of the campaign.

9. It's all very well to build new housing, but we should also rehabilitate neighborhoods that have (**deteriorated, garbled**) through neglect.

10. He was trying to talk calmly, but his (**quavering, enlightened**) tones gave away his emotions.

11. I'm not saying that you shouldn't watch TV, but why (**recoup, squander**) so much of your time on those low-grade programs?

12. I wish there was a (**rivulet, statute**) that would forbid people to tell me the ending of a detective story!

13. Once a political leader has lost his reputation and his popularity, it is almost impossible for him to (**recoup, comport**) public confidence.

14. Early rifles had such a "kick" to them that inexperienced soldiers were often injured by their (**recoil, statute**).

15. The speaker's (**enlightened, staccato**) delivery truly reminded us of a jackhammer breaking up concrete.

16. In spite of the vast number of details in the United States Constitution, the document is remarkably (**relentless, concise**).

17. A person accused of a crime is not obliged to (**divulge, forestall**) anything that might be incriminating.

18. The clothing of the firefighters soon (**quavered, reeked**) of smoke and sweat.

19. (**Rivulets, Garbles**) of sweat ran down the faces of the men working in that terrible heat.

20. No matter where you go in the village, you will see cozy thatched cottages with neat little lawns and (**demure, relentless**) gardens.

Unit 12

Definitions

Note carefully the spelling, pronunciation, and definition of each of the following words. Then write the word in the blank space in the illustrative phrase following.

1. **appreciable**
(ə ′prē shə bəl)
(*adj.*) sufficient to be noticed or measured
lost an _____ amount of blood

2. **autocratic**
(ô tə ′krat ik)
(*adj.*) absolute in power or authority
a dictator's _____ control

3. **blanch**
(blanch)
(*v.*) to remove the color from; to make or turn pale; to parboil
_____ at the awful sight

4. **blasphemy**
(′blas fə mē)
(*n.*) an act, utterance, or writing showing contempt for something sacred
accused of _____

5. **brawny**
(′brô nē)
(*adj.*) strong, muscular
admire his _____ build

6. **concerted**
(kən ′sər tid)
(*adj.*) planned or performed in cooperation with others
a _____ drive to register new voters

7. **contend**
(kən ′tend)
(*v.*) to fight, struggle; to compete; to argue
_____ for first prize

8. **humane**
(hyü ′mān)
(*adj.*) kind, merciful
_____ treatment of animals

9. **illustrious**
(i ′ləs trē əs)
(*adj.*) very famous, distinguished
meet the _____ statesman

10. **intolerable**
(in ′täl ər ə bəl)
(*adj.*) unbearable
refuse to put up with such _____ behavior

11. **irreverent**
(i ′rev ər ənt)
(*adj.*) disrespectful
resent his _____ comments

12. **laborious**
(lə ′bôr ē əs)
(*adj.*) not easy, requiring hard work; hardworking
find it to be a most _____ task

13. **lithe**
(līth)
(*adj.*) bending easily, limber
as _____ and agile as a ballet dancer

14. **maltreat**
(mal ′trēt)
(*v.*) to abuse, use roughly or cruelly
_____ the puppy

15. **ponder**
(′pän dər)
(*v.*) to consider carefully, reflect on
_____ over the recent events

16. subversive
(səb ′vər siv)

(*adj.*) intended to undermine or overthrow; (*n.*) one who advocates or attempts to undermine a political system

confiscate the _____ pamphlets

17. synthetic
(sin ′thet ik)

(*adj.*) made or put together by people; (*n.*) something artificial

rayon, one of the first _____ fabrics

18. temperate
(′tem pər ət)

(*adj.*) mild, moderate

a _____ disposition

19. venomous
(′ven ə məs)

(*adj.*) poisonous; spiteful, mean

bitten by a _____ spider

20. wily
(′wī lē)

(*adj.*) sly, shrewd, cunning

a _____ trader

Completing the Sentence

From the words for this unit, choose the one that best completes each of the following sentences. Write the word in the space provided.

1. "Once upon a midnight dreary, while I _____ weak and weary over many a quaint and curious volume of forgotten lore—"

2. Mexico City is located deep in the tropics, but because of the altitude, its climate is _____ .

3. The typical gymnast doesn't have huge muscles like a weight lifter but rather a slim, _____ body.

4. Some _____ fibers are actually better than natural materials for certain purposes.

5. Instead of trying to accomplish something worthwhile on his own, the man spends too much time boasting about his _____ ancestors.

6. The bite of the rattlesnake and the sarcastic words of a supposed friend can both be _____ .

7. We learned too late that the _____ fox had escaped our trap by doubling back on his own tracks.

8. The mountain climbers had to _____ not only with the unfavorable weather but with the fatigue brought on by the altitude.

9. Only when the new drug was administered did the patient begin to show _____ signs of improvement.

10. In spite of his pose of being a "hard-boiled businessman," he is notably _____ in all his dealings with his employees.

11. When I said that the famous rock star was singing off-key, his devoted fans seemed to think I was guilty of _____ .

12. The years had _____ the auburn from her hair, which now resembled a crown of snowy white.

13. Students joined with faculty in a(n) _____ effort to increase the school's involvement in community affairs.

14. Far from boosting team pride, the new training regulations had a really _____ effect on the players' morale.

15. The _____ guide hoisted the canoe on his shoulders and carried it up the steep hill to the lake.

16. I resented the _____ manner in which he told us—without even asking for our opinion—what we should do to improve our situation.

17. When it was discovered that the unfortunate animals were being cruelly _____ , they were taken away by the ASPCA.

18. Our climb up the mountain was so _____ that we had to take a long rest before starting down.

19. I needed the job badly, but the working conditions in that company were so _____ that I finally had to quit.

20. Some people were amused and others were outraged by his lighthearted, _____ attitude toward the institutions of government.

| **Synonyms** | From the words for this unit, choose the one that is most nearly **the same** in meaning as each of the following groups of expressions. Write the word on the line given. |

1. to battle, dispute; to vie; to maintain, assert _____

2. profane, impious, sacrilegious, flippant _____

3. sympathetic, compassionate, kindhearted _____

4. to misuse, mistreat, harm, aggrieve _____

5. treasonous, traitorous; a revolutionary _____

6. domineering, dictatorial, tyrannical, bossy _____

7. artificial, ersatz _____

8. to think over, ruminate, contemplate _____

9. broad-shouldered, strapping, husky, burly _____

10. supple, flexible, pliant, lissome _____

11. arduous, difficult, strenuous, wearisome _____

12. perceptible, detectable; considerable _____

13. eminent, renowned, prominent, celebrated _____

14. clever, tricky, artful, foxy, cagey _____

15. joint, cooperative, combined, consolidated _____

16. to bleach, drain, wash out; to go white _____

17. nasty, malicious, virulent, malevolent _____

18. a curse, profanity, sacrilege, imprecation _____

19. composed, balanced, mellow, fair _____

20. insufferable, unendurable; outrageous _____

Antonyms　　From the words for this unit, choose the one that is most nearly **opposite** in meaning to each of the following groups of expressions. Write the word on the line given.

1. unknown, obscure, nameless, anonymous _____

2. patriotic, loyal, true-blue _____

3. immoderate, extreme, excessive, harsh _____

4. awed, respectful, devout, pious, deferential _____

5. cruel, merciless, unfeeling, brutal, heartless _____

6. natural, genuine _____

7. reverence, veneration, devotion, respect _____

8. to color, dye, infuse; to blush, flush _____

9. to yield, acquiesce, submit, relinquish _____

10. stiff, rigid, inflexible, taut _____

11. slight, trivial, inconsequential, negligible _____

12. dull-witted, dense; artless, straightforward _____

13. to coddle, pamper, indulge _____

14. democratic, egalitarian; lenient, permissive, indulgent _____

15. unorganized, unilateral, diffused _____

16. easy, effortless, facile _____

17. harmless, innocuous, benign _____

18. slight, frail, delicate, puny _____

12

Choosing the Right Word *Encircle the **boldface** word that more satisfactorily completes each of the following sentences.*

1. Is it (**irreverent, appreciable**) of me to suggest that the "great man" may not be as great as he thinks he is?

2. The explanation she offered for her failure to be present seemed to me far-fetched and (**humane, synthetic**).

3. As a public official, I have learned to expect criticism of my ideas, but not such (**venomous, temperate**) attacks on my character.

4. In a country as rich as ours, it is simply (**illustrious, intolerable**) that so many people live below the poverty level.

5. He has the reputation of being a (**laborious, wily**) coach who can win even with smaller, less experienced players.

6. With two such candidates (**pondering, contending**) for the same office, the voters can't go wrong, whomever they may choose.

7. Let's stop the name-calling and try to discuss our problems (**temperately, venomously**).

8. Some people criticized the judge as being "too lenient," but I thought he was simply being (**autocratic, humane**).

9. To devoted fans of celebrated stand-up comedians, the remark that "he's not very funny" is almost (**blasphemous, laborious**).

10. Is there any other animal in the world as graceful and (**subversive, lithe**) as the common house cat?

11. Isn't it amazing how the Adams family produced (**illustrious, intolerable**) men and women in so many fields of activity?

12. They were not very sympathetic in their care of the elderly patients, but I would not accuse them of (**irreverence, maltreatment**).

13. After completing the textbook, the writer faced the (**laborious, brawny**) job of compiling the index.

14. Advocates of American independence were regarded by Great Britain not as patriots but as dangerous (**subversives, synthetics**).

15. In those days, a dollar was a(n) (**concerted, appreciable**) sum, and was not to be spent lightly.

16. Even those of us not philosophically inclined like to (**contend, ponder**) occasionally over the meaning of life.

17. When the suspect (**concerted, blanched**) at the sudden accusation, his bloodless countenance as much as proclaimed his guilt.

18. All the nations of the world must make a(n) (**concerted, irreverent**) attack on the real enemies of mankind—poverty, ignorance, and disease.

19. We Americans believe that a government can be strong, resourceful, and efficient without being (**wily, autocratic**).

20. Many novels about football players or boxers are written in a style as (**brawny, concerted**) and athletic as the characters they portray.

Review Units 10–12

Analogies *In each of the following, encircle the item that best completes the comparison.*

1. **demure** is to **sedate** as
   a. illustrious is to obscure
   b. languid is to listless
   c. laborious is to agile
   d. despicable is to remarkable

2. **emancipate** is to **enslave** as
   a. impair is to consider
   b. render is to contribute
   c. garble is to confuse
   d. divulge is to conceal

3. **small** is to **diminutive** as
   a. big is to gigantic
   b. tall is to appreciable
   c. long is to concise
   d. large is to petite

4. **invincible** is to **conquer** as
   a. invisible is to hear
   b. inaudible is to listen
   c. inedible is to sell
   d. intolerable is to bear

5. **blasphemy** is to **irreverent** as
   a. envy is to content
   b. anger is to agreeable
   c. doubt is to skeptical
   d. pride is to humble

6. **wily** is to **fox** as
   a. energetic is to pig
   b. slippery is to eel
   c. docile is to mule
   d. intelligent is to sheep

7. **staccato** is to **music** as
   a. choppy is to prose
   b. extemporaneous is to oration
   c. synthetic is to plastic
   d. obtrusive is to art

8. **thinker** is to **ponder** as
   a. subversive is to recoup
   b. proponent is to advocate
   c. adept is to maltreat
   d. critic is to contend

9. **voice** is to **quaver** as
   a. eye is to wink
   b. nose is to sneeze
   c. head is to turn
   d. hand is to shake

10. **obtrusive** is to **unfavorable** as
    a. enlightened is to favorable
    b. temperate is to unfavorable
    c. erroneous is to favorable
    d. concerted is to unfavorable

11. **bleak** is to **hospitality** as
    a. wily is to cunning
    b. concise is to brevity
    c. slipshod is to care
    d. humane is to mercy

12. **reek** is to **unfavorable** as
    a. stench is to favorable
    b. fragrance is to unfavorable
    c. aroma is to favorable
    d. scent is to unfavorable

13. **forestall** is to **prevent** as
    a. blanch is to blush
    b. chide is to scold
    c. comport is to enjoy
    d. aspire is to deny

14. **spendthrift** is to **squander** as
    a. beggar is to save
    b. pickpocket is to invest
    c. banker is to embezzle
    d. miser is to hoard

15. **preamble** is to **document** as
    a. preface is to book
    b. prelude is to statue
    c. overture is to symphony
    d. prologue is to painting

16. **chore** is to **laborious** as
    a. feat is to cowardly
    b. achievement is to obtrusive
    c. deed is to commendable
    d. exploit is to daring

17. **venomous** is to **rattlesnake** as
    a. lithe is to cheetah
    b. diminutive is to elephant
    c. rugged is to butterfly
    d. brawny is to gnat

18. **rivulet** is to **wet** as
    a. mire is to dry
    b. plateau is to wet
    c. desert is to dry
    d. fire is to wet

R

Definitions   In each of the following groups, encircle the word that is most nearly **the same** in meaning as the introductory expression.

1. free from the power of another
demure   emancipate   render   divulge

2. projecting out or in the way
obtrusive   adept   staccato   quavering

3. voice disapproval of
squander   ponder   blanch   chide

4. showing disrespect for something sacred
brevity   reek   blasphemy   statute

5. think deeply
preamble   ponder   maltreat   contend

6. flexible and graceful
lithe   erroneous   invincible   wily

7. having sensible ideas
despicable   demure   enlightened   illustrious

8. disposed to doubt
appreciable   skeptical   relentless   bleak

9. contempt for something held sacred by others
rivulet   recoil   blasphemy   proponent

10. abuse cruelly
maltreat   forestall   squander   garble

11. small stream
proponent   rivulet   depreciation   subversive

12. introduction to a formal statement
mire   preamble   brevity   statute

13. of considerable size or quantity
slipshod   skeptical   appreciable   rugged

14. take advantage of
exploit   squander   ponder   aspire

15. performed or carried out together
brawny   concise   concerted   irreverent

16. harm or damage the value or effectiveness of
recoup   impair   contend   comport

17. extremely small
diminutive   laborious   synthetic   intolerable

18. spiteful or poisonous
extemporaneous   temperate   languid   venomous

19. dictatorial or despotic
humane   slipshod   autocratic   rugged

20. degenerate in quality, character, or value
deteriorate   aspire   contend   reek

Shades of Meaning   *Read each sentence carefully. Then encircle the item that best completes the statement below the sentence.*

In the arts, as in any field of endeavor, the laurels usually go to those who are as laborious as they are naturally gifted.   **(2)**

1. In line 2 the word **laborious** is used to mean
   a. difficult   b. wearisome   c. industrious   d. arduous

The naturalist produced an old wooden birdcall and with it expertly imitated the quaver of a meadowlark.   **(2)**

2. The best definition for the word **quaver** in line 2 is
   a. tremble   b. trill   c. shiver   d. cackle

Some scientists contend it is possible – even probable – that intelligent life not unlike our own exists elsewhere in the universe.   **(2)**

3. The word **contend** in line 1 most nearly means
   a. deny   b. struggle   c. vie   d. maintain

Before its mass production in the 1800s, soap was commonly made at home by a process that involved rendering animal fat.   **(2)**

4. The word **rendering** in line 2 is best defined as
   a. delivering   b. adding   c. submitting   d. extracting

When Boss Tweed ruled New York City in the 1860s, government floundered in a mire of corruption and graft.   **(2)**

5. In line 2 the word **mire** most nearly means
   a. tangle   b. mud slide   c. assortment   d. swamp

Antonyms   *In each of the following groups, encircle the word or phrase that is most nearly **opposite** in meaning to the word in **boldface type**.*

1. quavering
a. low-pitched
b. shaking
c. steady
d. high-pitched

2. synthetic
a. scientific
b. natural
c. sincere
d. artificial

3. recoup
a. gain
b. avenge
c. lose
d. reveal

4. irreverent
a. droll
b. respectful
c. lowly
d. honored

5. invincible
a. brave
b. vulnerable
c. peaceful
d. victorious

6. laborious
a. easy
b. difficult
c. long
d. brief

7. demure
a. cultured
b. strange
c. trite
d. bold

8. forestall
a. win
b. lose
c. prevent
d. bring about

9. garble
a. clog
b. medicate
c. clarify
d. injure

11. bleak
a. inviting
b. pale
c. abrupt
d. huge

13. brawny
a. nasty
b. husky
c. puny
d. tricky

15. impair
a. combine
b. disable
c. relate
d. improve

10. proponent
a. supporter
b. legislator
c. component
d. opponent

12. relentless
a. empty
b. poor
c. merciful
d. noisy

14. erroneous
a. correct
b. pleasant
c. slippery
d. mistaken

16. despicable
a. praiseworthy
b. cowardly
c. detestable
d. imaginary

Completing the Sentence — *From the following list of words choose the one that best completes each of the sentences below. Write the word in the space provided*

Group A

illustrious	despicable	comport	demure
adept	slipshod	autocratic	quaver
appreciable	brawny	render	divulge

1. Because of his _____ way of keeping records, he was never sure of which bills he had already paid.

2. How was I to know that he is the _____ scientist who won the Nobel Prize last year?

3. He refused to _____ how he had been able to enter our room without a key.

4. The boys' rowdy behavior did not _____ well with the solemnity of the occasion.

5. In Dickens's *Oliver Twist* we meet a band of young pickpockets and thieves, who, though tender in years, are already _____ in the art of larceny.

Group B

venomous	chide	recoil	skeptical
relentless	mire	rugged	despicable
garble	proponent	lithe	invincible

1. If looks could kill, the _____ glance she sent in my direction would have proved fatal.

2. In the pandemonium of battle, sailors manning the cramped gun decks of men-of-war were often injured by the _____ of their own cannon.

3. The physical fitness expert was a strong _____ of regular daily exercise.

4. Since I have been disappointed so often, I tend to be _____ about any plan that Vic proposes.

5. After visiting the concentration camp in 1945, she became a dedicated and _____ pursuer of Nazi war criminals.

Word Families

A. *On the line provided, write a **noun form** of each of the following words.*

EXAMPLE: venomous — **venom**

1. languid _____
2. bleak _____
3. diminutive _____
4. emancipate _____
5. contend _____
6. wily _____
7. erroneous _____
8. impair _____
9. invincible _____
10. rugged _____
11. skeptical _____
12. irreverent _____
13. concise _____
14. brawny _____
15. aspire _____
16. autocratic _____
17. maltreat _____
18. deteriorate _____
19. humane _____
20. obtrusive _____

B. *On the line provided, write a **verb** related to each of the following words:*

EXAMPLE: synthetic — **synthesize**

1. concerted _____
2. despicable _____
3. subversive _____

R

4. proponent _____

5. laborious _____

6. temperate _____

7. enlightened _____

8. depreciation _____

9. blasphemy _____

10. appreciable _____

11. obtrusive _____

12. extemporaneous _____

13. relentless _____

14. intolerable _____

15. irreverent _____

**Filling
the Blanks**

*Encircle the pair of words that best complete the
meaning of each of the following passages.*

1. I did everything I could to _____ his cunning attempts to
   undermine my authority in the company; unfortunately, he proved too
   _____ and persistent for me to anticipate all the time.
   - a. chide . . . impair
   - b. forestall . . . wily
   - c. divulge . . . slipshod
   - d. subvert . . . demure

2. Though a(n) _____ master might deal kindly and generously
   with the slaves, a cruel one would _____ and abuse them.
   - a. autocratic . . . impair
   - b. enlightened . . . emancipate
   - c. humane . . . maltreat
   - d. relentless . . . exploit

3. Her talents are just average, but she has _____ them to the
   fullest. On the other hand, he was given great natural abilities, but he has
   _____ them on trifles.
   - a. exploited . . . squandered
   - b. pondered . . . impaired
   - c. divulged . . . recouped
   - d. contended . . . forestalled

4. The _____ statistics cited in the magazine article certainly
   _____ its effectiveness. If the author had made sure that his
   figures were correct, his argument might have been more convincing.
   - a. bleak . . . quavered
   - b. laborious . . . enlightened
   - c. slipshod . . . rendered
   - d. erroneous . . . impaired

5. A ballerina's _____ and graceful figure contrasts sharply
   with a weight lifter's massively _____ physique.
   - a. demure . . . languid
   - b. lithe . . . brawny
   - c. diminutive . . . concise
   - d. slipshod . . . rugged

Analogies   *In each of the following, encircle the item that best completes the comparison.*

1. pensive is to **ponder** as
a. sardonic is to condone
b. incredulous is to believe
c. flippant is to suggest
d. skeptical is to doubt

2. irreverent is to **respect** as
a. irate is to anger
b. arbitrary is to sophistication
c. doleful is to joy
d. sterling is to wealth

3. brawny is to **strength** as
a. rugged is to genius
b. comely is to beauty
c. wily is to wisdom
d. lithe is to intelligence

4. illustrious is to **eminent** as
a. steadfast is to unflinching
b. cherubic is to devilish
c. ghastly is to humane
d. subversive is to obtrusive

5. words are to **garble** as
a. dreams are to succumb
b. hopes are to aspire
c. thoughts are to muddle
d. emotions are to forestall

6. chide is to **reprimand** as
a. squander is to salvage
b. abridge is to disentangle
c. recoil is to proliferate
d. compensate is to remunerate

7. emancipate is to **bondage** as
a. subjugate is to servitude
b. parole is to incarceration
c. liberate is to independence
d. adjourn is to convention

8. diffuse is to **concise** as
a. momentous is to significant
b. lackadaisical is to diligent
c. odious is to repugnant
d. lucrative is to obese

9. languid is to **vigor** as
a. bleak is to timeliness
b. sparse is to direction
c. stagnant is to motion
d. brazen is to intention

10. incessant is to **relentless** as
a. laborious is to arduous
b. superfluous is to essential
c. despicable is to credible
d. rabid is to apathetic

Shades of Meaning   *Read each sentence carefully. Then encircle the item that best completes the statement below the sentence.*

Students have for generations memorized and recited the pensive lines of Walt Whitman's great elegy "O Captain! My Captain!"   (2)

1. In line 1 the word **pensive** most nearly means
a. formal
b. thoughtful
c. melancholy
d. reflective

"Love is a spirit all compact of fire.
Not gross to sink, but light, and will aspire." (Shakespeare)   (2)

2. The word **aspire** in line 2 is used to mean
a. soar
b. yearn
c. seek
d. desire

Rugged weather had kept the fishing boats at their harbor moorings for the better part of a week.   (2)

3. The best definition for the word **Rugged** in line 1 is
a. Irregular
b. Rocky
c. Blunt
d. Stormy

CR

Fresh spinach must be blanched before it is sautéed for such dishes as eggs Florentine. (2)

4. In line 1 the word **blanched** is best defined as
a. whitened
b. discolored
c. seasoned
d. boiled briefly

That fortune hunters catch scent of her so quickly may be due to the fact that the heiress fairly reeks of money. (2)

5. The word **reeks** in line 2 most nearly means
a. spends huge amounts
b. smells unpleasantly
c. gives the impression
d. saves a great deal

Filling the Blanks *Encircle the pair of words that best complete the meaning of each of the following sentences.*

1. At the end of the grim novel, the spendthrift hero, who has recklessly _____ his entire fortune on riotous living, is buried in a _____ grave.
a. rejuvenated . . . vagrant's
b. impoverished . . . envoy's
c. relinquished . . . accomplice's
d. squandered . . . pauper's

2. Although the disastrous crash of 1929 did _____ many of those who had sunk money into the stock market, a few wily investors did eventually manage to _____ some or all of their losses.
a. impair . . . render
b. impoverish . . . recoup
c. reprieve . . . salvage
d. forestall . . . surmount

3. In verses that have resounded through the centuries, Homer recounts the daring _____ of the _____ heroes who fought so fearlessly beneath the walls of Troy.
a. exploits . . . intrepid
b. tirades . . . dissolute
c. statutes . . . subversive
d. hordes . . . militant

4. Reporters who are willing to tell a jury what they have learned but refuse to _____ their sources are _____ to be brought up on charges of contempt of court.
a. sully . . . immune
b. maltreat . . . concerted
c. console . . . fated
d. divulge . . . liable

5. Though I'm perfectly willing to put up with the occasional hour or two of _____ that my job involves, the prospect of spending my entire day on menial or unpleasant tasks is _____ .
a. larceny . . . daunting
b. fodder . . . repugnant
c. drudgery . . . intolerable
d. mire . . . despicable

Unit 13

Definitions *Note carefully the spelling, pronunciation, and definition of each of the following words. Then write the word in the blank space in the illustrative phrase following.*

1. ad infinitum
(ad in fə 'nī təm)

(*adv.*) endlessly

repeat a story _____

2. apportion
(ə 'pôr shən)

(*v.*) to divide and give out in shares

_____ the chores

3. bona fide
('bō nə fīd)

(*adj.*) genuine; sincere

a _____ masterpiece

4. buoyant
('boi ənt)

(*adj.*) able to float easily; able to hold things up; cheerful, hopeful

_____ kayaks bobbing down the rapids

5. clique
(klēk; klik)

(*n.*) a small, exclusive group of people

the ruling _____

6. concede
(kən 'sēd)

(*v.*) to admit as true; to yield, submit

refuse to _____ that she was right

7. congenial
(kən 'jēn yəl)

(*adj.*) getting on well with others; agreeable, pleasant

_____ companions

8. lofty
('lôf tē)

(*adj.*) very high; noble

_____ ideals

9. migration
(mī 'grā shən)

(*n.*) a movement from one country or region to another

the great _____ to the West

10. perceive
(pər 'sēv)

(*v.*) to be aware of through the senses, observe; to grasp mentally

_____ a change in her attitude

11. perverse
(pər 'vərs)

(*adj.*) inclined to go against what is expected; stubborn; turned away from what is good or proper

angered by his _____ attitude

12. prelude
('pre lüd)

(*n.*) an introduction; that which comes before or leads off

played the _____ to the opera

13. rancid
('ran sid)

(*adj.*) stale, spoiled

the sour odor of _____ butter

14. rustic
('rəs tik)

(*adj.*) countrylike; simple, plain; awkward; (*n.*) one who lives in the country

_____ cabins in the woods

15. sever
('sev ər)

(v.) to separate, divide into parts

_____ all ties with them

16. sordid
('sôr did)

(adj.) wretchedly poor; run-down; mean or selfish

the _____ conditions in the slum

17. untenable
(ən 'ten ə bəl)

(adj.) not capable of being held or defended; impossible to maintain

realized their arguments were _____

18. versatile
('vər sə təl)

(adj.) able to do many things well; capable of many uses

proved to be a _____ musician

19. vindicate
('vin də kāt)

(v.) to clear from hint or charge of wrongdoing; to defend successfully against opposition; to justify

_____ his honor

20. wane
(wān)

(v.) to lose size, strength, or power

watch the moon _____

Completing the Sentence

From the words for this unit, choose the one that best completes each of the following sentences. Write the word in the space provided.

1. We found it easy to float in the lake because the high salt content makes the water extremely _____ .

2. I am convinced that the Drama Club is run by a(n) _____ of students who reserve all the best roles for themselves!

3. It takes a really _____ athlete to win varsity letters in three different sports.

4. The accused clerk _____ himself by producing signed receipts for all the questioned items.

5. Since the theory is based on inaccurate and out-of-date information, it must therefore be regarded as _____ .

6. When the mayor failed to carry out his campaign promises, his popularity quickly _____ , and he failed to win reelection.

7. In 1776, the Continental Congress moved to _____ all political connections between the 13 colonies and Great Britain.

8. Isn't it boring when people go on and on about _their_ looks, _their_ clothes, and _their_ popularity _____ ?

9. New employees are assigned their duties by the office manager, who is responsible for _____ work among the staff.

CARLMONT HIGH SCHOOL TEXTBOOK

10. I realize that I made a bad mistake, but at least I possess the strength of character to _____ that I was wrong and apologize.

11. The oil, which had been inadvertently stored in a heated room, soon began to exude a rank odor that told us it had turned _____ .

12. It was only after we toured the area devastated by the explosion that we began to _____ how much damage had been done.

13. The Declaration of Independence first set forth the _____ standards to which we as a nation have ever since aspired.

14. Who would believe that this peaceful, _____ hideaway is only 25 miles from the inner city!

15. Dismissing all his rivals as impostors, the undefeated heavyweight boxer pronounced himself the only _____ contender for the crown.

16. It is a regrettable fact of our history that several Presidential administrations have been tainted by _____ scandals.

17. Although many of my friends seem to like him, I've never found him a particularly _____ companion.

18. The seasonal _____ of birds southward reminds us that we have come to the end of another summer vacation.

19. He is so _____ that he goes out of his way to do exactly what we don't want him to do.

20. That early cold spell proved to be a fitting _____ to one of the most severe winters of modern times.

Synonyms   From the words for this unit, choose the one that is most nearly **the same** in meaning as each of the following groups of expressions. Write the word on the line given.

1. an inner circle, coterie _____

2. rough, unsophisticated, countrified _____

3. adaptable, handy, all-around, many-sided _____

4. filthy, squalid; base, vile; seedy, sleazy _____

5. to acquit, absolve, exonerate; to advocate _____

6. to cut off, amputate; to break off, dissolve _____

7. to distribute, allot, parcel out, allocate _____

8. blithe, jaunty, lighthearted, animated _____

9. to diminish, decline, subside, dwindle _____

10. authentic, indisputable, legitimate, certified   _____

11. friendly, sociable, amiable, compatible   _____

12. indefensible, insupportable, groundless   _____

13. to acknowledge, grant, allow, assent   _____

14. elevated, towering; exalted, grand   _____

15. obstinate, contrary, mulish; wayward   _____

16. a preface, overture, prologue, "curtain raiser"   _____

17. a population shift, mass movement   _____

18. to notice, discern; to understand   _____

19. foul, rank, fetid, sour, rotten, putrid   _____

20. forever, unceasingly, incessantly, ceaselessly   _____

Antonyms   *From the words for this unit, choose the one that is most nearly* **opposite** *in meaning to each of the following groups of expressions. Write the word on the line given.*

1. disagreeable, surly; cold, standoffish   _____

2. to contest, dispute, gainsay, challenge   _____

3. an epilogue, postlude, aftermath   _____

4. citified, urban; sophisticated, suave   _____

5. to implicate, incriminate, condemn, convict   _____

6. downcast, depressed, gloomy, morose   _____

7. base, petty, low, sordid, despicable   _____

8. to miss, overlook, be blind to   _____

9. succinctly, concisely, tersely, briefly   _____

10. pure, noble; opulent, lavish   _____

11. to join, unite, weld together   _____

12. wholesome, fresh   _____

13. limited, specialized, restricted   _____

14. false, fake, bogus, spurious, counterfeit   _____

15. tractable, docile, amenable, yielding   _____

16. to grow, wax, amplify, balloon, increase   _____

17. irrefutable, impregnable, incontestable   _____

Choosing the Right Word   *Encircle the **boldface** word that more satisfactorily completes each of the following sentences.*

1. Leonardo da Vinci was a (**buoyant, versatile**) genius who excelled in many different fields of art and science.

2. My faith in that seemingly "ordinary" young girl was entirely (**vindicated, perceived**) many years later when she won the Pulitzer Prize in fiction.

3. The successful invasion of France in June, 1944 was only a (**prelude, clique**) to the great Allied victories that ended the war in Europe.

4. Because our tank forces had been destroyed, the position of the ground troops proved (**sordid, untenable**), and retreat was ordered.

5. Children are easily hurt and disappointed, but they are so (**buoyant, versatile**) that their bad moods rarely last long.

6. You are at a stage of life when you should begin to (**wane, sever**) the apron strings that tie you to your mother.

7. There are more than 100 members in the State Legislature, but the real power is held by a small (**clique, prelude**) of insiders.

8. A good politician must appear (**sordid, congenial**) even when he or she is feeling cross and unsociable.

9. The atmosphere in the tiny, airless cell soon grew as (**buoyant, rancid**) as the foul-smelling soup the prisoner was fed every night.

10. American society in recent years has been deeply affected by the steady (**migration, clique**) from the "inner city" to the suburbs.

11. Our problem now is not to (**sever, apportion**) blame for our failures but to find a way to achieve success.

12. Shakespeare's clowns are often simple (**cliques, rustics**) who are trying to behave like sophisticated men of the world.

13. I appreciate her interest in me, but I am annoyed by her tendency to offer criticism and advice (**bona fide, ad infinitum**).

14. The psychologist said that troubled young people often have a (**perverse, rancid**) impulse to do exactly what will be most injurious to them.

15. Good citizens should not sit by idly while the vitality of their community (**wanes, migrates**).

16. One of the aims of education is to enable us to (**perceive, sever**) the difference between what is truly excellent and what is second-rate.

17. He claimed to be an unselfish patriot, but we were aware that in reality he was acting from the most (**untenable, sordid**) motives.

18. When he came home from college for Christmas vacation, he treated us "high school kids" with (**congenial, lofty**) scorn.

19. He talks a great game of tennis, but I (**concede, wane**) nothing to him until he has shown that he can beat me on the court.

20. They will not be allowed to vote in the election because they are not considered (**ad infinitum, bona fide**) residents of this community.

Unit 14

Definitions

Note carefully the spelling, pronunciation, and definition of each of the following words. Then write the word in the blank space in the illustrative phrase following.

1. **annex**
(v., ə 'neks;
n., 'an eks)

(v.) to add to, attach; to incorporate; (n.) an attachment or addition

_____ the disputed territory

2. **cleave**
(klēv)

(v.) to cut or split open; to cling to

_____ the shield with one stroke

3. **cordial**
('kôr jəl)

(adj.) in a friendly manner, hearty; cheery; (n.) a liqueur

receive a _____ reception

4. **cornerstone**
('kôr nər stōn)

(n.) the starting point of a building; a fundamental principle or element

a _____ of our foreign policy

5. **debacle**
(di 'bäk əl)

(n.) an overwhelming defeat, rout; a complete collapse or failure

end in a _____

6. **devitalize**
(dē 'vīt ə līz)

(v.) to make weak or lifeless

_____ by the illness

7. **embroil**
(em 'broil)

(v.) to involve in a conflict or difficulty; to throw into confusion

could _____ our country in war

8. **exonerate**
(eg 'zän ə rāt)

(v.) to clear from a charge or accusation

evidence that _____ the defendant

9. **glib**
(glib)

(adj.) ready and fluent in speech; thoughtless, insincere

a _____ salesperson

10. **haphazard**
(hap 'haz ərd)

(adj.) by chance, not planned; lacking in order

unsuccessful in his _____ attempts

11. **improvise**
('im prə vīz)

(v.) to compose or perform without preparation; to construct from available materials

_____ an emergency shelter

12. **incite**
(in 'sīt)

(v.) to rouse, stir up, urge on

attempt to _____ a riot

13. **influx**
('in fləks)

(n.) a coming in, inflow

an _____ of frigid air

14. **pallor**
('pal ər)

(n.) an extreme or unnatural paleness

the _____ of illness

15. pedigree
('ped ə grē)
(*n.*) a list of ancestors, family tree; the history or origin of something

a racehorse's noble _____

16. precipitous
(pri 'sip ət əs)
(*adj.*) very steep

a _____ mountain trail

17. profuse
(prō 'fyüs)
(*adj.*) very abundant; given or flowing freely

_____ in his apologies

18. reconcile
('rek ən sīl)
(*v.*) to restore to friendship; to settle; to resign (oneself)

_____ two enemies

19. shackle
('shak əl)
(*v.*) to put into chains; (*n., usually pl.*) a chain, fetter

put _____ on the prisoner

20. threadbare
('thred bâr)
(*adj.*) shabby, old and worn

replacing his _____ suit

Completing the Sentence

From the words for this unit, choose the one that best completes each of the following sentences. Write the word in the space provided.

1. In the untended garden the weeds were so _____ that they all but smothered the few flowers that managed to blossom.

2. Of the millions of immigrants who came to America from all over the world, only the Africans arrived here in _____ .

3. People who are reasonably well satisfied with the government under which they live cannot be _____ to rise up against it.

4. He is certainly a(n) _____ talker, but does he have a firm grasp of the subjects he is discussing?

5. The heavy rains of June brought a(n) _____ of mosquitoes into the neighborhoods bordering the marshland.

6. His old-fashioned clothes were patched and _____ , but we could see that he had made every effort to keep them spotlessly clean.

7. The entertainer cleverly _____ limericks and other comic rhymes on subjects suggested by the audience.

8. His books are scattered around in such a(n) _____ manner that it is a mystery to me how he can find the ones he wants.

9. My dog Rover may look like a mutt at first glance, but in fact he has a distinguished _____ .

10. The Roman numeral MCMXCVI is inscribed on the commemorative plaque that adorns the _____ of the new building.

11. With one flashing stroke of his mighty axe, the skilled woodsman was able

to _____ the heavy branch from the tree trunk.

12. We certainly did not expect to receive such a(n) _____
greeting from someone who had been described to us as cold and
unsociable.

13. With all the worries I have on my mind at the moment, why would I want to

become _____ in other people's arguments?

14. After that humiliating loss to Henderson, can the Belleville squad rebound

from the _____ and regain its winning form?

15. With the Louisiana Purchase of 1803, Jefferson _____ a
vast territory that doubled the size of the nation.

16. As we grow older and perhaps wiser, we _____ ourselves
to the fact that we will never achieve all that we had hoped in life.

17. By proving that his 18th birthday came one day before the election,

Vincent was _____ of the charge of unlawful voting.

18. I saw nothing but peril in the prospect of trying to scale a cliff so sheer

and _____ that even expert climbers shied away from it.

19. Her deathly _____ and distraught expression told us she
had already received the tragic news.

20. She was so _____ by the illness that it was several weeks
before she could return to her job.

21. When Gwen was injured on the slopes, we had to _____ a
stretcher from our ski poles and jackets.

Synonyms   *From the words for this unit, choose the one that is most
nearly **the same** in meaning as each of the following
groups of expressions. Write the word on the line given.*

1. to entangle, ensnarl, involve   _____

2. superficial, pat; oily, unctuous, facile   _____

3. frayed, seedy, ragged, shopworn, trite   _____

4. to sever, halve, sunder; to adhere to, clasp   _____

5. random, accidental; slapdash   _____

6. a foundation, base, underpinning, support   _____

7. to spur, kindle, provoke, prompt, instigate   _____

8. handcuffs, bonds, irons; to manacle, enslave   _____

9. sheer, abrupt, sharp   _____

10. an inpouring, inrush, invasion _____

11. lineage, ancestry, genealogy _____

12. a disaster, calamity, fiasco _____

13. to ad-lib, play it by ear, wing it, extemporize _____

14. wanness, lividness, bloodlessness _____

15. to join, acquire, appropriate, procure _____

16. to unite, conciliate, "mend fences" _____

17. extravagant, lavish, bounteous, plenteous _____

18. hospitable, affable, warm, convivial _____

19. to absolve, acquit, vindicate, exculpate _____

20. to weaken, sap, enfeeble, enervate _____

Antonyms   *From the words for this unit, choose the one that is most nearly **opposite** in meaning to each of the following groups of expressions. Write the word on the line given.*

1. to plan, rehearse, practice, prepare _____

2. an outpouring, exodus, departure _____

3. gruff, unfriendly, unsociable _____

4. to separate, disconnect, disentangle _____

5. awkward, speechless, halting, tongue-tied _____

6. to free, liberate, emancipate _____

7. to implicate, incriminate, inculpate _____

8. a flush, blush; rosiness, bloom _____

9. sparse, scanty, meager, insufficient _____

10. deliberate, purposeful; orderly, meticulous _____

11. gradual, shallow, graded, incremental _____

12. to antagonize, alienate, drive a wedge between _____

13. a success, triumph, victory, coup _____

14. to enliven, stimulate, energize, excite _____

15. to check, curb, impede, restrain, smother _____

16. luxurious, plush, costly, sumptuous _____

Choosing the Right Word   *Encircle the **boldface** word that more satisfactorily completes each of the following sentences.*

1. The disaster was so great that the overcrowded hospital was forced to house some patients in a makeshift (**annex, influx**).

2. Although I had never even met her, the letters she wrote me were so (**cordial, glib**) that I felt we were old friends.

3. To seaside resorts, the annual (**influx, pallor**) of tourists marks the true beginning of the summer season.

4. We learned from the TV film that Spartacus was a Roman gladiator who (**reconciled, incited**) his fellow slaves to armed rebellion.

5. What we need is not *talkers* with (**glib, cordial**) solutions for all our problems, but *doers* who are prepared to pitch in and help.

6. We are tired of listening to those (**cordial, threadbare**) old excuses for your failure to keep your promises.

7. He is the kind of speaker who is more effective when he (**improvises, exonerates**) his remarks than when he reads from a prepared script.

8. True, he comes from an aristocratic family, but he won that promotion on the basis of merit, not because of his (**pedigree, cornerstone**).

9. In spite of all the progress made in recent years, we are still not entirely free from the (**shackles, profusions**) of prejudice and superstition.

10. How can he (**annex, reconcile**) his claim that he is a "good citizen" with the fact that he doesn't even bother to vote?

11. The elderly couple thanked me so (**haphazardly, profusely**) for the small favor I had done them that I was almost embarrassed.

12. The story of his unhappy childhood aroused our sympathy but did not (**exonerate, incite**) him from the charge of criminal assault.

13. With such a (**glib, haphazard**) way of keeping accounts, is it any wonder that your budget is a disaster area?

14. Separation of powers is one of the (**shackles, cornerstones**) upon which the American form of government is built.

15. The President said in his inaugural address that we must not become (**embroiled, exonerated**) in the quarrels of other nations.

16. Many of our foodstuffs are so (**annexed, devitalized**) by the processing operations that they lose both taste and nutritional value.

17. My campaign for the class presidency ended in an utter (**influx, debacle**) when I forgot my speech as I was about to address the assembly.

18. In a time of unrest and bewildering change, it is more important than ever to (**incite, cleave**) to the basic principles that give meaning to our lives.

19. Runaway inflation can cause a (**glib, precipitous**) decline in the value of a nation's currency.

20. The famous actor applied a layer of ashen makeup to simulate the ghastly (**pedigree, pallor**) of a ghost.

Unit 15

Definitions

Note carefully the spelling, pronunciation, and definition of each of the following words. Then write the word in the blank space in the illustrative phrase following.

1. abase
(ə 'bās)

(v.) to lower in esteem, degrade; to humble

refuse to _____ oneself

2. actuate
('ak chü āt)

(v.) to move to action; to impel

_____ by selfish motives

3. avert
(ə 'vərt)

(v.) to turn aside, turn away; to prevent, avoid

_____ his eyes

4. boorish
('bür ish)

(adj.) rude, unrefined; clumsy

offended by his _____ remarks

5. brunt
(brənt)

(n.) the main impact, force, or burden

bear the _____ of the attack

6. combatant
(kəm 'bat ənt)

(n.) a fighter; (adj.) engaged in fighting

separate the _____

7. dormant
('dôr mənt)

(adj.) inactive; in a state of suspension; sleeping

awakening the _____ buds

8. dubious
('dü bē əs)

(adj.) causing uncertainty or suspicion; in a doubtful or uncertain state of mind, hesitant

a _____ claim

9. harangue
(hə 'raŋ)

(v.) to deliver a loud, ranting speech; (n.) a loud speech

an intemperate _____

10. harry
('har ē)

(v.) to make a destructive raid on; to torment, harass

_____ the defenseless villagers

11. impenitent
(im 'pen ə tənt)

(adj.) not feeling remorse or sorrow for errors or offenses

an _____ thief

12. knave
(nāv)

(n.) a tricky, deceitful, or unprincipled fellow

swindled by a _____

13. legion
('lē jən)

(n.) a large military force; any large group or number; (adj.) many, numerous

joined the Foreign _____

14. liberality
(lib ə 'ral ə tē)

(n.) generosity, generous act; breadth of mind or outlook

renowned for her _____

15. plaintiff
('plān tif)

(n.) one who begins a lawsuit

interview the _____ in the case

16. probe
(prōb)

(*v.*) to examine, investigate thoroughly; (*n.*) an investigation; a device used to explore or examine

_____ the source of the funds

17. protract
(prō ′trakt)

(*v.*) to draw out or lengthen in time or space

a ruse to _____ the trial

18. quarry
(′kwär ē)

(*n.*) a place from which stone is taken; something that is hunted or pursued; (*v.*) to cut or take from (or as if from) a quarry

work in the local marble _____

19. spurn
(spərn)

(*v.*) to refuse with scorn, disdain

decide to _____ the offer

20. subterfuge
(′səb tər fyüj)

(*n.*) an excuse or trick for escaping or hiding something

a _____ to avoid admitting guilt

Completing the Sentence

From the words for this unit, choose the one that best completes each of the following sentences. Write the word in the space provided.

1. The entire boardwalk at the beach was smashed to bits when the full

   _____ of the hurricane struck it.

2. In A.D. 79, the sudden and violent eruption of a volcano that had been

   _____ for many years destroyed Pompeii in two days.

3. His sudden fainting spell was a(n) _____ to get out of taking me to the Spring Dance!

4. Fortunately, the loud and generally _____ behavior of a few of the guests did not spoil the party for the rest of us.

5. Divers from the salvage ship will try to _____ the ocean floor where the Confederate warship sank in 1863.

6. As a lawyer for the _____ , you will have full opportunity to cross-examine the witnesses for the defendant.

7. The police were quickly ordered to the scene as a precautionary measure

   to _____ a threatened riot.

8. At Julius Caesar's funeral, Shakespeare tells us, Mark Antony stirred up the

   Roman mob with a ringing _____ .

9. Why should you _____ yourself by begging to be admitted to a club made up of snobs and phonies?

10. Isn't friendship with a person who mistrusts you of _____ value?

11. The soldiers of the mighty Roman _____ were organized in battle units called cohorts and maniples.

12. We learned that the bizarre sequence of events was _____ by an accidental tug on the switching device.

13. His many donations of large sums of money to organizations dedicated to relieving world hunger are evidence of his _____ .

14. The bloodhounds pursued their human _____ through the swamps.

15. Our planned stopover in Denver was unexpectedly _____ when a blizzard prevented us from leaving the city for days.

16. On the surface she seemed stubbornly _____ , but secretly she regretted the damage her thoughtlessness had caused.

17. The two _____ fought it out with words rather than with fists.

18. The Mississippi riverboats were home to crooks and _____ of every description, from cardsharps to confidence men.

19. Because his feelings were hurt, he _____ any attempts on my part to provide help.

20. Bands of guerillas _____ the straggling soldiers as they retreated in disarray.

21. The "Speakers' Corner" in London's Hyde Park is home to soapbox orators who _____ idlers and passersby.

22. After his talents had lain _____ for many years, he suddenly produced the masterpiece on which his reputation is based.

Synonyms   *From the words for this unit, choose the one that is most nearly **the same** in meaning as each of the following groups of expressions. Write the word on the line given.*

1. remorseless, unrepentant, incorrigible   _____

2. a tirade, diatribe; to rant, lecture   _____

3. largess, magnanimity, broad-mindedness   _____

4. prey, game, victim; an excavation, pit, mine   _____

5. to turn down, reject, decline, snub, repudiate   _____

6. vulgar, crude, uncouth, ill-mannered, gauche   _____

7. to prolong, extend, elongate, spin out   _____

8. a rascal, rogue, scoundrel, miscreant   _____

9. to explore, scrutinize; an inquiry; a detector   _____

10. a multitude, host, throng; a division, regiment _____

11. a soldier, warrior, disputant; hostile, battling _____

12. a complainant, accuser _____

13. to badger, pester, hound; to pillage, ravage _____

14. to trigger, incite, impel, instigate _____

15. resting, still, quiescent _____

16. a dodge, blind, ruse, deception, artifice _____

17. questionable, suspect; unsettled, undecided _____

18. to stop, deflect, ward off; to preclude _____

19. to lower, humiliate, prostrate, demean _____

20. the main force, impact _____

Antonyms   *From the words for this unit, choose the one that is most nearly **opposite** in meaning to each of the following groups of expressions. Write the word on the line given.*

1. to accept, welcome, greet _____

2. a hunter, predator, pursuer _____

3. a defendant, the accused _____

4. certain, positive; indubitable, reliable _____

5. awake, active, lively, productive _____

6. stinginess, miserliness, narrow-mindedness _____

7. to elevate, ennoble, exalt _____

8. a civilian; neutral, peaceful _____

9. to contract, compress, concentrate _____

10. the aftershock, aftermath, repercussion _____

11. ashamed, remorseful, contrite, apologetic _____

12. suave, urbane, polished, courtly, well-bred _____

13. few, sparse; a squad, platoon _____

14. to conceal, hide; a cover-up, whitewash _____

15. a whisper, murmur, undertone _____

16. to invite, induce, provoke, cause _____

Choosing the Right Word *Encircle the **boldface** word that more satisfactorily completes each of the following sentences.*

1. A pack of reporters (**spurned, harried**) the Senator with pointed and persistent questions even as he was being whisked into his limousine.

2. Since the prisoner remained defiantly (**impenitent, boorish**), the review panel saw no reason for granting him parole.

3. We demand that the committee be made up of legislators who will (**probe, actuate**) fearlessly into the causes of the energy crisis.

4. He pretended to be speechless with anger, but we recognized this as a (**subterfuge, harangue**) to avoid answering the charges against him.

5. How can that heartless beauty (**combat, spurn**) my offers of devotion!

6. When the referee called back a touchdown by the home team, he had to bear the (**probe, brunt**) of the crowd's anger.

7. After World War II, the United States and the Soviet Union became locked in a(n) (**protracted, actuated**) struggle known as the Cold War.

8. Let us not (**avert, spurn**) our attention from the sufferings of the people living in the slums of our community.

9. At a time when we need good will and cooperation, nothing will be gained by an emotional (**quarry, harangue**) about old abuses and mistakes.

10. It is written in the Bible that "whosoever shall humble himself shall be exalted, and he that shall exalt himself shall be (**dormant, abased**)."

11. A new popular singing idol will often (**actuate, abase**) changes in clothing fashions.

12. Since his absurd scheme was never really intended to harm us, we regard him as more of a fool than a (**quarry, knave**).

13. For many years after the Civil War, thousands of (**combatants, legions**) in the great battle of Gettysburg met in annual reunions.

14. The dinner to celebrate the 50th anniversary of Mrs. Roth's teaching career was attended by a (**legion, probe**) of her former students.

15. I think that we can settle this dispute in a friendly way, without either of us becoming a defendant or a (**quarry, plaintiff**).

16. People who think only of themselves, with no concern for the feelings of others, are bound to be (**brunt, boorish**).

17. Your (**liberality, subterfuge**) is to be admired, but it must be controlled so that it is not out of proportion to your means.

18. The detective story was so cleverly constructed that the character whom we took to be the pursuer turned out to be the (**quarry, brunt**).

19. During the Great Depression millions of Americans were out of work as much of the nation's productive capacity lay (**dormant, impenitent**).

20. We began with confidence in his success in the election, but as he made one mistake after another, we grew more and more (**dubious, abased**).

Review Units 13–15

Analogies *In each of the following, encircle the item that best completes the comparison.*

1. **moon** is to **wane** as
a. sun is to shine
b. volcano is to erupt
c. planet is to revolve
d. tide is to ebb

2. **liberal** is to **open hand** as
a. taciturn is to green thumb
b. dour is to glad hand
c. stingy is to tight fist
d. talkative is to closed mouth

3. **vindicate** is to **exonerate** as
a. incite is to arouse
b. perceive is to ignore
c. spurn is to accept
d. embroil is to roast

4. **prelude** is to **opera** as
a. overture is to novel
b. preface is to sculpture
c. footnote is to report
d. prologue is to play

5. **shackle** is to **slave** as
a. helmet is to quarterback
b. crown is to king
c. beret is to fool
d. tiara is to artist

6. **sever** is to **apart** as
a. apportion is to together
b. improvise is to apart
c. reconcile is to together
d. actuate is to apart

7. **war** is to **combatant** as
a. game show is to contestant
b. debate is to mediator
c. boxing match is to spectator
d. footrace is to panelist

8. **untenable** is to **hold** as
a. inedible is to cook
b. inflammable is to hear
c. indomitable is to wound
d. immobile is to move

9. **boor** is to **rude** as
a. skinflint is to profuse
b. miser is to cordial
c. knave is to wicked
d. plaintiff is to impenitent

10. **pallor** is to **ghost** as
a. red is to knave
b. tan is to sunbather
c. blue is to plaintiff
d. green is to recluse

11. **sordid** is to **unfavorable** as
a. perverse is to favorable
b. congenial is to unfavorable
c. versatile is to favorable
d. buoyant is to unfavorable

12. **rancid** is to **butter** as
a. tepid is to tea
b. pasteurized is to milk
c. aromatic is to coffee
d. tainted is to water

13. **skyscraper** is to **lofty** as
a. mansion is to sordid
b. log cabin is to rustic
c. car wash is to glib
d. quarry is to dubious

14. **annex** is to **more** as
a. influx is to less
b. cornerstone is to more
c. eclipse is to less
d. debacle is to more

15. **protract** is to **duration** as
a. enlarge is to scale
b. reduce is to diet
c. concede is to size
d. cleave is to length

16. **threadbare** is to **suit** as
a. obsolete is to model
b. bald is to tire
c. scratched is to surface
d. latent is to talent

17. **legion** is to **many** as
a. migration is to few
b. brunt is to many
c. clique is to few
d. probe is to many

18. **dormant** is to **volcano** as
a. fertile is to valley
b. lukewarm is to bath
c. rundown is to building
d. fallow is to field

Definitions *In each of the following groups, encircle the word that is most nearly **the same** in meaning as the introductory expression.*

1. accept as true
   actuate   concede   exonerate   improvise

2. sap someone's strength
   devitalize   incite   probe   reconcile

3. musical introduction
   pedigree   influx   migration   prelude

4. lessen in size or extent
   vindicate   sever   perceive   wane

5. remain faithful
   exonerate   embroil   concede   cleave

6. country dweller
   rustic   perverse   bona fide   dormant

7. discover through the senses
   concede   perceive   spurn   avert

8. unprincipled or deceitful person
   combatant   knave   plaintiff   liberality

9. the object of a hunt
   annex   reconcile   abase   quarry

10. unable to be defended
    versatile   dormant   haphazard   untenable

11. steeply sloping
    sordid   congenial   precipitous   buoyant

12. involve in difficulties
    spurn   protract   avert   embroil

13. anything that prevents free action
    cornerstone   shackle   subterfuge   debacle

14. very large number
    clique   legion   pallor   brunt

15. lacking depth and forethought
    untenable   versatile   glib   rancid

16. cut off completely
    devitalize   improvise   sever   wane

17. marked by lack of order or direction
    boorish   haphazard   lofty   profuse

18. unrepentant
    impenitent   cordial   versatile   bona fide

19. shabby or overused
    lofty   ad infinitum   dubious   threadbare

20. reject with contempt
    harangue   harry   apportion   spurn

Shades of Meaning *Read each sentence carefully. Then encircle the item that best completes the statement below the sentence.*

Only a fool would regard as bona fide the declarations of friendship offered by so shameless a double-dealer as he. (2)

1. In line 1 the phrase **bona fide** is best defined as
a. proven
b. sincere
c. certified
d. bogus

The peace commission invited representatives of the combatant parties to talks aimed at bringing the bloodshed to an end. (2)

2. The word **combatant** in line 1 most nearly means
a. warring
b. neutral
c. diplomatic
d. wounded

Of as much interest as the exquisite workmanship of the ancient silver goblet was its notorious pedigree. (2)

3. The best definition of the word **pedigree** in line 2 is
a. breeding
b. family
c. price
d. history

In my opinion the auctioneer's assistant was far too boorish to be entrusted with objects so fragile and costly as those. (2)

4. In line 1 the word **boorish** most nearly means
a. rude
b. clumsy
c. young
d. snobbish

Though the two politicians claimed to be reconciled, there were strong hints that some hard feelings remained. (2)

5. The word **reconciled** in line 1 is best defined as
a. resigned
b. allied
c. restored to friendship
d. victorious

Antonyms *In each of the following groups, encircle the word that is most nearly **opposite** in meaning to the word in **boldface type**.*

1. quarry
a. marble
b. hunter
c. deer
d. mine

2. spurn
a. accept
b. reject
c. encourage
d. discourage

3. liberality
a. friendliness
b. stinginess
c. conservatism
d. reactionary

4. rustic
a. urban
b. crude
c. wrong
d. isolated

5. profuse
a. expensive
b. sparse
c. active
d. gruff

6. buoyant
a. swimming
b. dry
c. depressed
d. expensive

7. lofty
a. heavy
b. lowly
c. level
d. uneven

8. migrate
a. fly
b. develop
c. lose
d. remain

9. apportioned
a. undivided
b. emptied
c. sold
d. bought

10. incite
a. rebel
b. befriend
c. alarm
d. discourage

11. abase
a. strike out
b. cover
c. elevate
d. stall

12. cordial
a. urban
b. mellow
c. ruddy
d. hostile

13. dormant
a. quiescent
b. active
c. willing
d. present

14. sever
a. slice
b. finish
c. polish
d. join

15. concede
a. dispute
b. permit
c. review
d. follow

16. haphazard
a. risky
b. deliberate
c. random
d. delightful

Completing the Sentence
From the following list of words choose the one that best completes each of the sentences below. Write the word in the space provided.

Group A

clique	pedigree	influx	apportion
wane	lofty	haphazard	versatile
prelude	incite	shackle	subterfuge

1. His influence over us _____ from the moment we realized that he was tricky and insincere.

2. My mother decided to _____ among her children the responsibilities involved in running the household.

3. His _____ methods of work in the lab did not please the supervisor, who expected technicians to be skilled and conscientious.

4. The coach's arguments with the referee seemed to _____ the crowd to the point of violence.

5. I resent the _____ attitude which he takes toward people he considers his "inferiors."

Group B

probe	debacle	migration	buoyant
dormant	sordid	rustic	harangue
liberality	ad infinitum	avert	profuse

1. Instead of describing the pleasures of her summer at the lake, Stephanie delivered a(n) _____ about the evils of motorboats.

2. Since we have run out of money, our plan to buy new bicycles will have to remain _____ for the time being.

3. It is generally agreed that the _____ from Asia of the people who were first to inhabit North America occurred during the last Ice Age.

R

4. Our government is committed to preventing a repetition of the horrendous economic _____ of the 1930s.

5. A Senate committee will _____ alleged waste in military spending.

Word Families

A. *On the line provided, write a* **noun form** *of each of the following words.*

EXAMPLE: annex — **annexation**

1. dormant _____

2. boorish _____

3. profuse _____

4. vindicate _____

5. buoyant _____

6. concede _____

7. congenial _____

8. perceive _____

9. rancid _____

10. rustic _____

11. sever _____

12. apportion _____

13. cordial _____

14. exonerate _____

15. devitalize _____

16. lofty _____

17. perverse _____

18. versatile _____

19. reconcile _____

20. improvise _____

B. *On the line provided, write a* **verb** *related to each of the following words.*

EXAMPLE: combatant — **combat**

1. buoyant _____

2. perverse _____

3. migration _____

4. rustic _____

5. dubious _____

**Filling
the Blanks**   *Encircle the pair of words that best complete the
meaning of each of the following passages.*

1. Though urban life may suit some people to a tee, I have always found a
   _____ environment more _____ .
   a. lofty . . . protracted
   b. sordid . . . perverse
   c. cordial . . . haphazard
   d. rustic . . . congenial

2. We can go ahead with this project just as soon as we know we have the
   money to finance it in the bank. Unfortunately, the plan must remain
   _____ as long as the necessary financial resources are
   _____ .
   a. untenable . . . profuse
   b. dormant . . . dubious
   c. sordid . . . haphazard
   d. bona fide . . . perverse

3. "You'll usually win a debate if your arguments are valid and convincing," I
   observed. "But if your position is _____ , you'll eventually
   be forced to _____ defeat."
   a. untenable . . . concede
   b. dubious . . . spurn
   c. bona fide . . . avert
   d. glib . . . improvise

4. Over the years, the _____ of our patrons and sponsors has
   kept the wolf from our door more than once. Without their generous
   support, I honestly don't know how our little theater company would have
   _____ disaster.
   a. clique . . . reconciled
   b. versatility . . . spurned
   c. liberality . . . averted
   d. migration . . . shackled

5. Most dictators don't just address their audiences; they _____
   them. Their words are not meant to soothe or enlighten; they are designed
   to _____ the listener to violence and hatred.
   a. harangue . . . incite
   b. probe . . . harry
   c. apportion . . . reconcile
   d. improvise . . . embroil

6. As Great Britain's power and prestige began to _____ and
   lose their luster, subject peoples all over the empire rose up to demand
   release from the onerous _____ that bound them so firmly
   to the motherland.
   a. cleave . . . subterfuges
   b. pall . . . cornerstones
   c. wane . . . shackles
   d. concede . . . cliques

7. Before the curtain goes up on the first act, the orchestra plays a short
   _____ depicting in musical terms the _____
   ideals of the high-minded knight who is the hero of the opera.
   a. debacle . . . buoyant
   b. prelude . . . lofty
   c. brunt . . . glib
   d. pedigree . . . threadbare

Analogies   *In each of the following, encircle the item that best completes the comparison.*

1. brawny is to **build** as
a. comely is to age
b. diminutive is to size
c. prim is to weight
d. pensive is to shape

2. shackle is to **unfetter** as
a. subjugate is to emancipate
b. vindicate is to exonerate
c. compensate is to remunerate
d. assimilate is to escalate

3. influx is to **exodus** as
a. breach is to rift
b. statute is to law
c. realm is to metropolis
d. advent is to departure

4. tenacious is to **relinquish** as
a. diligent is to toil
b. unflinching is to recoil
c. incredulous is to doubt
d. relentless is to perceive

5. dormant is to **activity** as
a. diffuse is to vigor
b. obtrusive is to focus
c. stagnant is to movement
d. concise is to punch

6. vagrant is to **migrate** as
a. combatant is to contend
b. pauper is to dissent
c. accomplice is to prattle
d. knave is to meander

7. impenitent is to **atone** as
a. invincible is to conquer
b. sardonic is to jeer
c. pugnacious is to fight
d. irreverent is to honor

8. sparse is to **profuse** as
a. intricate is to superfluous
b. garbled is to lucid
c. grievous is to sordid
d. preposterous is to exorbitant

9. devitalize is to **rejuvenate** as
a. impair is to damage
b. proliferate is to snowball
c. deteriorate is to rally
d. fortify is to bolster

10. miserly is to **liberality** as
a. timid is to pugnacity
b. persistent is to tenacity
c. brazen is to temerity
d. genial is to cordiality

11. tirade is to **harangue** as
a. anarchy is to order
b. business is to drudgery
c. quandary is to dilemma
d. epilogue is to preamble

12. skeptic is to **dubious** as
a. customer is to irate
b. coward is to intrepid
c. host is to boorish
d. crybaby is to doleful

13. wane is to **dwindle** as
a. estrange is to reconcile
b. garble is to muddle
c. incinerate is to inundate
d. hamper is to facilitate

14. hatchet is to **cleave** as
a. scalpel is to probe
b. rasp is to saw
c. ax is to hew
d. shovel is to sever

15. bona fide is to **bogus** as
a. biased is to prejudiced
b. cunning is to wily
c. perilous is to dangerous
d. authentic is to spurious

16. quarry is to **hunter** as
a. booty is to marauder
b. message is to envoy
c. protest is to militant
d. larceny is to brigand

17. goods are to **shoddy** as
a. possessions are to subversive
b. methods are to slipshod
c. finances are to sordid
d. clothes are to haphazard

18. extemporaneous is to **improvise** as
a. erroneous is to rectify
b. heterogeneous is to exploit
c. synthetic is to fabricate
d. versatile is to protract

19. intolerable is to **endure** as
a. untenable is to maintain
b. unbridled is to grasp
c. invincible is to hoard
d. unflagging is to enjoy

20. buoyant is to **float** as
a. autocratic is to warp
b. plastic is to bounce
c. erratic is to spring
d. elastic is to recoil

21. reek is to **smell** as
a. breach is to sight
b. hew is to taste
c. rasp is to sound
d. feign is to touch

22. course is to **erratic** as
a. claim is to spurious
b. handwriting is to illegible
c. publication is to posthumous
d. pitch is to wild

23. militant is to **act** as
a. circumspect is to hurry
b. surly is to behave
c. sprightly is to loiter
d. pensive is to think

24. heterogeneous is to **uniformity** as
a. sardonic is to bite
b. terse is to edge
c. diffuse is to focus
d. paramount is to clout

25. admonish is to **mild** as
a. prattle is to severe
b. revile is to mild
c. reprimand is to severe
d. taunt is to mild

26. surmount is to **triumph** as
a. usurp is to defeat
b. abridge is to triumph
c. succumb is to defeat
d. deadlock is to triumph

Shades of Meaning

Read each sentence carefully. Then encircle the item that best completes the statement below the sentence.

The lot that saw the most spirited bidding of the evening was a set of hand-cut eighteenth-century cordial glasses. (2)

1. In line 2 the word **cordial** is best defined as
a. hospitality
b. liqueur
c. friendship
d. ceremony

Engineers used robotic probes equipped with radiation meters to check the interior of the stricken reactor. (2)

2. The word **probes** in line 1 most nearly means
a. private investigators
b. cross-examinations
c. detectors
d. trial balloons

The scullery maid used a scuttle to carry coal from the bin in the cellar to the kitchen stove. (2)

3. In line 1 the word **scuttle** is used to mean
a. scurry
b. sink
c. wagon
d. pail

Language students soon discover that in every tongue there are expressions impossible to render satisfactorily in another. (2)

4. In line 2 the word **render** most nearly means
a. reproduce
b. extract
c. memorize
d. submit

CR

"It is my burning hope," quoth he, "that never come the day
When from my face thou shouldst avert thy noble azure gaze." **(2)**
    (A.E. Glug, *The Clodyssey* IV, 471–472)

5. The word **avert** in line 2 is best defined as
   a. avoid   c. preclude
   b. turn away   d. detour

**Filling
the Blanks**   *Encircle the pair of words that best complete the
meaning of each of the following sentences or sets of
sentences.*

1. Dense woods intersected by small streams and _____ give
   the area in which I live a decidedly _____ appearance.
   a. precipices . . . perennial   c. rivulets . . . rustic
   b. mire . . . impoverished   d. interims . . . repugnant

2. There are some people who might not be so moved by the sight, but I still
   _____ in horror and disgust when I see old film clips of
   Adolf Hitler _____ his followers at the Nuremberg rallies of
   the 1930s.
   a. dilate . . . inciting   c. succumb . . . maligning
   b. recoil . . . haranguing   d. feint . . . impelling

3. The _____ in the case were seeking _____
   for damage they claimed the defendants had done to the lawn and garden
   in the course of putting a new wing on the house.
   a. plaintiffs . . . compensation   c. catalysts . . . depreciation
   b. brigands . . . maltreatment   d. incorrigibles . . . remuneration

4. When the refrigerator began to _____ like overripe cheese,
   I checked its contents for a rotten egg or some _____
   butter.
   a. blanch . . . pliant   c. reek . . . rancid
   b. feign . . . bleak   d. defray . . . mediocre

5. If the Kaiser and his saber-rattling cronies had been less _____
   in their attitudes, the First World War and the horrible waste of human life it
   entailed might both have been _____ .
   a. pugnacious . . . averted   c. circumspect . . . forestalled
   b. boorish . . . actuated   d. opinionated . . . facilitated

6. Every Friday afternoon of summer, millions of urban Americans join the
   _____ to our beaches and shorelines in a determined and
   sometimes wholly unsuccessful attempt to replace an unbecoming winter
   _____ with a healthy tan.
   a. expulsion . . . prognosis   c. venture . . . cubicle
   b. advent . . . pedigree   d. exodus . . . pallor

7. The play ends happily, however, when one of the gods descends from heaven in a fiery chariot to _____ the knotted threads of the plot and _____ the lovers from the horrible death to which they have been condemned.

a. incinerate . . . supplant
b. rectify . . . hew
c. defray . . . succumb
d. disentangle . . . reprieve

8. In 1980, a violent volcanic eruption transformed the _____ alpine terrain around Mount St. Helens into a barren wasteland as _____ and uninviting as any lunar landscape.

a. relentless . . . obtrusive
b. laborious . . . slipshod
c. staccato . . . subversive
d. rugged . . . bleak

9. During the _____ , people throughout Europe strove to _____ their minds from the bonds of obsolete ideas and attitudes that often harked back to the Dark Ages, hundreds of years before.

a. Age of the Autocrats . . . render
b. Skeptical Era . . . divulge
c. Enlightenment . . . emancipate
d. Great Depreciation . . . mire

10. Although I had tried my best to _____ the tasks involved in the project as evenly as possible, I found to my horror that those who were most capable had, as usual, been forced to bear the _____ of the workload.

a. reconcile . . . influx
b. exonerate . . . pallor
c. improvise . . . cornerstone
d. apportion . . . brunt

Final Mastery Test

I. Selecting Word Meanings

*In each of the following groups, encircle the word or expression that is most nearly **the same** in meaning as the word in **boldface type** in the introductory phrase.*

1. **admonish** the child
   a. dress   b. teach   c. praise   d. warn

2. **efface** a wrong
   a. discover   b. wipe out   c. hide   d. apologize for

3. a **perennial** favorite
   a. old-fashioned   b. recent   c. temporary   d. enduring

4. **subjugate** the enemy
   a. torture   b. release   c. kill   d. defeat

5. **dissolute** behavior
   a. unsuccessful   b. stylish   c. immoral   d. modest

6. **jeer at** our efforts
   a. examine   b. reject   c. criticize   d. ridicule

7. a firm **adherent**
   a. enemy   b. outsider   c. supporter   d. student

8. a **semblance** of order
   a. appearance   b. lack   c. result   d. opposite

9. an **irate** guest
   a. sociable   b. welcome   c. talkative   d. angry

10. a brief **altercation**
    a. shower   b. argument   c. relief   d. statement

11. an **intrepid** camper
    a. tireless   b. strong   c. fearless   d. skilled

12. **revile** the driver
    a. adore   b. train   c. pay   d. abuse

13. made a **trite** remark
    a. stale   b. witty   c. original   d. in bad taste

14. **rectify** an impression
    a. explain   b. make   c. correct   d. confirm

15. **daunted** by their threats
    a. encouraged   b. ridiculed   c. destroyed   d. intimidated

16. a child's **prattle**
    a. clothing   b. outlook   c. play   d. talk

17. **brazen** conduct
    a. shameless   b. modest   c. deadly   d. acceptable

18. a major **exodus**
    a. entrance   b. discussion   c. departure   d. battle

19. an **impoverished** neighbor
    a. learned   b. poor   c. beloved   d. unfriendly

20. a **lucid** explanation
    a. clear   b. inadequate   c. learned   d. foolish

II. Synonyms

In each of the following groups, encircle the two words or expressions that are most nearly **the same** *in meaning.*

21. a. institute   b. end   c. improve   d. begin

22. a. increase   b. venture   c. escalate   d. sever

23. a. supporter   b. proponent   c. opponent   d. plaintiff

24. a. rugged   b. rustic   c. pliant   d. rough

25. a. sweet   b. candid   c. outspoken   d. alert

26. a. skeptical   b. relentless   c. well-educated   d. doubting

27. a. rancid   b. garbled   c. confused   d. latent

28. a. scream   b. draw back   c. avert   d. recoil

29. a. destroy   b. build up   c. annihilate   d. torture

30. a. liability   b. conciseness   c. brevity   d. prelude

31. a. protest   b. quaver   c. waste   d. squander

32. a. introduction   b. tirade   c. catalyst   d. preamble

33. a. advent   b. expulsion   c. arrival   d. opposition

34. a. profuse   b. scarce   c. sincere   d. plentiful

35. a. awkward   b. skilled   c. concerted   d. adept

III. Antonyms

In each of the following groups, encircle the two words that are most nearly **opposite** *in meaning.*

36. a. commandeer   b. actuate   c. hoodwink   d. terminate

37. a. emancipate   b. fortify   c. shackle   d. taunt

38. a. glib   b. lofty   c. abased   d. alien

39. a. lucid   b. opaque   c. lithe   d. rabid

40. a. languid   b. illustrious   c. haphazard   d. circumspect

41. a. embroil   b. disentangle   c. defray   d. abscond

42. a. apportion   b. rejuvenate   c. incite   d. devitalize

43. a. annex   b. reek   c. surmount   d. succumb

44. a. tenacious   b. repugnant   c. comely   d. cumbersome

45. a. versatile   b. bona fide   c. bogus   d. biased

FMT

IV. **Supplying Words** *In each of the sentences below, write in the blank space the*
in Context *most appropriate word chosen from the following list.*

Group A

abridge	relentless	depreciation	malign
pilfer	untenable	impair	shoddy
terse	dilemma	taunt	wily
recoup	stagnant	immunity	exorcise

46. All that we heard from him was the _____ message, "I have
arrived."

47. So there was my _____ : either to keep working at a job I hated,
or to quit and find myself unemployed and all but penniless.

48. The suspect agreed to testify against the other conspirators in exchange for
_____ from prosecution.

49. His job was to _____ the two-volume biography into a single,
medium-sized book.

50. Then they began the _____ pursuit of the escaped criminal that
was to last for many weeks.

51. He who begins by _____ pennies may end by stealing millions.

52. As he presented his explanation of the causes of inflation, his position seemed to
me weak and _____ .

53. Lack of practice will certainly _____ your tennis game.

54. Not until later did I realize how his _____ strategy had saved us
from defeat.

55. A piece of furniture that costs so little must be _____ in its
construction.

Group B

predispose	despicable	incessant	spasmodic
wane	access	exorbitant	intricate
bleak	realm	interim	flippant
impel	apex	debris	relinquish

56. As night came on and it became much colder, the courage of the runaways
_____ .

57. The President stands at the very _____ of power in our national
government.

58. Although I am no public speaker, I feel _____ to say a few words
in his defense.

59. In the _____ between the two semesters, we will enjoy a brief vacation.

60. Scattered all over the beach was _____ from the wrecked ship.

61. Do you realize how _____ a job it is to reschedule the programs of hundreds of students?

62. We felt rather gloomy as we looked out at the _____ winter scene.

63. Their charge for preparing a tax return is so _____ that I am going to do the work myself.

64. The _____ chatter of the birds kept us awake for many hours.

65. His _____ wisecracks were clever but in bad taste.

| V. | **Words That Describe People** | *Some words that describe people are listed below. Write the appropriate word on the line next to each of the following descriptions.* |

accomplice	**buoyant**	**irreverent**	**alien**
brawny	**unflinching**	**arbitrary**	**enlightened**
opinionated	**autocratic**	**despicable**	**momentous**
impenitent	**sterling**	**vagrant**	**knave**

66. The poor homeless man trudged through the city streets, hoping to find a night's lodging. _____

67. She is well informed on social problems, and takes a humane, forward-looking attitude toward them. _____

68. Tom is a big, strong fellow with muscles that he hasn't used yet. _____

69. George III of England believed that it was his right to rule the American colonists with an iron hand. _____

70. Laura always looks on the bright side of things and refuses to be gloomy, even when the situation is discouraging. _____

71. The police arrested the man who had assisted the bank robber by acting as a lookout. _____

72. In my opinion, Tom fails to show the proper respect for things that many people consider sacred. _____

73. Since he was convinced that he had done no wrong, Rod felt no pangs of conscience. _____

74. The pioneers faced many hardships without thought of turning back. _____

FMT

75. She is set in her ideas and refuses even to consider that she may be wrong.

_____

VI. Words Connected with Occupations *The words in Column A may be applied to occupations and professions. In the space before each word, write the **letter** of the item in Column B that best identifies it.*

Column A	**Column B**
_____ **76.** improvise	a. a physician's forecast
_____ **77.** fodder	b. a defense attorney's forte
_____ **78.** envoy	c. material in a junkyard
_____ **79.** statute	d. oil painting
_____ **80.** rebuttal	e. often done by jazz musicians
_____ **81.** salvage	f. offered by a clergyman
_____ **82.** probe	g. representative of our government abroad
_____ **83.** consolation	h. head of a school
_____ **84.** prognosis	i. used by a farmer to feed livestock
_____ **85.** fabricate	j. law passed by the state legislature
	k. job of Senate investigating committee
	l. put together parts, as in a factory

VII. Word Associations *In each of the following, encircle the word or expression that best completes the meaning of the sentence or answers the question, with particular reference to the meaning of the word in **boldface type**.*

86. We can apply the word **meander** to
a. rivers and arguments
b. victories and defeats
c. sellers and buyers
d. plaintiffs and defendants

87. A story that goes on **ad infinitum** is
a. short and snappy
b. pointless
c. too long
d. worth repeating

88. A person who seeks **asylum** is looking for
a. an orphan to adopt
b. an easy job
c. public office
d. protection

89. Which nickname would a **doleful** person be most likely to have?
a. Sad Sam
b. Big John
c. Little Mo
d. Broadway Joe

90. We may apply the word **dormant** to
a. a poem and a song
b. a talent and a volcano
c. the moon and the stars
d. shackles and freedom

91. The word **horde** might be used to describe
a. an efficient group of workers
b. an individual working alone
c. an invading army
d. a symphony orchestra

92. A word closely associated with **pauper** is
a. incorrigible
b. inquisitive
c. invariable
d. impoverished

93. Which of the following might apply to a person who is **mediocre**?
a. illustrious
b. immortal
c. inadequate
d. sterling

94. Which of the following events *cannot* occur **posthumously**?
a. signing one's will
b. an increase in one's fame
c. being awarded a medal
d. the sale of one's house

95. An argument that is **opaque** is lacking in
a. facts
b. sincerity
c. lucidity
d. strong language

96. An **invincible** team is one that has never known
a. the joy of victory
b. the agony of defeat
c. the fear of flying
d. injury or illness

97. You might say **adieu**
a. when someone sneezes
b. when you arrive
c. when you leave
d. when you step on someone's toes

98. Which of the following would specifically *not* apply to a typical **metropolis**?
a. bustling
b. crowded
c. perilous
d. rustic

99. A country in a state of **anarchy** lacks
a. arts and sciences
b. law and order
c. fun and games
d. food and drink

100. If you say that your vocabulary program has been **arduous**, you mean that it has been
a. demanding
b. too easy
c. worthwhile
d. a lot of fun

Building with Word Roots

Units 1–3

pon, pos—to put, place

This root appears in **predispose** (page 11). The literal meaning is "to put away before," but the word now means "to incline" or "to make susceptible." Some other words based on the same root are listed below.

component	**disposition**	**juxtapose**	**superimpose**
composite	**impose**	**repository**	**transpose**
depose	**interpose**		

From the list of words above, choose the one that corresponds to each of the brief definitions below. Write the word in the space at the right of the definition, and then in the illustrative phrase below the definition.

1. to place between, to come between   _____

    _____ an objection at that moment

2. made up of distinct parts; combining elements or characteristics; such a combination ("*put together*")   _____

    a _____ drawing of the suspect

3. one's temperament; a tendency, inclination; a settlement, arrangement   _____

    a person with a pleasing _____

4. to put out of office; to declare under oath (*'to put down''*)   _____

    a plot to _____ the king

5. a part, element   _____

    replace one of the _____ of the system

6. a place where things are stored or kept   _____

    a safe _____ for our company records

7. to place side by side or close together ("*to place next to*")   _____

    _____ two items for comparison

8. to establish by force; to take advantage of ("*to place on*")   _____

    _____ a fine on the offender

9. to interchange positions; to shift   _____

    _____ the music into another key

10. to put or place upon or over something else   _____

    _____ a second image over the first

From the list of words on page 131, choose the one that best completes each of the following sentences. Write the word in the space provided.

1. The attic is a(n) _____ for anything that we are unwilling to part with.

2. You will not be able to repair this old television set until you discover which of its

_____ is not in working order.

3. I could never be friends for long with a person who has such a jealous and

intolerant _____ .

4. The novel's main character is a(n) _____ portrait of several of the author's college friends.

5. New York is a city where wealth and poverty are strikingly _____ .

6. I am not going to do you that favor because you have _____ once too often on my good nature!

7. When his misconduct was discovered, he was _____ from his office as president of the association.

8. I soon discovered the mess that can be made of old plaster walls when you try to

_____ a water-based paint over an oil-based paint.

9. When she misspells a word, she usually writes all the correct letters, but she

_____ some of them.

10. When the student discussion threatened to become an argument, the teacher

_____ his own list of possible solutions.

Units 4–6

ten, tain, tin—to hold, keep

This root appears in **tenacious** (page 42), which means, literally, "full of holding power." Some other words based on the same root are listed below.

abstention	**detention**	**retinue**	**tenor**
containerize	**pertain**	**sustenance**	**tenure**
detainee	**pertinacity**		

From the list of words above, choose the one that corresponds to each of the following brief definitions. Write the word in the space at the right of the definition, and then in the illustrative phrase below the definition.

1. the means of support or subsistence; nourishment   _____

drew _____ from her faith

2. the time during which something is held; a permanent right to an office or position after a trial period   _____

a President's _____ in office

3. to have reference to; to be suitable; to belong, as an attribute or accessory

_____

evidence that _____ to the case

4. stubborn persistence; determined adherence to an idea or plan

_____

pursued the scheme with _____

5. a body of followers, group of attendants

_____

a king followed by his _____

6. the act of doing without; refraining

_____

_____ from fatty foods

7. confinement, holding in custody

_____

a place of _____

8. to package in large standardized containers to facilitate shipping and handling

_____

_____ the cargo

9. the flow of meaning through something written or spoken, drift; the highest adult male voice

_____

an operatic role for a(n) _____

10. a person held in official custody

_____

a political _____

From the list of words on page 132, choose the one that best completes each of the following sentences. Write the word in the space provided.

1. When their food supplies ran out, the desperate survivors turned to roots and berries for _____ .

2. He sticks to his opinions with such _____ that I have given up trying to change his mind about anything.

3. The crane operator swiftly transferred the _____ cargo from the ship's hold to the flatcars of the freight train.

4. The teacher suggested reference works in which I might look for material that _____ to the topic of my research paper.

5. The people showed their disapproval of both candidates running for office by widespread _____ from voting.

6. His overriding hope is that during his _____ in office, our city will meet the needs of its people.

7. We gathered from the _____ of his remarks that he differs from us on this issue.

8. During the war, special facilities were set up to house _____ suspected of being security risks.

9. _____ after hours was once a prevalent method of punishment in schools.

10. The all-state basketball star had a(n) _____ of hangers-on who turned his head with endless praise.

Units 7–9

pel, puls—to drive

This root appears in **impel** (page 64), which means "to drive on." Some other words based on the same root are listed below.

compulsion	**expel**	**propulsion**	**repellent**
dispel	**impulsive**	**pulsate**	**repulse**

From the list of words above, choose the one that corresponds to each of the brief definitions below. Write the word in the space at the right of the definition, and then in the illustrative phrase below the definition.

1. to drive away, scatter _____

a wind that _____ the clouds

2. something that thrusts or drives away; disgusting _____

an effective insect _____

3. to drive or beat back; to reject rudely or coldly _____

_____ the enemy attack

4. the use of force; the imposition of one's will on another _____

take only under _____

5. to throb, beat, quiver _____

blood _____ through our veins

6. a driving forward or onward _____

safe means of _____ through the water

7. easily moved, acting on whim (*"driven on"*) _____

a(n) _____ child

8. to put out (*"to drive out"*) _____

_____ from the courtroom

From the list of words above, choose the one that best completes each of the following sentences. Write the word in the space provided.

1. During the busy hours of the day, the city seems to _____ with activity, as though it were alive.

BWR

2. The _____ teenager gave all his money to the street beggar.

3. In one of the funniest scenes in the play, the heroine cleverly _____ the disagreeable advances of an unwanted suitor.

4. The manager threatened to have the unruly group _____ from the theater.

5. Only time will tell whether the speaker was successful in _____ the fears of the community regarding an atomic energy plant.

6. We had to use a long pole as the only means of _____ when the paddle of our canoe broke in the swampy water.

7. The lawyer for the plaintiff argued that since the agreement had been signed under _____ , its provisions were not binding.

8. I find her threatening tone of voice and abusive language when she speaks to the children so _____ that I cannot bear being in her presence.

Units 10–12

spec, spic—to look

This root appears in **despicable** (page 77), which means "that which is to be looked down at." Some other words based on the same root are listed below.

aspect	**perspicacious**	**respective**	**specter**
conspicuous	**prospective**	**retrospect**	**speculate**
introspection	**prospectus**		

From the list of words above, choose the one that corresponds to each of the brief definitions below. Write the word in the space at the right of the definition, and then in the illustrative phrase below the definition.

1. a phantom, apparition; a fearful image or threatening possibility   _____

      a frightening _____

2. to reflect, meditate; to buy or sell at risk   _____

      _____ about the meaning of life

3. looked forward to, expected   _____

      my _____ sister-in-law

4. an examination of one's own thoughts and feeling ("*looking within*")   _____

      given to _____

5. an appearance; a side or view; the direction something faces   _____

      a different _____ of the matter

6. belonging to each; individual (*"looking back and forth"*) _____

   their _____ rooms

7. noticeable, drawing attention _____

   a large, _____ building

8. a printed description of a forthcoming book, stock, etc. (*"a looking ahead"*) _____

   read the _____

9. keen in observing and understanding (*"able to see through"*) _____

   a(n) _____ observer

10. with reference to the past; a survey of the past (*"a looking back"*) _____

   seen in _____

From the list of words on page 135, choose the one that best completes each of the following sentences. Write the word in the space provided.

1. Only through painful _____ was he able to understand why he was so eager to become class president.

2. I can see now in _____ where I went wrong and created the conditions for our failure.

3. At present, scientists can only _____ about the forms of life that may exist elsewhere in the universe.

4. The most pleasing _____ of this matter is that we will be working together for a worthwhile cause.

5. When the drought continued into a second year, government officials were faced with the terrible _____ of famine.

6. It's hard not to be _____ in a crowd when you're 6 feet, 8 inches tall and weigh 285 pounds!

7. You cannot make solid plans for the future on _____ earnings.

8. When we have all the facts before us, we will be in a better position to judge the _____ merits of the candidates.

9. Before investing in the securities of that corporation, you would do well to make a careful study of its _____ .

10. Then he made a(n) _____ observation that illuminated the whole problem for us.

Units 13–15

vert, vers—to turn

This root appears in **versatile** (page 101). The literal meaning of this word is "able to be turned." In modern use it now refers to the ability to turn from one task to another with ease. Some other words based on the same root are listed below.

adversity	**conversion**	**invert**	**version**
aversion	**diverse**	**reversion**	**vertigo**
conversely	**divert**		

From the list of words above, choose the one that corresponds to each of the brief definitions below. Write the word in the space at the right of the definition, and then in the illustrative phrase below the definition.

1. different, differing from one another, unlike   _____

have _____ interests

2. to turn aside; to entertain, amuse   _____

_____ one's attention

3. a return to a former state, belief, or condition; a reversal   _____

a _____ to former practices

4. a particular form of something; an account of an incident   _____

wanted to hear her _____ of the story

5. dizziness; giddiness (*"a turning feeling, as in the head"*)   _____

suffer an attack of _____

6. in reverse order, relation, or action; contrarily   _____

acted out the sequence _____

7. to turn upside down; to change direction   _____

_____ a glass

8. a strong dislike; a thing disliked (*"turning against"*)   _____

my pet _____

9. distress, misfortune, hardship   _____

a victim of _____

10. a change in condition or belief (*"turning toward"*)   _____

the _____ of ice into water

From the list of words above, choose the one that best completes each of the following sentences. Write the word in the space provided.

1. The drainage ditch will _____ water from the pond into the nearby fields.

2. This collection contains the works of a large and _____ group of poets.

3. Any student of logic will tell you that deductive reasoning runs not from the specific to the general but, _____ , from the general to the specific.

4. To prevent a _____ to his former depressed state, we redoubled our efforts to keep him in good spirits.

5. Her _____ toward cats is so strong that she refuses to visit friends who have cats in their homes.

6. Even the sight of a toy ship bobbing in a backyard pool can give me an attack of

_____ .

7. Even someone with the extraordinary patience of Job would find it hard to bear all

the _____ that has come my way this year.

8. The factory owners decided that the _____ of the old machinery would cost more than replacing it with new equipment.

9. As reflected in the waters of the lake, the row of lime trees that grew on the bank

appeared to be _____ .

10. Sally's _____ of the song is so different from the one I'm used to that it hardly seems like the same tune.

Index

The following list includes all the base words presented in the various units of this workbook, as well as those introduced in the *Vocabulary of Vocabulary* and *Building with Word Roots* sections. The number after each item indicates the page on which it is introduced and defined, but the words also appear in exercises on later pages.

incessant, 41
incinerate, 31
incite, 105
incorrigible, 36
incredulous, 64
influx, 105
inscribe, 64
institute, 59
interim, 54
interpose, 131
intolerable, 87
intrepid, 31
intricate, 41
introspection, 135
inundate, 54
invert, 137
invincible, 77
irate, 20
irreverent, 87

jeer, 15
juxtapose, 131

knave, 110

laborious, 87
languid, 77
larceny, 31
latent, 36
legion, 110
liability, 59
liberality, 110
literal, 4
lithe, 87
lofty, 100
lucid, 41
lucrative, 15

malign, 54
maltreat, 87
marauder, 20
meander, 54
mediocre, 15
metaphorical, 4
metropolis, 54
migration, 100
militant, 36
mire, 77
momentous, 54
monologue, 64
morose, 36
muddle, 10

obesity, 20
obstreperous, 54

obtrusive, 77
opaque, 36
opinionated, 10

pallor, 105
paramount, 36
pauper, 20
pedigree, 106
pejorative, 4
pensive, 54
perceive, 100
perennial, 10
perilous, 55
perspicacious, 135
pertain, 132
pertinacity, 132
perverse, 100
pilfer, 20
plaintiff, 110
pliant, 31
pompous, 32
ponder, 87
posthumous, 41
prattle, 36
preamble, 78
precipice, 32
precipitous, 106
predispose, 11
prefix, 3
prelude, 100
preposterous, 59
prim, 41
probe, 111
profuse, 106
prognosis, 65
proliferate, 16
proponent, 82
propulsion, 134
prospective, 135
prospectus, 135
protract, 111
pugnacious, 59
pulsate, 134

quarry, 111
quaver, 82

rabid, 59
rancid, 100
rasping, 65
realm, 59
rebut, 37
recoil, 82
reconcile, 106
recoup, 82

rectify, 32
reek, 83
rejuvenate, 60
relentless, 83
relinquish, 11
remunerate, 60
render, 78
repellent, 134
repository, 131
reprieve, 32
reprimand, 37
repugnant, 65
repulse, 134
respective, 135
retinue, 132
retrospect, 135
reversion, 137
revile, 32
rift, 20
rivulet, 83
rugged, 78
rustic, 100

salvage, 11
sardonic, 41
scuttle, 65
semblance, 21
servitude, 37
sever, 101
shackle, 106
shoddy, 55
skeptical, 78
slapdash, 37
slipshod, 78
sordid, 101
sparse, 60
spasmodic, 11
specter, 135
speculate, 135
sprightly, 55
spurious, 11
spurn, 111
squander, 83
staccato, 83
stagnant, 37
statute, 83
sterling, 60
subjugate, 16
subterfuge, 111
subversive, 88
succumb, 37
suffix, 3
sully, 16
superfluous, 42
superimpose, 131

supplant, 42
surly, 55
surmount, 21
sustenance, 132
synonym, 1
synthetic, 88

tantalize, 16
taunt, 42
temperate, 88
tenacious, 42
tenor, 132
tenure, 132
terminate, 21
terse, 16
threadbare, 106
tirade, 55
tone, 4
transpose, 131
trite, 21

unbridled, 11
unflinching, 16
untenable, 101
usurp, 21

vagrant, 55
venomous, 88
venture, 60
versatile, 101
version, 137
vertigo, 137
vindicate, 101

wane, 101
warp, 60
wily, 88